THE CHALMERS RACE

THE CHALMERS
RACE

Ty Cobb, Napoleon Lajoie, and the
Controversial 1910 Batting Title
That Became a National Obsession

RICK HUHN

Foreword by CHARLES C. ALEXANDER

University of Nebraska Press
Lincoln and London

Library of Congress
Cataloging-in-Publication Data
Huhn, Rick, 1944–
The Chalmers race: Ty Cobb,
Napoleon Lajoie, and the
controversial 1910 batting title
that became a national obses-
sion / Rick Huhn; foreword
by Charles C. Alexander.
pages cm
Includes bibliographical
references and index.
ISBN 978-0-8032-7182-1
(cloth: alk. paper)
ISBN 978-0-8032-7376-4 (epub)
ISBN 978-0-8032-7377-1 (mobi)
ISBN 978-0-8032-7375-7 (pdf)
1. Baseball—United States—
History—20th century. 2. Batting
(Baseball)—United States—
History—20th century. 3. Cobb,
Ty, 1886–1961. 4. Lajoie,
Napoleon, 1874–1959. I. Title.
GV863.A1H84 2014
796.357'6409041—dc23
2013035015

Set in Lyon by Laura Wellington.
Designed by Nathan Putens.

*To my wife, Marcia, who constantly provides
spirit and meaning to my life*

HIPPODROME

Hip"po*drome\, v. i. [imp. & p. p. -dromed; p. pr. & vb. n. -droming.]
(Sports) To arrange contests with predetermined winners. [Slang, U.S.]
—*Webster's Revised Unabridged Dictionary*, ©1996, 1998 MICRA, Inc.

Contents

Foreword

CHARLES C. ALEXANDER

Most of today's baseball fans, especially younger ones, understand the 1919 World Series fix—universally known as the Black Sox Scandal—as the singular sin against the integrity of America's oldest and most cherished team sport. Yet, as the growing number of people who have undertaken careful study of baseball's long history are aware, other questionable and often high-smelling episodes punctuate the sport's past—from the bribes gamblers paid Louisville players to throw the 1879 National League pennant race (and their subsequent banishment) to recent and ongoing revelations of the use of steroids and other performance-enhancing drugs by players seeking an edge in strength and endurance. In short, dishonesty in its many forms has been a remarkably persistent feature of what was long hailed as the National Pastime.

Rick Huhn's book is about what used to be called a "hippodrome." Taken from the names of chariot race courses in ancient Greece and later of various circuses and theaters, "hippodrome" became a commonly used term in the late nineteenth- and early twentieth-century United States to denote athletic events—usually baseball and prizefighting—that appeared not on the up-and-up, as fake rather than the real thing. Such was the case with the finale of the 1910 American League batting race between Detroit's Ty Cobb and Cleveland's Napoleon Lajoie. Both men were future Hall of Famers and outstanding performers in baseball history. What was at stake was not only the distinction of being the top man in batting average (then considered baseball's most significant offensive statistic), but winning the prize of a brand new Chalmers 30 touring car. That was the clever promotional scheme of Hugh Chalmers, a mostly forgotten pioneer in the emerging auto industry who offered a new 30 to the player with the highest average in the Major Leagues.

The competition for the Chalmers 30 brilliantly served Hugh Chalmers's purpose by creating mounting national interest in the batting races in the two leagues as well as in his "motor cars" (as the first generation of automobiles was called). Today, when many big-league players are multimillionaires, offering a new automobile as the prize for winning a batting title or any other achievement would seem of little consequence. But in 1910, when average family income in the United States was less than $1,000 per year, very few Americans had the wherewithal to purchase an automobile at even the $450 or $500 for which cheaper models were selling. The Chalmers 30, advertised for $1,500, was a hugely expensive item in the eyes of most people. Although the 30 wasn't Hugh Chalmers's top-of-the-line car (his 40 retailed for $2,750 and his "limousine" model for $3,000), it was an appealing prize, even for Cobb, who, like a growing number of professional ballplayers and other notables, had already acquired one or more early automobiles. (Each of which, with the exception of Henry Ford's inaugural Model T in 1908, had the steering wheel located on the *right side*.)

By September 1910 Connie Mack's Philadelphia Athletics were far ahead of everybody in the American League; Detroit, which had won three straight pennants (and lost each World Series) would finish a distant third, while Cleveland ended up fifth. Whatever suspense remained had to do with the race for the Chalmers 30, and it was obvious it would be decided in the American League between Cobb and Lajoie, whose averages remained in the upper .300s week after week. (The Philadelphia Phillies' Sherwood Magee, who batted .331, led the National League.) As Rick Huhn reminds us, few players could have been more unlike in temperament and playing style. Ty Cobb, in his fifth year in the Majors but still only twenty-three, was a native Georgian, a lean, high-strung, fiery competitor who slapped and pushed the ball to all fields and ran bases with abandon. He was driving for his fourth consecutive batting championship. A fifteen-year Major

Leaguer, Napoleon Lajoie ("Larry" to his baseball peers) turned thirty-five in September 1910. He was a native New Englander, usually easygoing, a big man for his time who was known as a "hard hitter"—a player who hit the ball as solidly and as far as anybody in the Majors. Having given up the burden of managing the Cleveland team, Lajoie was enjoying his best year since winning his third batting title in 1904.

Cobb had few friends on the teams he played for (and managed, 1921–26) during his twenty-four years in the big leagues, and his aggressive, hell-bent style aroused the ire of fans everywhere in the American League except Detroit—and sometimes even there. Lajoie was generally well liked by teammates and by fans around the American League. In his home city, he was wildly popular, so popular that the Cleveland team was named in his honor—the "Naps." Yet while Cobb often went out of his way to cultivate the favor of sportswriters and was usually a good interview, Lajoie, poorly educated and less articulate than Cobb, didn't like dealing with writers, nor were they fond of him.

At greater or lesser length, a number of people have written about the 1910 Cobb-Lajoie competition for the batting title and the Chalmers 30, including the present writer. But no one before Rick Huhn has examined so thoroughly the background, progress, and ins and outs of that American League season, which climaxed with the scandalous, season-ending doubleheader in Sportsman's Park in St. Louis between Cleveland and the local Browns. Unlike other scandals—the 1879 Louisville mess; an attempt to bribe the umpires before the 1908 pennant-deciding New York Giants–Chicago Cubs game; the effort by a Giants coach and player to bribe Philadelphia's shortstop near the end of the 1924 season; and of course, most famously, the 1919 World Series fix—what happened in 1910 involved neither money nor gamblers. It was more akin to the New York team's sloppy play in 1891 in losing five late-season games to the Boston National Leaguers, thereby helping Boston beat out Chicago for the pennant, and Minnesota outfielder Steve Brye's letting George Brett's fly ball drop safely in the last game of the 1976 season, which enabled Brett to edge Kansas City teammate Hal McRae for the American League batting title (a distasteful little episode that Huhn discusses toward the end of his book).

The 1910 scandal resulted from prejudice and favoritism: prejudice toward Cobb, favoritism toward Lajoie. Despite vigorous denials from Browns manager Jack O'Connor, other Browns, and Lajoie himself, it was obvious at the end of the doubleheader in St. Louis that the Browns had deliberately permitted Lajoie to make eight hits in nine times at bat so that he could narrowly beat out Cobb for the batting championship— and the Chalmers 30. What followed was a complex series of events, well covered by Huhn. The whole business infuriated Byron Bancroft "Ban" Johnson, the American League's imperious president. Johnson and Cobb already had a troubled relationship that would worsen in the coming years. In 1909 Johnson had warned Cobb about being overly aggressive on the base paths, especially after he had spiked Philadelphia third baseman Frank Baker in a critical series. But Johnson—determined to clear up the fiasco created in St. Louis before the start of the World Series between the Athletics and the Chicago Cubs—had the league's secretary do some creative refiguring and then proclaimed Cobb the champion with a final average of .384944 to Lajoie's .384084. Hugh Chalmers executed a neat public-relations gesture, awarding a Chalmers 30 to *both* Cobb and Lajoie, the ceremony for which took place before the first game of the World Series.

Having cleared up the outcome of the batting race, Ban Johnson had Browns owner Robert Hedges fire O'Connor and then banished from Organized Baseball both O'Connor and pitcher Harry Howell, who had repeatedly gone to the Sportsman's Park press section to try to cajole the scorer into giving Lajoie still another hit on a fielder's choice. O'Connor, one of the more rascally figures of that period, had gained a reputation early in his playing career as a dirty and insubordinate player and as a drinker and carouser. In 1891 the president of the then–Major League American Association expelled him from that league, although he resurfaced in the National League the next season. Never more than an average player (mostly as an outfielder and catcher), O'Connor remained in the National League for twelve years, then joined New York in the American League, and ended his playing career with the Browns, becoming their manager in 1910. In 1901 and 1902, when he was a part-time player with Pittsburgh, O'Connor acted as Ban Johnson's clandestine agent in luring several members of his team to jump to Johnson's newly formed American League. So until that doubleheader in St. Louis, Johnson had no reason to dislike O'Connor and in fact had reason to be grateful for his undercover work in Pittsburgh. Nonetheless, at Johnson's behest he was gone, thus giving him the dubious distinction of being the only man ever kicked out of two major leagues.

Rick Huhn makes three particularly significant contributions to the story of the 1910 Cobb-Lajoie competition. The first is his incisive examination of the unreliable and often haphazard scoring of hits and errors in that period and for a long time thereafter—despite continual calls from various quarters for systemization of the scoring process. In 1910, as Huhn shows, on a given day newspapers in different cities would likely publish varying batting statistics.

Second, Huhn provides a detailed and original account of the trial of the lawsuit Jack O'Connor brought in St. Louis against owner Hedges, who, he claimed, had actually hired him for two years. O'Connor believed he was thus entitled to $5,000, the amount he had been paid in 1910. Huhn, a retired attorney and the first to examine the transcripts of the trial of O'Connor's suit, brings a sure hand to his analysis of how the trial proceeded.

The controversy over what happened in 1910 was largely forgotten for almost seventy years, until several researchers went back over the whole 1910 American League season, studying what Cobb and Lajoie had done game by game. They discovered a number of discrepancies in Johnson's official batting figures and concluded that in fact Lajoie had outhit Cobb .384 to .383. That revelation, published in 1981 in the *Sporting News*, may have mattered little if at all to most baseball fans, but it mattered a great deal to people who insisted on getting baseball's records exactly right. Now it seemed incontrovertible that Cobb's previously accepted run of twelve batting titles in thirteen seasons (Tris Speaker clearly beat him out in 1916) was actually only eleven in thirteen seasons. It was still an amazing record, but Cobb's brilliant career had lost just a bit of its luster. Official Baseball, however, meaning the Commissioner's Office and the National Baseball Hall of Fame, has continued to recognize Cobb as the

1910 winner. Huhn's analysis of this resurgent controversy—his third significant contribution—provides a fine denouement to his book.

Rick Huhn thus gives us a vivid account of a hotly controversial episode in baseball history, centering on two of the game's greatest players. But his book is also about a time when Organized Baseball was a far smaller universe, in which personalities and personal relations often were critical determinants in how things were done—or not done. It was also a time when Ban Johnson, as American League president and the dominant figure on the ruling three-man National Commission, wielded power in a way nobody else in baseball could before 1920, when the club owners created the office of commissioner and gave virtually dictatorial authority to Kenesaw Mountain Landis. Since then, no league president has possessed the kind of power that Johnson, increasingly frustrated with his subordinate role in the 1920s, had once had. Rick Huhn's book is splendid baseball history. It ought to be read by anyone the least interested in the game's checkered past.

Preface

Today the home run is baseball royalty. The arc of the bat followed by the sound of wood on leather rivets attention to one location, all eyes following the seamed white sphere as it lifts higher and higher until it clears the fence, sending base runners in unfettered motion and the batter on a four-cornered journey home. The excitement that mighty swing of the bat creates is undeniable. For current fans of the game, it seems it was always so, but that is not the case. There was a time when a mere base hit ruled on high. A time when a two-man race for a batting crown and its accompanying bounty—a sleek, fast-moving piece of motorized steel— captivated the sports world, topping even the forthcoming World Series in fan interest. That the race involved perhaps the game's most popular player versus its most controversial and least liked, and that both men were star performers of the highest order, only added spice to the mix. String out the intrigue to the last weekend of the baseball season. Take the suspense to the last at bats in a pair of games one sports columnist of the day described as having "the same standing among sportsmen as a limburger cheese might enjoy at a perfume bazaar,"[1] and even fabled home-run duels between the likes of Maris and Mantle and Sosa and McGwire might pale in comparison. For in 1910 it was Napoleon "Larry" Lajoie versus Ty Cobb, a classic confrontation between old and new, arguably the two best players in the American League, that held sway. The base hit, that most basic offensive weapon, not the home run or anything in between, held baseball in its grasp. When the 1910 batting race was over—and there are some who say it still is not—the game had been tainted. But that was owing to the foibles of man, not the game itself. And that should not serve to deter a reexamination or even a salute to a time when, like the mighty home run today, the base hit was the king of baseball. This book is about that time, those men, and that season.

THE CHALMERS RACE

Prologue

They don't hand you anything in baseball.
—Napoleon Lajoie

The Tigers' center fielder peered out onto the Comiskey Park playing field from his seat on the bench. His team was about to lose yet another close game. His mind likely drifted elsewhere. His work for the day—no, for the year—was done. The last gasp for the three-time defending American League champion Detroit Tigers had come and gone weeks ago. One more out and the Tigers would fall eighteen games behind the pennant-clinching Philadelphia Athletics. Two more games and the 1910 regular season would be over as well. For Ty Cobb, however, the regular season ended today. His two hits in three at bats had underscored and confirmed what he now knew to be almost certainly true. In two days he would be crowned the American League's batting champion for the fourth time in a row, salvaging something quite important to the highly competitive outfielder from an otherwise dismal season. And this year the coveted batting title would be topped with its own special brand of icing: a prize to end all prizes. This season the player with the highest batting average in Major League Baseball would drive away in a brand new automobile. Cobb had sat in a similar model just a few weeks earlier, his chief adversary, Napoleon "Larry" Lajoie, across from him in the back seat, only inches away. At the time there was no way to tell which of the two might finish on top. Cobb was confident in his skills and staying power, but not

1

overconfident. He thought he might have to continue the fight to the last bitter out. He traveled to Chicago prepared to do just that if necessary, but now, after his performance today, he would no longer have to finish out the season. Moments later, the last out made, sealing a 2–0 White Sox win, he gathered his bats and his glove and quickly left the stadium. His teammates could play this out; he had more interesting work ahead.

When questions later arose about the reasons for Cobb's early departure and absence, he was frank. He owed no apology and told reporters, "So far as my leaving the team before the end of the season is concerned, I can say this: I asked manager [Hugh] Jennings ten days before the season closed to give me permission to leave the team, as I wanted to pack up and take an automobile trip to Philadelphia and play with the All Stars. I had planned not to go to Chicago, but the race for the prize was close, and so I went to Chicago and played two games."[1]

Indeed, while his team played out its final games, Cobb hightailed east to join a cast of American League stalwarts chosen to test the pennant-winning Athletics. Their task was to make sure the Athletics did not grow stale while waiting for the Chicago Cubs, first-place finisher in the rival National League, to play out what had been a controversial staggered schedule. Some speculated that the anomaly by which the Nationals finished their season several days after the Americans was profit driven, to permit the National League franchises an opportunity to reel in a Columbus Day gate the equal of July 4. Whatever the reason, the fact remained that a fine young A's outfit managed by the wily Connie Mack was left waiting for the start of the World Series. While they waited, a team that included a number of the American League's best traveled to Philadelphia to school them. It was the first time a squad was formed for such a purpose. In addition to Cobb, the formidable group included, among others, speedy outfielder Clyde Milan, infielder Kid Elberfeld, catcher Gabby Street, and pitcher Walter Johnson of the Washington Nationals; outfielder Tris Speaker and infielder Jake Stahl of the Boston Red Sox; and pitcher Ed Walsh of the White Sox.

By the time the Tigers took the field the next day, Cobb had already returned to Detroit and boarded a ship steaming across Lake Erie, headed for Buffalo. Once there his itinerary took him by automobile—by far his favorite mode of transportation and a source of endless fascination and fun—to Philadelphia. He had every intention of arriving in Philadelphia in time to take the field for the first exhibition contest on October 11. Alas, his auto broke down in Kingston, New York.[2] He thus missed the first game, arriving by train in time to play the next day and crack out three hits, as the All-Stars added worry lines to Mr. Mack's furrowed face by winning for the second time. By then Cobb too wore a frown. For by the time he had arrived in the City of Brotherly Love, he was experiencing an automobile problem of an entirely different sort.

The seeds of Cobb's car problem may have been germinating for some time. Two years earlier, in October 1908, the regular season had ended in triumph for his Tigers. Not so for their Great Lakes' rivals, the Cleveland Naps. On October 4 of that year, the Naps had begun a season-ending three-game series in St. Louis, arriving in Missouri locked in a tight pennant race with the Tigers and the White Sox. At that point, they trailed the league-leading Detroiters by a game and a half, having failed to follow up a perfect-game gem pitched by Addie Joss with a knockout punch to the White Sox. The hometown Browns had been another pennant contender, but by this point they had been eliminated from contention and were merely playing out the string. Although a three-team race offered many final scenarios for the combatants, the Tigers and White Sox finished their season facing each other. Thus, the Naps' margin for error was quite slim. Nonetheless, a sweep would at least give them a fighting chance, perhaps even seal a first-ever pennant for the Cleveland club.

Given the same circumstances, some baseball clubs with nothing really left to play for might have eased up—nothing fraudulent mind you, just not playing at full tilt. The 1908 edition of the St. Louis Browns was not such a team. In the first game of this final series, played on a Sunday, the teams battled hard and were tied 1–1 as Cleveland's Bill Hinchman batted with two out and two on in the Naps' half of the ninth. Runners Addie Joss on third and Bill Bradley on second were off at the crack of the bat as Hinchman grounded sharply through the box. The Browns' aging shortstop,

Bobby Wallace, raced over, made a terrific stop behind second, and threw off balance to first. The throw appeared to pull Browns first baseman Tom Jones off the bag, meaning Hinchman was safe. At least Jones thought so as he watched Joss cross the plate with the lead run and threw home to make sure Bradley did not try to also score and give the Naps a two-run lead. It was only at this point that umpire Jack Egan, an arbiter who had arrived midgame owing to travel difficulties and who had a stormy history with the Naps, let everyone in on his secret. He had called Hinchman out at first. The Naps stormed the field and pleaded almost endlessly, but to no avail. Even some loyal Browns fans joined the chorus of protest. The score, however, remained tied. It did not change that day. At the end of eleven innings, the game was called a tie, to be replayed as the first game of a doubleheader the next day. The Naps had fought gamely, perhaps even won, yet they were absolutely no closer to their goal.

When the score arrived from Chicago, the Naps could only shake their heads and dream of what might have been. Chicago was the winner, 3–1. To win the pennant, the Naps now had to win their three remaining games. There was no longer any margin for error. A Naps loss combined with two Sox wins meant Chicago moved on to the World Series. A Naps loss and a Tigers win gave Detroit their second flag in a row.

The next day again found the Browns just as they should have been: playing as if it were their pennant chances at stake. They sent veteran Bill Dineen to the mound. The Naps countered with right-hander Glenn Liebhardt. The Browns jumped on top with a run in the first. The Naps tied it up in the fifth. In the sixth the Naps committed two errors leading to a pair of runs. The Browns made the lead stand and ended the Naps' pennant chances with a 3–1 victory. The win meant absolutely nothing to the Browns. The loss meant everything to the Naps, a club that had yet to taste a league title. To make matters worse, Detroit shut out the White Sox that same afternoon. Ty Cobb and his mates had locked up their second straight pennant.

At season's end, despite wins in their final two games with the Browns, there was no cheer in the Naps' locker room. Easily the most dejected Cleve-lander was the team's manager, popular hitting star and team namesake

Nap Lajoie. He had just completed the fifteenth season of a playing career that had seen him achieve nearly every goal imaginable, save one. He had never played on a pennant winner, never savored the ultimate team goal. The season just completed had offered him his best chance yet. The final season standings, including the replay of the tie, left his club a game behind the Tigers in the loss column. Making it even more frustrating, each team had won ninety games. The Tigers benefitted by playing one fewer game owing to a rainout that required no makeup under then-existing rules. The final percentages found Detroit less than one close shave ahead at .588, Cleveland at .584.

Now approaching thirty-four years of age, Lajoie had to wonder how many more chances he would have to win it all. He knew he could not come any closer and still come up short. And this time, unlike so many others, he had to shoulder a major part of the blame. In a bone-crushing 3–2 loss to the White Sox in the Naps' home finale, Lajoie, usually a sure-handed second baseman, dropped a throw from his catcher. The fumble opened the door to a pair of runs. Later in the game, the Naps' manager had a golden chance to redeem himself. Standing at the plate with the bases loaded, two out and a full count, the normally aggressive hitter took a fastball right down the middle for a called third strike. The fact that Lajoie already had a pair of doubles to his credit that afternoon and that the pitcher he faced was Chicago's ace, Ed Walsh, pitching in relief, did nothing to mollify the Naps' slugger. Then, in the backbreaking loss to the Browns in the replay game, the fielding bug again struck Lajoie. This time he made a throwing error that led to the runs which ultimately resulted in defeat and elimination.

Some said Napoleon Lajoie cried after his team came a cropper in 1908. Even if he didn't actually shed a tear, there is no doubt his team's demise left the bitterest taste of his career. He said later, "I honestly believe that the 1908 race . . . took more out of me than three ordinary seasons."[3]

The pain etched in deep furrows across the face of the Naps' leader in the waning days of 1908 did not go unnoticed by the local St. Louis press. Billy Murphy, a baseball writer for the *St. Louis Star*, wrote that he saw Lajoie at the Planters Hotel after the 3–1 loss to the Browns. The Naps' player-manager was "a broken-hearted and bitter man. His team was preparing to depart for home, instead of leaving for Chicago to participate in the world's series. This is one hurt that time will never heal."[4]

Now it was 1910 and a full two years had passed. Once again the Naps, no longer managed by Lajoie, found themselves playing the Browns in the last games of the season. True to Billy Murphy's prediction, Lajoie had not forgotten how the Browns, playing for nothing in 1908 as the season wound to a close, had backed down nary an inch when a victory for him meant so much. "You can take it from me that they don't hand you anything in baseball," he told the press. "Two years ago we could have won the American league [*sic*] pennant by taking both games of a double-header from St. Louis. Members of the St. Louis team were pulling for us to win the flag. But did they hand us both games and the flag? Not on your life. They buckled down, worked their heads off, won one of the games, and beat us out of the bunting in one of the hardest races in the history of the game."[5]

Lajoie indeed remembered 1908. Perhaps so did some of the Browns. The outcome involved the same teams, albeit a totally different race—individual in nature—and a unique prize. Nonetheless, this time around, in 1910, the Browns wanted to do their part to ensure the popular Lajoie achieved a markedly different result and attained the prize at stake.

Chapter One

I'll sit here alone.
—Napoleon Lajoie

It was a well-rested, high-spirited bunch of baseball professionals who took in the festivities at Detroit's Gayety Theatre on the evening of October 4, 1910. The Gayety held baseball nights from time to time. This was the final one of the season. The visiting Cleveland Naps and home-standing Tigers had just spent a lazy afternoon staring at raindrops, a number of them playing cards, none chasing fly balls or curve balls at Bennett Park. The scheduled affair would have been the Tigers' next to last game with the Naps and their next to last home game to boot. These last few games meant little to either team, although the Tigers still had a shot at second place in the American League. Each had been eliminated from the 1910 pennant race some time ago. Fan interest now—and there was still plenty—centered on the individual batting race between Ty Cobb and Nap Lajoie. The rainout game this late in the season meant a double-header the next day and the final meeting of the season between baseball's leading hitters. Reports from the Gayety do not indicate whether either man was in attendance. The next day, however, both players, in a bizarre meeting to say the least, were together before the game even started. The pregame event getting attention from players and fans alike was the unveiling of a 1911 Chalmers 30 touring car. The all-black topless sedan stood like a silent sentry behind the left-field wall down Bennett Park's third base line. Some months before one of these horseless carriages had been offered to the player who finished with the highest batting average in the Major Leagues for the 1910 season. At some point, as the teams finished their on-field pregame preparations, a news photographer spotted the pair of odds-on favorites for the treasured object, Messrs. Cobb and Lajoie, approaching the vehicle. In a few days one of these men would undoubtedly own the machine. Praising his good fortune, the lucky photojournalist ran after the rivals and poised for a shot, but not before asking the players to take a seat in the car. They obliged, both climbing in the rear. This, of course, would not do. Which one, the photographer asked, would sit in front?

"I'll sit here alone," said Lajoie, referring to the back seat.

"Me, too," said Cobb.

And there they remained.

"I'm not superstitious," said Cobb. Lajoie just smiled. Cobb patted the upholstery. "Pretty soft stuff this, Larry."

"Well, anyway, they will never get two handsomer looking chaps in this car. Mr. Photographer, go ahead," said Lajoie.

By this time a crowd had gathered to observe the scene.

"Do you think you will win?" someone asked Cobb.

"I'm not saying a word," replied the Tigers' outfielder. "I'm just trying."[1]

In the days that followed, the strange photo of the two rivals sitting abreast in the rear seat of the Chalmers they each cherished found its way onto sports pages around the country. Each man's refusal to take the wheel in the other's presence and the kind words each expressed about the other to the press in the days leading up to this final meeting of the season, merely served to belie that each one for his own personal reasons strove mightily to drive away with the valued vehicle in hand. That these were two of baseball's fiercest competitors only underscored the endeavor. That today, more than a hundred years later, there is no clear-cut winner just adds to the intrigue and the fun.

At least one baseball fan had to be extremely pleased about all the fuss in Detroit that early October afternoon. His name was Hugh Chalmers.

When the photographs of ballplayers Cobb and Lajoie appeared on sports pages around the nation, his company's automobile became recognized as their coveted prize. The competition between the pair was turning the brand into a household name. In Chalmers's eyes, this was exactly how he meant the contest to play out.

Some three years earlier, Hugh Chalmers's participation in a venture of this sort would have seemed far-fetched. Although by 1910 the American automobile had been in existence for more than a decade, Hugh Chalmers's involvement in the still fledgling industry had come about much more recently. For Chalmers had been in Detroit only since 1907. Before that he lived in Dayton, Ohio, where he was born in 1873. He was enrolled in the local public school system, but he remained there only until age fourteen, when he left to find work. Soon he was employed as an office boy at the downtown sales office of one of Dayton's most important corporations, the National Cash Register Company (NCR). He also studied bookkeeping and stenography at a night school.

It was not long before Chalmers's strong work ethic gained favor at NCR, launching him on his career path. One who took note of Chalmers's potential was John H. Patterson. It never hurts to impress the big boss, and Patterson was number one at NCR. He was the company's founder and president. Furthermore, he was a well-known leader in the burgeoning field of marketing. Patterson, who had a reputation as a tough sell, liked what he saw in Chalmers and asked him to become a member of his sales team. But before Hugh could represent the company in the field, he had to pass an NCR training regimen personally designed by Patterson. Pass it he did. At the tender age of eighteen, Chalmers was an NCR salesman. A mere two years later, he was promoted to sales agent, a position that carried with it a sales territory in his home state of Ohio.

Promotions came quickly for the company's fast-rising stars, of which Hugh Chalmers was one. At twenty-four he was Ohio's district sales manager. In this position he supervised some twenty-four salesmen and agents. A year later he was an assistant sales manager. According to his biographer, he "was credited with creating one of the finest sales organizations in the world!"[2]

The next jump for the still young Chalmers was a big one. Patterson appointed his protégé, who was only twenty-seven, to vice president and general manager of the entire company. He was now second only to Patterson himself. Chalmers remained in this position for the next seven years, continuing to hone his marketing skills and gain a national reputation. By 1907 Chalmers had mastered the art of public speaking, an attribute that fit nicely with his innate charm and winning personality. At age thirty-four, the NCR executive's sales and marketing skills were earning him a king's ransom. His annual salary of $72,000 was enormous for the time, higher than that of the U.S. president.

Given his relative youth and high-level skills, it seemed nothing could derail Chalmers's advance, but that was not the case. Hugh's popularity with his fellow workers soon brought him into conflict with his one remaining boss, John Patterson. When his coworkers asked Chalmers to approach Patterson about the latter's increasingly autocratic rule, the result was Hugh's dismissal amid a general shake-up at NCR.

It now seemed that Chalmers's shooting star was reentering the Earth's atmosphere at warp speed. But news that was met with shock and dismay in some business circles was met in others with a smile. Some of the men Chalmers had impressed as he climbed the ladder of success at NCR took his sudden misfortune as their opportunity to lure him into what they hoped would be an arrangement of mutual benefit. One of these men, Fred Bezner, formerly worked with Chalmers at NCR and knew him well. Bezner had left the cash register company before the shake-up. He was now aligned with three other men, all near the age of thirty, in the business of automobile manufacturing. Bezner and his cohorts, who included Roy Chapin, one also impressed with Chalmers's marketing acumen, now held an interest in the Thomas-Detroit Motor Company, manufacturer of the Thomas-Detroit automobile. These men were extremely ambitious. Their goal was to purchase their own auto company, but they lacked the finances to do it by themselves. Bezner and Chapin saw Chalmers, an expert marketer with his own financial assets, as a perfect fit. Here was someone who could help them realize their dream. Despite the obvious risks of such a venture in an industry that was little more than a minefield for the uninitiated, Bezner and associates moved forward, offering Hugh Chalmers a proposal they hoped he could not refuse.

The deal the Bezner group hoped to broker required the men to purchase the Thomas-Detroit Motor Company by obtaining substantial shares from E. R. Thomas. The company had been founded in 1906 in Buffalo, New York, by Thomas, the builder of the well-known Thomas Flyer, as well as Bezner, Chapin, Howard Coffin, and James Brady. The latter four had earned their spurs in the auto industry by working for Ransom E. Olds and the Olds Auto Works of Detroit. The Thomas-Detroit was manufactured and marketed by Thomas through his parent company in Buffalo, a setup Bezner and colleagues hoped to change. The deal offered Hugh Chalmers was an intriguing one. He would be given the opportunity to purchase a substantial amount of E. R. Thomas's interest in Thomas-Detroit. In addition, within two years he would earn a guaranteed annual salary of $50,000.[3] Once the details were worked out, he agreed. By 1908 Hugh had made Detroit his home, and there he owned a bundle of stock and was president of what was now called the Chalmers-Detroit Company.

In 1909 Chalmers-Detroit manufactured and sold two models designated by their horsepower, the 30 and the 40. The 30, with its four-cylinder thirty-horsepower chassis on a 110-inch wheelbase, was the lower-priced model and was marketed as such. The five-passenger touring car was lightweight, European in style, and sold for $1,500, placing it in the midprice range. As soon as Hugh Chalmers joined the company, he set out to use his marketing talents to make the company's two models household names. One way to attract attention was by entering the vehicles in various racing competitions that were popular in that period. The Chalmers-Detroit vehicles, particularly the 30, won a number of races, including the prestigious Glidden Trophy. Increases in sales followed. The company was earning a nice dividend.

Despite the company's success, some of those involved in the venture were restless. Bezner and his group, in particular inventive-types Coffin and Chapin, felt they were still not where they wanted to be: designing and manufacturing their own vehicle. In early 1909 the group was able to pursue its dream when it received major funding from an uncle of a former associate. The wealthy uncle was Detroit department store owner Joseph L. Hudson. The new group formed the Hudson Motor Car Company. Chalmers was given an interest in the new venture, and progress was made in the design and manufacture of a low-cost vehicle under the Hudson name. By December 1909, however, the splinter group felt so comfortable with its decision to form a separate company that it sold its Chalmers-Detroit stock to Hugh and bought out his interest in Hudson. Thus, by late 1909 Chalmers was in complete control of Chalmers-Detroit. In early January 1910 the company became the Chalmers Motor Company.

As the driving force behind his own company, Hugh Chalmers looked around and saw competition on every side. The infant auto industry was growing whiskers. To keep up with his competitors and sell a substantial number of cars, Chalmers felt the need to market in new and innovative ways. He had already sufficiently and successfully mined the racing circuit. Major wins lured prominent buyers such as the Vanderbilts, the Rockefellers, a Russian grand duke, and the emperor of Japan.[4] Now he came up with yet another idea.

Hugh Chalmers loved few things as much as he loved his family—he was married with four children—and his job.[5] He had little time left for anything else. But he did make room for at least one more love interest. Chalmers had a particular fondness for the increasingly popular game of baseball. His interest in the game had not gone unnoticed. In September 1909 Hugh spoke to a national meeting of advertising colleagues and illustrated many of his points with references to baseball. The baseball weekly *Sporting Life*, in reporting on the gathering, noted that "the automobile manufacturer [Chalmers], who drew a salary larger than the President of the United States while he was at Dayton with the National Cash Register, is a base ball enthusiast. He understands the game. When he was talking about the most important adjunct to advertising success called 'copy' he said: 'No copy writer can hit it off right all the time no more than a shortstop can go through a hard championship season and accept every fielding chance offered him!'"[6]

Indeed, Hugh Chalmers liked baseball. Like the automobile, the sport was growing in stature and popularity day by day. Baseball and advertising—Chalmers had connected them in that speech in 1909. The illustration caught the eye of a reporter and bought him a free bit of promotion in a national baseball publication. Why stop there? He had already decided that advertising and professional sports made for a natural coupling. Chalmers now saw an opportunity to marry the two. In 1910 he envisioned a plan to promote baseball and at the same time sell Chalmers autos. It would be good for his business. It would be good for the sport. All he needed to do was float the idea and sell it to the men who led what was fast becoming America's national game.

Not one to pussyfoot around, Chalmers went right to the top. In 1910 the "top" when it came to baseball was the National Commission. The commission had been formed in 1903, when the existing National League reluctantly accepted the fledgling American League as a second professional Major League and went about setting up a system to administer the bilateral result. That system, still in place in 1910, consisted of a three-member committee: The president of each Major League and a third member elected by the first two to serve as chair. Since the commission's inception, the chair had been August "Garry" Herrmann, president of the Cincinnati Reds of the National League. In 1910 Byron Bancroft "Ban" Johnson, the driving force behind the development of the American League and its establishment as a Major League, served as the junior circuit's one and only president. The National League president was Thomas J. Lynch, newly elected as a compromise candidate and a former National League umpire.

In addition to his executive position with the Reds, Garry Herrmann was a part owner. The Cincinnati resident was a jovial sort who mixed local politics with a strong yen for German sausages and beer. If there were worries that Herrmann's National League background would tip the scales in the direction of the old, established league, they were misplaced. Herrmann and Ban Johnson had become fast friends when the latter lived in Cincinnati and worked as a sportswriter. In fact, Herrmann voted Johnson's way more often than not, making the American League's chief executive baseball's most powerful man.

It was to the National Commission that Hugh Chalmers took his latest marketing scheme. In its March 3 edition, the *Sporting News*, baseball's second weekly newspaper, in a story datelined Cincinnati, reported that Reds' president Herrmann and his commission were reviewing a proposal from "an enterprising automobile manufacturing concern" that would reward "the best batsman in the major leagues this season" with one of the manufacturer's automobiles, a prize worth $1,500. The article speculated that the offer placed Herrmann on the horns of a dilemma. If he chose a National League player, he would face charges of "partisanship." But, if he leaned toward an American Leaguer, "that old, rank, unfounded accusation that he is toadying to Ban Johnson will be sprung." The writer figured that to avoid an issue, Herrmann would appoint a panel of newspapermen to make the choice, since it appeared "to be the only safe thing for him to do."[7]

The newspaper need not have worried. By March 12 *Sporting Life* was reporting that National League president Lynch held a communication from the auto manufacturer offering a vehicle to "the champion batsman of each major league."[8] It is perhaps from this short report that so much confusion arose over exactly what the Chalmers Motor Company offered Major League Baseball in 1910. Only one vehicle was to be awarded, and that to the single leading batsman in all of Major League Baseball.[9] This was further clarified when the National Commission met in special session on Friday, March 25, in Cincinnati. The automobile offer was only one of many topics discussed, and certainly not the most pressing or important. The tabling of a decision on the reinstatement request of Chicago Cubs' catcher Johnny Kling was front and center. Nonetheless, the offer from Chalmers garnered its share of news type.

In response to Chalmers's offer, the National Commission issued the following notice to all Major Leaguers: "This is to notify all major league players that the Chalmers Detroit Motor Company of Detroit, Michigan has offered through the National Commission, a Chalmers '30' motor car to the champion batsman of the National and American leagues for the season of 1910. This is a car that sells for $1,500. The winner will be given the privilege of selecting any particular type he might want—that is to say, a touring car, a pony tonneau, or a roadster—and full equipment."

The notice then went on to list the conditions for eligibility. In a nutshell, to be eligible for the award by season's end, an infielder or outfielder must have 350 "credited" (official) times at bat, a catcher—in deference to how the strenuous nature of the position affected regular play—250 times at bat, and a pitcher 100 times at bat. If a player played more than one position, it made no difference; however, nothing was said about a catcher (or a pitcher for that matter) who played other positions during the season. The prize would be awarded at the 1910 World Series, if possible.[10] As an aside, it was reported that secretaries John Heydler of the National League, formerly its interim president, and Robert B. McRoy of the American would compile the official averages.[11]

Although the stakes had never been higher, this was not the first time an award had been given to the baseball player with the highest average in the Major Leagues. In 1908 the George "Honey Boy" Evans Cup (named for and presented by the singer/songwriter best known for penning that old favorite "In the Good Old Summer Time") was presented to top batter Honus Wagner of the National League's Pittsburgh Pirates. In 1909 the prize went to Ty Cobb.[12] Each contest had run its course without a hitch. Nevertheless, in time, despite the fine track record, the members of the National Commission would say that when they issued their March 25, 1910, notice they harbored grave concerns about how wise it was to offer a valuable prize to participants in a game that depended so much on grace and good sportsmanship. But they had done just that, continuing to base the awarding of the prize on a simple statistic. No reservations were expressed at the time. The rules were brief and to the point. The player with the highest batting average would rule the day by virtue of a number, not open to interpretation. Politics would play no part. Personalities would play no part. Everyone—players, umpires, team officials, and fans alike—could look in a column and clearly see the winner. What could be fairer? What, indeed!

Chapter Two

There is a certain charm about .300.
—Gavvy Cravath

By 1910 automobiles were no longer an uncommon sight on the American scene. Nonetheless, owning a vehicle was still considered a luxury. The idea of winning one, even for a ballplayer at the top of his game and pay grade, was an exciting prospect. Thus it did not take the best hitters, those with a legitimate chance to drive home a nice, new Chalmers, long to offer their opinion on Hugh Chalmers's proposal.

Any list of the "best" everyday players heading into the 1910 season started with Ty Cobb and Honus Wagner. The pair and their teams had squared off against each other in the 1909 World Series, which was won by Wagner's Pirates in seven games. Furthermore, each had been the winner of the 1909 batting title in his respective league and a "Honey Boy" Evans Cup. Cobb, the fiery twenty-three-year-old outfielder from Royston, Georgia, ended the year batting .377 for his third consecutive batting title. Wagner had carried a .339 mark at season's end. At age thirty-six, the veteran shortstop was still considered by most the best player in the National League and—before the ascendancy of Cobb—by many as the top player in the entire game.

The owner of one if not more vehicles already, Cobb gauged the level of interest among his contemporaries and jumped into the Chalmers fray early on. He told *Baseball Magazine*, "The offer of an automobile is awakening a lot more enthusiasm among both players and fans than any trophy which could be offered. I would much rather win an automobile than any other prize. I hope to be lucky enough to own a new Chalmers car next fall."[1] Wagner, who had purchased his first automobile in 1907 and become friends with automobile entrepreneur extraordinaire Henry Ford, took a more laid-back approach, careful lest he express too much self-interest in the prize.[2] He told the same magazine that a "motor car for the leading batsman has the usual medals beaten a mile. It is a very generous offer on the part of Mr. Chalmers."[3]

To be sure, the list of candidates for "the leading batsman," as Honus Wagner put it, did not end with Cobb and "The Flying Dutchman." There were a number of qualified candidates, perhaps even a few dark horses. The list included Eddie Collins, the young Columbia University graduate who, after searching for a position to play on Connie Mack's rising Philadelphia Athletics squad, finally found a home at second base in 1909. He batted .347 that season, second only to Cobb. Another youngster to watch was Tris Speaker; all of twenty-one, the graceful Boston Red Sox outfielder by way of Texas was just getting started in 1909, when he finished sixth in the American League batting race with a .309 average.

The American League had at least one dark-horse candidate for the 1910 Major League batting title, but he was by no means a rookie. Napoleon Lajoie was a seasoned veteran for the Cleveland Naps—the team's name no coincidence at all. The Cleveland second baseman had already finished atop the American League in batting three times—four if you count 1902, when he batted .378 but had only 385 at bats in eighty-seven games. On the other hand, Lajoie had earned his last title in 1904, when he was but thirty and in his prime. In addition, the burden of both managing and play-ing had taken its toll. In both 1907 and 1908 the man no small number of observers considered baseball's premier hitter had seen his average fall below .300. But that was then and this was now. Frustrated with below par personal accomplishments and his team's performance on the field and in the standings, Lajoie resigned as manager of the Naps in the middle of 1909. The move had the desired effect. He ended the season third in the league, batting .324. No one knew whether the man many called "Larry," who would enter the 1910 season at thirty-five years of age, was on his way back up or merely treading water before the inevitable slide, but no one was willing to count him out either.

Over in the National League, there was Sherwood "Sherry" Magee of the Philadelphia Phillies. Born and bred in Pennsylvania, Magee had a .270 batting average in 1909, his lowest figure since he had become an outfielder for the Phillies in 1904. Yet his age—he was twenty-five entering the season—and a .328 average in 1907 kept him in the forefront when one predicted success for 1910 hitters in the race for the Chalmers. Another legitimate candidate was outfielder Mike Mitchell of the Cincinnati Reds. In 1909 the Ohio native enjoyed his best season at the plate to date, batting .310. The figure was good enough for second place behind Wagner. Teammate Dick Hoblitzell was a first baseman who had finished third at .308. He was only twenty-one years old, whereas Mitchell was twenty-nine. Both men figured to catapult off their fine 1909 seasons and make a serious run for the top. Other possibilities based on their finish in the 1909 batting race included second baseman Larry Doyle of the New York Giants (fourth, .302), his infield teammate Al Bridwell (fifth, .294), and Kitty Bransfield, the Phillies' first baseman.

Of course any player, even a pitcher, who met the at-bats qualification for his position was a potential winner of a new Chalmers. One's performance in previous seasons made no difference, nor did the perception of fellow players, the media, or the fans. The winner need not be the best ballplayer that season for his team or in his league. He need simply hit safely in enough at bats to outpoint everyone else. Kitty Bransfield was particularly instructive on that point. His batting average with the Pittsburgh Pirates bounced around so much that despite a promising start to his career, he was traded in 1905 from the Pirates to the Phillies. In the Quaker City, his batting inconsistencies continued. The first baseman hit only .233 in 1907 but then raised his average seventy-one points in 1908. His .304 average that season placed him fourth in the league. He kept it up in 1909 and finished sixth at .292. Thus, as Kitty had shown, every able-bodied man on a 1910 Major League roster could be considered a legitimate contender for what would become known as the Chalmers Award.

Today a player's batting average is considered only one of many indicators of his true hitting ability and value to his team. Statistical measures such as slugging percentage and on-base percentage are generally recognized as much truer yardsticks.[4] One's batting average appears much lower in the lineup of baseball stats. In 1910, however, batting average was the key statistic, and it was not surprising that the Chalmers Award would be based on it. Even today, according to Alan Schwarz, author of *The Numbers Game*, batting average is the game's most famous statistic.[5]

By 1910 "batting average"—at least in its present form, hits divided by at bats—had been around for thirty-eight years. The seed from which all baseball statistics sprung, the box score, first appeared in the *New York Morning News* on October 22, 1845.[6] A more recognizable statistical record of the game, authored by a young, serious-minded reporter for the *New York Clipper* named Henry Chadwick, began appearing in the late 1850s. The English-born Chadwick evolved over the years into a champion of many facets of the game. His strongest and most lasting contributions, however, may well have been to the development of baseball statistics.

In the earliest stages, baseball statistics emphasized fielding and base running at the expense of hitting. Only runs and outs were recorded as far as that phase of the game was concerned. Base hits were not counted. Pitching was totally ignored. Chadwick had an ultimate goal for his numbers game. The bearded reporter/statistician wanted to use the various averages culled from his box scores to measure a player's value to his team and thus separate the special player from the ordinary. The rules of the game could change over time, he knew, but the cold hard numbers would provide consistency to the sport and ring true.[7]

Of course, numbers could be twisted in so many ways that eventually they could deceive or even lie. In time hitting statistics, often created by Chadwick, increased in popularity, soon eclipsing all others. And just like those other statistics, these new hitting stats could deceive. The results for two increasingly popular hitting statistics, "hits per game" and "total bases per game," were tilted in favor of those placed higher in the batting order. In 1870, according to Alan Schwarz, the *Clipper* began recording times at bat. Two years later Chadwick received a letter from a fan of the game from Washington DC. One H. A. Dobson suggested rating hitters by dividing hits by at bats. Chadwick liked it. In fact, he likèd the formula and resulting statistical measure so much that he declared it the best statistic yet. In the 1872 edition of the *Beadle*, his annual baseball guide, Chadwick wrote, "According to man's chance, so should his record be. Then what is true of one player is true of all."[8]

Batting average had arrived, anointed—though not created—by the acknowledged father of baseball statistics as the reigning king of baseball yardsticks. By the early 1870s baseball was gaining great popularity. The descriptions of games were carried in word and box score by newspapers across the land. Year by year the interest in individual player statistics grew. Batting average, easy to figure out, understand, and compare, was a lock for the most popular statistic. In 1876 the National League player with the highest batting average was considered its batting champion. By 1910, a decade into an established two-league structure, the league secretaries kept the official tally, performing the function at the behest, if not the direction, of each league's president. During the season, some individual newspapers kept and reported unofficial figures as well, whereas others subscribed to the services of a reporting firm. Twenty papers or so regularly featured the tabulations of George L. Moreland of Pittsburgh.[9] The statistics of each player, including pitchers, normally appeared in the sports sections of Sunday editions of most newspapers nationwide, and a separate box containing league leaders in batting average appeared daily in many of these same papers as well. Thus, at any time during the 1910 season, it would be quite easy to view the progress of the players as they vied for the Chalmers. A fan need only remember one simple statistical number of a player and judge it against that of all others. He could root for his favorite and against all rivals. It made for interest in individual performance over and above interest in team performance and stood ready-made for a race for a grand prize.

Batting average as a key statistic earned kudos from the game's finest players. Just about everyone, fan or not, knew that anyone who hit .300 or above was a fair-country hitter. Outfielder Gavvy "Cactus" Cravath once said, "There is a certain charm about .300. If a man hits it he is a star, if he doesn't he isn't." Tris Speaker apparently agreed, pointing out that players would fight "tooth and nail" to boost their average above .300 because they recognized the prestige associated with that level of hitting.[10]

However, individual player statistics such as batting averages were not without detractors. Even Chadwick grew concerned, fearing that publishing the statistical results of games "is calculated to drive players into playing for their records rather than for their side."[11] Adding a grand prize to the mix could only increase the risk of individual performance overriding the team as the primary concern. In a lengthy season—the teams were scheduled to play 154 games in 1910—there would be times when the need to wait for the right pitch to hit would clash with the need to swing at a bad pitch to protect a runner trying to steal. A situation might call for a batter to work a pitcher for a walk. If a hit meant a car, would the batter be tempted to swing away? The players would deny it to a man, but the concern was real. As the years passed, so did Chadwick's angst. Had he unleashed a monster? He apparently believed he had, as he publicly complained that the situation had deteriorated to the point that base hits "had a certain market value."[12]

Chadwick was not alone. A Boston paper decried "the growing and prevalent custom of papers in printing the averages of the players."[13] The paper called for a protest. The hue and cry went unheeded, certainly by Hugh Chalmers, the National Commission, and the countless newspapers across the country that trumpeted individual statistics—batting averages, in particular—on a daily basis.

Batting average as a standard of evaluation had its list of critics as well. One who had the vehicle to make his views known to the baseball world was F. C. Lane, a writer and later editor for *Baseball Magazine*, a monthly publication devoted to baseball. Lane was no lightweight. He was a graduate of Boston University and performed graduate work there, as well as at Boston University Law School and the Massachusetts Institute of Technology. Writing out of Boston, Lane was not pleased that the Chalmers Award would be given to the player with the highest batting average. In Lane's view, batting average was a "worse than worthless" way to rate and rank hitters. Although written in 1916, the following quote from Lane could just as easily have been written in 1910 and explains his objections in a nutshell: "Would a system that placed nickels, dimes, quarters and fifty cent pieces on the same basis be much of a system whereby to compute a man's financial resources? . . . And yet it is precisely such a loose, inaccurate system which obtains in baseball and lies at the root of the most popular branch of baseball statistics."[14]

Lane's was an argument that made sense to many. Yet an argument against change was that by uniformly using the batting average to rank players over the years, you would have a tool that could be used to compare the players of one era to another. That argument was propounded as late as 1922 by Irving E. "Sy" Sanborn, the veteran writer for the *Chicago Tribune*. Writing in Lane's baseball monthly and agreeing with the editor that batting average offered little in meaningful guidance for determining a ballplayer's value, he asserted that "at least it has the merit of uniformity." But then he revealed a big caveat, one that perhaps had eluded Hugh Chalmers and the National Commission in March 1910. Sanborn pointed out that the statistic's one saving grace—"uniformity"—was useful only "if the official scorers are unprejudiced."[15]

Bias on the part of official scorers? Was Sy Sanborn, a close friend of Ban Johnson, the most powerful man in baseball, kidding? He most certainly was not. There was no question that official scorers would be an important factor in the quest for the Chalmers. By basing the award on hitting safely, there would be no way around it. Scoring would determine a hit as opposed to an error, a sacrifice rather than an out. And, unfortunately, the system employed by Major League Baseball was open to question.

In 1910 "official" scorers were selected and paid—usually a small amount—by the local club to work home games. Those chosen were almost always reporters from one of that city's newspapers. The scorer sat through the game, kept score, and afterward forwarded his results to the league secretary. Unlike umpires, who worked out in the open under the type of scrutiny usually afforded only scheming politicians and escaping prisoners, official scorers were rarely identified and their length of service was often short.

The selection process would not have been so bad if the reporters chosen to officially score the game were experts at or properly trained for the job they had been selected to perform. Such was not the case. There was no uniformity of training; in fact, there was really no formal training at all. Experience and knowledge were gained exclusively on the job and with no apparent supervision. Thus, the official scorer determined how each play was scored and did so without either verification or review by any higher authority. He was also in essence an employee of the home team. If he wanted to continue to earn a stipend, which was usually in addition to his reporter's pay, he should well remember who was footing the bill. This was not all that difficult since, as hard as he might work to set aside his personal opinion, a sports reporter was at heart a fan of his home team. If baseball's ruling authorities thought the system could avoid abuse, they were sorely mistaken. They had developed and perpetuated a system calculated to ignore the human element.

One who recognized the frailties in the system and attempted to bring them to light was one who should have known best: baseball's keeper of the statistics, George Moreland. Moreland's columns of statistics appeared each week in papers everywhere. The product of baseball scorers provided his livelihood. He therefore had an interest in making sure that what he reported each week was accurate and essentially fair. His job was complicated by the fact that many newspapers scored their own games through the assigned reporters, often with differing results. Thus Moreland yearned for a uniform system of scoring.

Writing in 1908 in *Baseball Magazine*, Moreland, described by the publication as a "statistical expert," stated a universal truth. He wrote, "One of the reasons that there is not more uniform scoring is from the fact that there is not a uniform scoring system." Noting that the present system might have worked in the early days, before squeeze plays, sacrifices, and the like, he argued that more complicated rules cried out for a better system. His solution: the leagues should select a set amount of "efficient" scorers and assign them to games around the two circuits just like they assigned umpires. Moreland said his piece well over a year before Chalmers offered his 30. Maybe he was anticipating the race for the "Honey Boy" Evans Cup, or perhaps he was just prescient when he offered that his plan would combat one of the "greatest evils in baseball, favoritism." For Moreland believed it "a certainty that scorers in different cities that have the honor of having a player on their team who is likely to lead the league in batting are not going to give that particular player the worst end of the deal."[16]

Baseball's moguls ignored Moreland's smoke signals. Entering the 1910 season, the system for scoring remained intact. The only way any serious problems would arise was in the unlikely event of a particularly close race in which one hit either way could make a significant difference. Instead the moguls took a "what me worry" attitude and then settled back for an uneventful batting race—one like that of the previous season, when no one came closer than thirty-eight points to Tyrus Raymond Cobb.

Chapter Three

The auto selling game is nothing for a ball player.
—Ty Cobb

It is fair to say that even if by 1910 the attention of the baseball world was not focused on Tyrus Raymond Cobb all the time, it was riveted on the Tigers' young outfielder most of the time. Much of that attention derived from his ability to hit a baseball like no other and then run the base paths with ferocity unmatched by any player to that time. An almost equal dose was derived from Cobb's antics, sometimes downright outrageous, both on the field and off, that angered opposing players, their fans, and on occasion even his own teammates. Thus, it was no small matter in Detroit and elsewhere that in early March 1910 a report in the *Detroit Free Press* assured local fans that the Tigers' prize possession was already under contract with the team. The report stated that the previous October, shortly after the team's losing effort in the 1909 World Series, team president Frank Navin presented Cobb a contract with a blank line for salary and Cobb had signed it. Navin then immediately filled in the salary, showed it to Cobb, and was rewarded with a smile.[1] Although the ballplayer would publicly deny the amount, it is said that the new contract called for Cobb to receive $9,000 per year for three years. This placed Ty in the nosebleed section when it came to high salaries; only veteran Honus Wagner received more.[2]

By paying top dollar for his services, the Tigers by all rights could have expected Cobb, who wanted nothing to do with the inconvenience of spring training, to at least just this once report on time to the team's training site in San Antonio and join his team in preparing for a new season. He was asked to report around mid-March. A report in the *Free Press* indicated that Cobb had written and assured his manager, Hugh Ambrose "Hughie" Jennings, that he would be in camp by March 20.[3] By the end of the month, he still had not shown, but now he revealed why. He was busy selling cars. Sometime during the fall of 1909, Cobb had purchased an auto dealership. He was an authorized dealer of the Hupmobile with a showroom on Broad Street in his adopted hometown of Augusta, Georgia.[4] In addition to welcoming his first offspring, Tyrus Raymond Cobb Jr., born January 30, Ty had enjoyed a busy off-season learning the game of golf, hunting, and selling automobiles. He had just not sold enough of the latter to make a comfortable exit. At the outset he assured fans that his absence was not related to his contract terms: "The only differences between myself and the Detroit club are those four autos you see on this floor. . . . I surely will be on hand when the bell rings."[5]

Apparently, Cobb wasn't letting any grass grow under his feet in Augusta. In his defense, he always kept himself in tip-top shape in those days, and in fact, when Boston's National League entry stopped in Augusta for a game with the local Minor League team, Cobb was on the field playing for the locals. Shortly thereafter it was reported that the outfielder took to bed; the strain of his training regimen and work at his dealership had been too much. Not to worry—he would catch up with the Tigers in Nashville as they played themselves north in final preparation for their season.[6]

Augusta was a particularly appropriate place for Ty Cobb to make his 1910 playing debut. The city had played an important part in the early playing career of the now firmly entrenched big leaguer, and Cobb was a local hero. Ty was born on December 18, 1886, in The Narrows, Banks County, Georgia, but he grew up in Royston, about seventy-five miles northeast of Atlanta and some eighty-five miles from Augusta. His father, William Herschel Cobb, was a schoolteacher who married Ty's mother, Amanda, when she was but twelve years old. As an educator, W. H. Cobb held high hopes for his children, particularly Ty. In his mind, a career in law or medicine would have been a good fit for his firstborn. Alas, as often happens, the father's hopes and dreams for his son did not track well with a boy who had the intelligence but not the interest in academic achievement, especially when there were other activities that interested him much more. The one activity that eventually came to overshadow all the others was baseball.

From his earliest days, Ty exhibited a competitive drive that when combined with superior athletic talent, portended greatness. At the same time, it carried a thinly veiled threat of destruction for anyone who stood in his way or his wake. Cobb's biographer, Charles C. Alexander, describes an incident that occurred when the boy was in the fifth grade. One of Cobb's male classmates missed a word in a spelling bee, which found the boys in the class faced off against the girls. Cobb physically attacked the young man who had flubbed the word. He had cost Ty's team a victory.[7] Years later Cobb expressed a philosophy that had been second nature all his life: "I was a man who saw no point in losing, if I could win."[8]

Another life-shaping philosophy became so much a part of Cobb that he wore it like his skin—white skin, that is. The youngster grew up in a portion of the country that tolerated blacks, worked and even played with them. But they were to be subservient at all times, taking pains to obey orders from the superior white man, and by all means, they were to know their place. When it came to a man with a hair-trigger temper like Cobb, if your skin was black, you stepped across that line at your own risk.

Before long Ty's stubborn disposition and interest in baseball would collide with his father's desire for him to follow a more traditional and respected career path. Despite an intense longing to please his father and win his respect, the youth felt the time had come to make a break.

Royston had two town baseball teams: the Rompers for the younger players and the Reds for the adults. Initially, the fourteen-year-old Ty Cobb played for the Rompers, but when an opportunity presented itself to play as a fill-in for the Reds, he took advantage of it with all of his usual gusto. The older, more experienced Reds took notice. Cobb was asked to travel with the team. His father reluctantly granted his approval. Again young Cobb's play stood out, and the acclaim he received for his initial successes, particularly at this higher level of play, only strengthened his resolve to make baseball the central part of his life.

In 1903 Ty received encouragement from a fellow ballplayer to give professional ball a try. The South Atlantic (Sally) League was newly formed. It was a Class C league with six teams in Georgia and neighboring states. Cobb wrote to all and received in return a letter from one, the Augusta entry, the Tourists, inviting him at his own expense to a tryout. Now the easy part was over. The hard part would be convincing Professor Cobb. However, after a monumental struggle, that highest hurdle was achieved. The professor even provided Ty with sufficient expenses to try to win a job he must have hoped the son would never attain.

Although he did not play in an exhibition game, Cobb was still with the Augusta team on opening day, and he earned a start when injury to a regular left the manager a player short. Despite an impressive performance—a single and double in four at bats—he was cut from the team. He learned of a semipro team that needed players in Anniston, Alabama. He yearned to go, to give it at least one more try, but he felt compelled once again to seek his father's consent. He telephoned him, expecting a quick hook. He received just the opposite. His father told him to go on to Alabama and in closing offered what he might have intended as words of encouragement but that could as easily have been taken as a final warning: "Don't come home a failure." Ty took it as the former. Years later he told readers that his father's words were a "blessing," adding, "My father put more determination in me than even he knew."9 The conversation formed another large chunk of the burning cauldron that would become the mature Ty Cobb.

The league in which Anniston's team played was an unsanctioned "outlaw league," meaning it was not recognized by Organized Baseball's National Commission. It was, however, a cut or two above town ball, and moreover, its players received pay for their trouble. Here the newly energized Cobb flourished, leading the league in hitting. His fine play was noticed as far away as Augusta. Three months after Cobb began playing in Anniston, Augusta's Tourists, by then under new management, extended Cobb an invitation to return, which he readily accepted. He finished the season with the Tourists batting .237, not as bad as it might seem in a league where hits were hard to come by. Batting average notwithstanding, Cobb was offered a contract by the Tourists for the 1905 season. He agreed, but only after successfully doing a little negotiating on his own behalf.

It just so happened that as they had in 1904, the Detroit Tigers made Augusta their 1905 spring training base. While there, they played exhibition games with the Tourists in exchange for the right of claim to any Tourist player they wanted for their own. In 1904 Cobb had not played against the Tigers, but he certainly played against them in 1905. The big leaguers took notice of his live bat and aggressive style on the base paths. Germany Schaefer, the Tigers' flaky second baseman, remarked that Cobb was "the craziest ballplayer I ever saw."[10] Still, when the 1905 season began, Cobb remained a member of the Augusta Tourists, a regular in the outfield on a less than mediocre team that bored its fans and its regular right fielder to boot. Only after the team's veteran outfielder and captain George Leidy took over and took Cobb under his wing—providing wise counsel and individualized training—did Cobb begin to channel his talent in the direction of the big leagues.[11]

By July 1905 Cobb was playing better ball than anyone in the Sally League. Scouts for the Tigers and other big league teams regularly attended his games. His play earned him a substantial raise. Then, in early August, the young man suffered a personal tragedy. He learned via telegram that his father had been shot and killed—by his mother no less. Amanda Cobb said that her husband had told her he would be away overnight.[12] Hearing noises on the rooftop and seeing someone attempting to open the bedroom window, she grabbed a firearm and shot the supposed intruder, who turned out to be William.[13] A plausible reason for William's presence on the roof was the rampant rumor in Royston that summer of his wife's infidelity. Professor Cobb may have feigned travel in order to catch his wife in the act of an evening with a lover.

Mrs. Cobb was charged with voluntary manslaughter but eventually acquitted by a jury that was never told of the alleged marital infidelity. Ty, who was not particularly close with his mother, was now left to carry on without the person he loved and admired most. Rather than dampen his spirit, however, the loss only deepened his resolve to succeed. By dominating the game of baseball, the game Ty loved, like no one else, he would prove to all that his father had been correct in allowing him to pursue this avenue in life.

The best place to prove his case was in Augusta, and a few days later, Cobb was back with his team. But not for long, for by the end of August, he learned his services had been purchased by the Detroit Tigers, by then a second-division team beset by injuries and looking for an infusion of new blood. In a period of just a few weeks, eighteen-year-old Cobb had lost his father and gained a big league job. If only he could have shared the news with the person who had mattered the most.

In Detroit the Sally League's batting champion—Ty ended up with a league best .326—played in all the Tigers' remaining games. From the start local fans were impressed with their brand new left-hand batting, right-hand throwing outfielder. His .240 batting average and occasional flashes of brilliance impressed his Tigers bosses, if not so much his new teammates. He received a raise and looked forward to his first spring training in 1906 as a Major Leaguer.

When Cobb reported to Augusta in March 1906, he probably assumed that he would no longer be considered a rookie ballplayer in the eyes of his teammates. As a rookie in 1905, Cobb had received hazing. It was after all a baseball tradition. It is doubtful he accepted it; rather he endured it. In his mind, by 1906 it would all be over, a thing of the past. This was not, however, how his Tiger teammates saw it. The treatment he received that year, beginning in training camp, was far worse than what he had experienced in his brief time with the Detroit club the previous season. Rather than reaching out to embrace his teammates he withdrew, often eating by himself, away from the others. One thing seems certain: Cobb had made an enemy on the team, and it was the wrong one—the popular outfielder, Matty McIntyre. In 1905 McIntyre, an entrenched northerner who was born in Connecticut and grew up on Staten Island, was a regular Tigers outfielder who played in 131 games for the third-place finishers. The situation with McIntyre was complicated in the spring of 1906 by the arrival of David Jefferson "Davy" Jones, a young outfielder who was purchased in the off-season from Minneapolis of the American Association, an upper-level minor league. Since the veteran slugger Sam Crawford was firmly entrenched in one outfield position, Cobb, Jones, and McIntyre were left to vie for the remaining two places on the field. Early on in the competition, Cobb suspected that McIntyre had enlisted many on the team to make it particularly difficult for him to succeed. He was probably correct, given the intensity of the hazing.

In addition to hostile teammates that spring, Cobb dealt with his mother's trial for murder and a case of tonsillitis, which resulted in surgery. Thus it was little wonder that when the Tigers opened their season at home in Bennett Park, Cobb was the odd man out among the team's four outfielders. A few games later, however, Sam Crawford injured his leg, and Ty was in the starting lineup to stay. His starting role exacerbated the tension between him and Matty McIntyre. As a result of the problems with his teammates, Cobb became a loner. Although pitcher "Wild" Bill Donovan and new teammate Davy Jones made passes at friendship, Ty lived by himself, took meals alone, and generally spent his off-field time by himself. In the early portion of the 1906 season, the Tigers played well, and Cobb's batting average was among the best in the league. By midseason Cobb's average had tailed off. It appears that despite his grittiness, the pressure he placed on himself and the lack of support from his teammates had taken a toll. Bill Armour announced in mid-July that his young outfielder had problems with his stomach and was headed back to Detroit for a rest. A week later surgery was performed on what probably was an ulcer. More may in fact have been at work here. After studying the contemporary reports, Cobb biographer Alexander believes his subject suffered "some kind of emotional and physical collapse."[14]

Cobb's absence, as well as other players' injuries and weak pitching, pushed the Tigers into an August swoon. Although Cobb returned to form in early September, the season concluded with the Tigers in sixth place. Just before the season ended, Cobb and McIntyre went at it again. They stood in the outfield pointing fingers at each other as a single rolled to the outfield fence and resulted in a two-run, inside-the-park home run. The Tigers' pitcher at the time was Ed Siever. He was a confirmed McIntyre supporter and Cobb hater. Once in the dugout, Siever hurled invectives at

Cobb. Later that evening the quarrel continued at the team hotel. Although Cobb apparently did his best to avoid a physical confrontation, when Siever continued to antagonize him, he went on the attack, administering a severe beating to the overmatched Siever. Although the fight did nothing to help the cause with his fellow players, according to biographer Richard Bak, the "ferocity of Ty's counterattack did more than serve notice to the anti-Cobb group to keep their distance. It also underscored an elemental cruel streak in Cobb's nature, a flaw that would create countless unflattering headlines over the coming years."15 Furthermore, it brought a particularly sour end to a year of disillusionment for a future superstar. His .316 batting average, attained in ninety-eight games, was good enough for sixth in the league, but even a competitor such as Ty might have traded a few of those points for one or two good friends on his own team.

The sixth-place finish cost manager Bill Armour his job. His replacement, Hughie Jennings, a thirty-eight-year-old veteran ballplayer and an important cog in the famous Baltimore Orioles' machine of the 1890s, became the sixth Tigers' manager in seven years. The choice would bear fruit for the team and its young slugger, but not before additional strife. When Cobb arrived in Augusta in March to begin training for the 1907 season, one of Jennings's first acts was to meet with the outfielder and attempt to counsel him on becoming a part of the team. The lecture apparently did not take. A few days later, when Ty arrived at the ballpark where the team trained, he was approached by a black groundskeeper named "Bungy." The man had known Cobb from his prior playing days in Augusta and apparently was excited to see him. When he extended his hand by way of greeting, Cobb pushed it away. When Bungy again came close, Cobb slapped him and chased him toward the clubhouse. The man's wife, who was in the area, began yelling at the enraged Cobb, who then turned on her, grabbing her and trying to choke her.

Several Tigers players were in the area and saw the ruckus. Among them was Charley Schmidt, a catcher who had once stepped into the ring for a boxing exhibition against heavyweight contender Jack Johnson. Like Cobb, he was from the South, but he disliked any male who would hurt a woman, no matter the color of her skin. Unlike Cobb, the catcher was popular with his teammates. He stepped forward, words were exchanged, and the two men began to fight. Teammates stepped in to separate the pair as Hughie Jennings looked on in wonder, realizing his message to Cobb had gone unheeded.

Jennings was no fool. He knew that Cobb possessed the skills necessary for stardom. Nonetheless, he and Tigers management saw an opportunity to exchange the difficult outfielder for a veteran player with considerable skills and at the same time rid themselves of a cancer that could destroy any hopes of team success. Acting quickly—in fact, mere hours after Cobb's incident with the groundskeeper—Jennings contacted the manager of the rival Cleveland Naps, Napoleon Lajoie, proposing a trade of Cobb for Naps outfielder Elmer Flick. In 1905 Flick had led the American League in batting with a .308 average. He had bettered that in 1906 by three points. He had yet to sign his contract for 1907, and the Tigers were now offering Lajoie an extremely viable option. The Naps' field general and star second baseman did not bite. He had heard the stories about Cobb and his difficult disposition. He turned down the Tigers' offer. Flick signed with the Naps three days later and played well in 1907. In subsequent years he produced little. He was finished with baseball by 1910, although his career résumé eventually placed him in the Hall of Fame. Cobb, on the other hand, was just getting started.

Hughie Jennings listened to one more offer for Cobb—this from the New York Highlanders—but turned it down and prepared to move forward with the temperamental outfielder on his roster. Ty was not so sure. He now demanded a trade, but the ship had sailed.

No one then knew it, but Cobb and his Tigers were about to have a banner year. Still, there was one unresolved matter. An article had appeared in an Atlanta newspaper in which Cobb allegedly claimed he would win a fight with Charley Schmidt or, for that matter, any of his Tigers teammates. Although Cobb would deny the claims attributed to him, Schmidt was determined to accept the challenge. He stood five feet eleven inches and weighed a rock-solid 200 pounds, substantially more than the six-foot-one-inch, 175-pound Cobb, and thoroughly thrashed him, breaking Ty's nose. Cobb missed several exhibition games and then returned to a different atmosphere. Apparently, the fact that he had taken his beating like a man finally won him points with his teammates. Perhaps that is what happened, perhaps not. A shift of player personnel by Jennings might have helped just as much. As the Tigers began play in 1907, the ever-popular Matty McIntyre won a starting position in left field over Davy Jones. McIntyre could no longer blame Cobb for his lack of playing time. Cobb now played right field, and Sam Crawford patrolled center.

The newly constituted Tigers of 1907 were a winning proposition. They won their first American League pennant with a record of 92-68. Ty Cobb, running, fielding, and hitting with reckless abandon, was a major factor in their success. He carried off an American League batting crown with an average of .350. His 212 base hits led the league as well. Even a dismal performance when he hit but .200 in the World Series, an event lost by the Tigers to the National League's Chicago Cubs four games to none with one tie, failed to extinguish the flame that was Cobb. His teammates now put up with him, even though they still did not much like him. The Detroit press and the team's fans, in contrast, adored him. Even newspaper writers and fans loyal to the opposition gave grudging admiration at the same time they, and the Tigers' playing opponents, took a dim view of his intimidating tactics, like sliding into bases spikes high, ready to fight in the blink of an eye.

During the 1907–8 off-season, Cobb found time to become engaged to a lass from Augusta and stir up yet another hornet's nest by holding out for a three-year contract at $5,000 per year. The fact that veteran star Sam Crawford readily signed and returned his contract for $4,000 and the other Tigers players had reached agreement without fuss merely served to further distance Ty from his teammates. When he finally capitulated, inking a one-year $4,000 deal, one of the first things he purchased was a brand new Chalmers two-seater.[16]

Despite a slow start, the 1908 Tigers were in the thick of the American League race by midseason and well on their way to their second-straight American League championship. Apparently, Cobb's teammates put aside their disdain for his preseason salary antics because on the whole the Tigers, including Cobb, were an amicable bunch. Unfortunately, as the young

Tigers outfielder enjoyed yet another stellar season on the playing field, the dark side of his personality resurfaced. This time the circumstances were revealed publicly in a Detroit municipal courtroom.

The incident, occurring early in the season, took place when Cobb was leaving the Hotel Pontchartrain, one of his favorite downtown Detroit hangouts. As he left the hotel, he stepped on fresh asphalt. The laborers who had installed the coating were still in the area. One of them, Fred Collins, a black man, angrily told Cobb to step away from the area. Additional words were exchanged, Cobb punched the man, and then he left. Collins filed charges, and a few days later, Cobb was in municipal court attempting to defend his actions and claiming that "the Negro" had offended him.[17] Once again it was a case of a black man who, in Cobb's view, didn't know his "place." The judge heard Cobb's not-guilty plea, found him guilty, and then suspended the sentence. Cobb later paid Collins seventy-five dollars to avoid a civil lawsuit and the incident was over, but not before it added to the growing stain on Ty's record.

How this affair affected Cobb's tenuous relationship with his teammates is unknown. However, in August, while his team was still in the throes of a pennant race, Cobb's impulsiveness and egotism struck again. This time it involved an affair of the heart. On August 2, a day after a Sunday afternoon loss to the Boston Red Sox at Bennett Park in Detroit, Cobb left the city by train for Augusta, where two days later he married seventeen-year-old Charlie Marion Lombard. Cobb's exit from Detroit, his team, and the American League pennant race was totally unexpected and unannounced. He returned to his team and the field on August 9, much to the delight of the Tigers' fans if not his fellow players. Sam Crawford spoke about the matter years later: "He just walked out and left us flat in midseason."[18]

Once he was back on the playing field, Cobb's batting average tailed off a bit, but he and his teammates still had enough gas in the tank to win a zany pennant race that saw the Chicago White Sox and Cleveland Naps, as well as the Tigers, enter the final weekend of the season with a chance to carry off the flag. The National League race was even more wild and woolly, given Fred Merkle's monumental base-running blunder. In the end, the Cubs prevailed over Merkle's Giants in a replay of a controversial incomplete game, setting up a repeat of the 1907 World Series. Cobb ended the year with a batting average of .324. He led his league for the second consecutive season in that category, as well as in hits and several other hitting categories. But none of these feats meant anything in the 1908 World Series. Although Cobb hit much better than he had in 1907, the Tigers lost once more to the Cubs by a count of four games to one.

During the off-season Cobb indulged in his growing fascination with the automobile. Shortly after the World Series, he attended automobile races in Atlanta and then embarked on a trip that began in New York City and wound its way south by motor caravan to culminate with a stop in Winston, North Carolina. During the trip Cobb and others promoted a national "good roads" campaign. Needless to say, he was the main attraction.[19]

Cobb reported to San Antonio for 1909 spring training in relatively good stead with his teammates and showing great affection for manager Hughie Jennings. Before long, however, he was engaged in a war of words with catcher Lou Criger, a fine defensive catcher who had played a good portion of his career with the Boston Americans but now served time behind the plate for the St. Louis Browns. When Criger bragged to the local newspapers that he had Cobb's number, Cobb issued a challenge. He would steal a base at Criger's expense the next time they met. He did so, and the competition continued throughout the season. On one occasion Cobb caught Criger with his spikes as he slid into home plate. The feud mainly concerned Criger, who moved to another club for the following season, but many of his Browns teammates remained and had long memories.

A more serious spiking incident occurred during the 1909 regular season. Once again the Tigers were in the thick of an American League pennant race. This time around their chief rivals were manager Connie Mack and his Philadelphia Athletics. In August the rivals faced off in Detroit in a three-game series. Early in the first game, Cobb attempted to steal third base on what turned out to be ball four. As Athletics third baseman Frank Baker attempted to tag Ty with the ball resting in his bare hand, Cobb's spiked right shoe sliced into Baker's forearm, producing a small cut. Baker's teammates stormed the field, demanding Cobb's ejection. He remained in the game, as did a bandaged Baker. Later in the game, Cobb slid into second base, toppling the Athletics' young second baseman Eddie Collins. It seemed just part of an intense late-season game. Both incidents might have blown over had it not been for an uncharacteristically heated protest from the normally reserved Connie Mack. When Mack called Cobb one of baseball history's dirtiest players, it did not go unnoticed, particularly by league president Ban Johnson, who issued a stern warning to Cobb. Later Johnson reviewed the evidence and backed down. When the dust settled, however, the accusations served only to further sully an already tarnished reputation, and according to Cobb, the incident "always stuck in my craw."[20]

A few days later, another particularly ugly incident occurred, this time in Cleveland. Cobb, returning late from an evening of theater and supper, engaged in a verbal spat with yet another black hotel employee. This time the fracas involved an elevator operator who, to Cobb's Southern sensibility, had stepped out of line. Cobb slapped the man and then confronted the hotel's black night watchman when he intervened. The night watchman clubbed Cobb with his nightstick. As the pair, now on the floor, continued to tussle, Cobb pulled a knife from his pocket and slashed out at his adversary. The night watchman in turn pulled a pistol and struck Cobb once more before others intervened. The night watchman claimed injuries, sought criminal charges, and filed a civil lawsuit against the Tigers' outfielder. The incident was widely reported outside of Detroit, less so in home environs. Tigers management, in particular Frank Navin, offered the night watchman a cash settlement, and for a small sum, he dropped all charges. The Cleveland police authorities, however, refused to buckle under and threatened to arrest Cobb the next time he set foot in Ohio.[21]

The atmosphere was still charged when Cobb and his mates traveled to Philadelphia for a crucial four-game series with the Athletics. By the time the team arrived, Cobb had received numerous threats. An already boiling cauldron was heated further by the local press. Fully aware of the rising tensions, the city of Philadelphia, wanting no part of the threatened violence, sent a significant police force to shiny new Shibe Park. They, as well as just about every other spectator, paid particular attention to right field, where a nervous Cobb plied his trade. Following a hitless first game, Cobb returned to the hotel. Later that evening he took a walk, winning friends when he entered the teeth of a confrontational throng that opened a path to allow him—the enemy—through. Ty further ingratiated himself with the locals as the series resumed, and he began to perform in his usual relentless style. The suddenly adoring fans were even willing to forgive Cobb when he spiked one of their heroes, shortstop Jack Barry. Although the Athletics took the crucial series three games to one, by season's end the Tigers once again stood atop the American League standings. The Athletics finished three and a half games in arrears.

This time around the Tigers' World Series opponents were the Pittsburgh Pirates, led by shortstop Honus Wagner. In the eyes of many fans, the 1909 Series would quite simply be Cobb versus Wagner. For his considerable troubles, Cobb had captured his third-consecutive league batting crown, finishing the season with a .377 average—more than thirty points higher than runner-up Eddie Collins—and leading his league in almost every other batting category too. Few in baseball history had ever performed as well offensively. Wagner was no slouch with the bat either. Now in his tenth season with the Pirates, the stout shortstop had just won his sixth National League batting title with an average of .339. It figured to be a mighty battle between two of baseball's finest talents. Nonetheless, World Series titles are won by teams, not individuals. In this instance Wagner played much better than Cobb, but the Tigers played their best World Series yet, almost securing their first world title. Still, their fine overall effort was not quite good enough. The Detroiters succumbed to the Pirates, four games to three. The third World Series loss in a row left Cobb chagrined. He later lamented, "I was too young when that part of my career happened."[22]

During his World Series travels, the still-young Cobb had carefully skirted the borders of neighboring Ohio. A few days after the Series ended, Cobb appeared in Cleveland, accompanied by Navin and legal counsel, to plead not guilty to felonious assault. Later that fall he agreed to a plea bargain whereby he pled guilty to assault and battery and paid a fine of a hundred dollars and costs.[23] His legal woes behind him, baseball's greatest player and most notorious scoundrel needed only to report to the Tigers'

1910 spring camp to add to his growing legend. Just a few unsold cars now stood in the way.

The 1910 edition of Ty Cobb did not link up with his team in Nashville as advertised, but instead hooked up with them in Evansville, Indiana, a few days later. On April 8 he manned right field and banged out a pair of hits in a Tigers victory over the locals. That same day he told reporters he was finished with the business of selling automobiles. According to Cobb, in March his dealership's sales fell somewhere between $12,000 and $17,000. He felt he would have sold even more vehicles in April. He told the *Free Press*, "The auto selling game is nothing for a ball player, because it gets good just when he should be reporting and making ready to earn his baseball salary."[24]

As the Tigers played their way to Detroit to prepare for a season home opener with Cleveland, they stopped for an exhibition game in Cincinnati with the Reds of the National League. Perhaps as a little incentive for those players interested in winning a batting title, Hughie Jennings and several other players rode to the field in a Chalmers Pathfinder.[25] Cobb was one of those on board, and this man who loved speed both on the base paths and the roadway was almost certainly aware that a Chalmers vehicle had recently finished first in a ten-mile handicap race run at Daytona Beach, Florida. It was equally certain that Ty Cobb probably needed a new Chalmers vehicle less than any ballplayer in the Major Leagues, yet he wanted one the most, not for its value but for what its addition to his growing fleet signified.

Chapter Four

I have never had any enemies off the field.
—Napoleon Lajoie

Although the chase for the 1910 league titles and the world championship began in mid-April, it would take several weeks for the leaders in the race for the Chalmers to emerge. Nonetheless, the path to the Major League batting title—one fraught with potholes—began in the ballparks of each of the sixteen Major League teams. One portion of the plot played out in the batter's box and the other in the press box, where the official scorer weighed in.

The practice of compiling and maintaining a statistical record of each season's play was still relatively new to the game. The National League began keeping official batting average statistics and several other statistics for individual players in 1903. The American League followed suit in 1905.[1] An article written in 1913 discussed what went on behind the scenes in Organized Baseball. The article, written by F. C. Lane of *Baseball Magazine*, included a description of the method the National League used for keeping individual records. The baseball official responsible for tracking individual and team statistics was the league secretary, in this case John Heydler.

The official scorer for the home team in any particular game—keep in mind that individual was almost always a local sports reporter, untrained and appointed by the home team in no uniform fashion—was required to make a daily report of those games to which he was assigned. Once received by the league secretary each report was reviewed, columns were added up and checked for accuracy, and the winning and losing pitchers were identified. Whereas the numbers themselves were not open to interpretation, the decision as to which pitcher won or lost the game was open to interpretation and sometimes became a matter of judgment. The figures were transferred to a ledger for each individual player. What resulted for each Major League season was a separate sheet documenting on a day-by-day basis the hitting and fielding accomplishments of each person who batted in a game that season. Each pitcher's various pitching statistics were kept on a separate sheet on a day-by-day basis as well. The entries were made using red or black ink. Black ink was used for home games and red ink for statistics generated on the road.

Team records were also kept on a separate form. The idea was to cross-check the team records with the individual statistics in order to discover and eliminate errors. Umpires provided separate reports on each game, although these reports did not concern themselves so much with statistics as with particular events that occurred in the individual game, such as how the players and teams behaved.[2]

National League Secretary Heydler described his duties as follows:

According to the baseball rules every official scorer forwards his report of the game to the secretary of the league generally immediately after the contest. The records must reach the office not later than five days after a game, otherwise there is a penalty of $2 for such an offence. The records are all sent in on printed sheets prescribed by the rules.

The Secretary has no right to alter the report in any way so far as base hits or errors are concerned. The only instance where anything is left to his judgment is the decision in certain cases crediting a pitcher with a win or loss of a game. . . . But the secretary has no authority to further alter the reports submitted to him in any other way. He merely compiles the records which are sent him and in the fall sends out the final averages.[3]

The procedure outlined by Heydler was in place in 1912. However, there is no reason to believe the procedure was any different in 1910. Nor is there any reason to believe that the methods prescribed by the National League differed from those of Ban Johnson's American League. In that league, official statistics were kept—at least through 1910—by league secretary Robert McRoy.[4] When McRoy was hired away from the jewelry business by President Johnson in 1900, he was still a teenager. Born in Chicago on July 8, 1882, and raised in that city, McRoy teamed up with Johnson the same year the latter's Western League, headquartered in the Windy City, became the American League. By 1908 *Sporting Life* described McRoy as "one of the rising young men of base ball." The newspaper considered him "quiet" and "unobtrusive" and "yet he is shrewd, discreet and diplomatic in high degree. . . . In the compilation of averages, also, is young McRoy expert."[5] By the end of 1910 McRoy would need these attributes and more just to stay afloat.

From opening day the problems with compiling stats and filing reports began to unfold. In unseasonably warm Detroit, where more than fourteen thousand fans, or "cranks" as they were called back then, attended, Cleveland drew first blood with a 9–7 win over the Tigers in ten innings. The warm weather apparently agreed with the batters for both sides. There were a total of twenty-four hits.

According to box scores in newspapers around the country, including the so-called official box score carried by the *Sporting News*, Ty Cobb, batting third and playing right field, had a pair of doubles in five trips to the plate for his day's work. However, when Cobb's statistics for the day were entered into the record back at league offices in Chicago by Robert McRoy, he was credited with three hits. Apparently unbeknownst to the other sportswriters in attendance who were tracking the game for their respective papers, a play in the third inning that was scored as an error by some writers was ruled a hit by the sportswriter assigned as official scorer.[6]

Inconsistencies in reporting of game statistics like that of the Detroit-Cleveland matchup of opening day occurred and recurred throughout the season, adding confusion and creating uncertainty until the end of the season and beyond in the race for the Chalmers. No one, not players, club officials, sportswriters for the many newspapers then existing, or interested baseball fans rooting for their favorite players on their hometown teams, could read a box score at work or in the comfort of his or her living room—even the boxes in the *Sporting News* carrying the very imprimatur of the league offices—and take comfort in the accuracy of the statistics contained therein. That is because one eyewitness scorer's sacrifice or error might be another's hit, one's count of four at bats someone else's mistaken three, and on and on. Thus, the summary of box scores resulting in standings of league leaders kept independently by some newspapers or purchased by others from a subscription service, such as George Moreland's of Pittsburgh, was tainted as well. The only ones who would know the whole story when it came to who was actually the leading hitter average-wise in the Major Leagues at any one time were the league secretaries. And they weren't talking until the season was over—that is, except for one time in mid-July, when, as was its custom, the American League, through Robert McRoy, released its list of the official batting averages in the league through games of July 4.

Up until midseason, interest in who was leading the Majors in batting was rather limited, confined to the occasional remark hidden in the column or postgame notes of one writer or another. One item in the *Detroit Free Press* mentioned that prior to the home opener in Detroit, the Chalmers Company sponsored a luncheon at the Hotel Pontchartrain. Almost certainly scheduled to drum up some early publicity, the affair was attended by sportswriters of both Cleveland and Detroit newspapers, including Henry P. Edwards, the well-respected sports scribe for the *Cleveland Plain Dealer*.[7] Another tidbit in *Sporting Life* in mid-May mentioned that fans in Cleveland were betting Lajoie would win the car, while Detroit fans were placing their dollars on Cobb, this because the pair had been among their league's leaders in average from the start.[8] A few weeks later, Tris Speaker of Boston's Red Sox was added to that mix by this same baseball weekly as he climbed up the batting chart. In the National League, the early thoroughbreds were Sherry Magee of the Phillies, the Reds' Dode Paskert, and Fred Snodgrass of the New York Giants. The impact of Snodgrass's high average as it related to the batting race—on June 25 he was reportedly at .439—was cushioned by his limited play. At that point, more than two months into the season, he had batted "officially" but forty-one times, whereas Paskert had a more substantial log at 115 at bats and Magee even more at 149.

Then, in July, the individual American League averages through games of July 4 as reported by official scorers and added up by the league's secretary—the only bean counter who mattered—were released. Now interest began to intensify. Those on top of that league's standings, as well as those in the senior circuit plodding along with their "unofficial" numbers, finally knew who they were really competing against, and those below knew whom they must pass, and at what hitting pace, to have a chance for a new car. On top in the American League was Napoleon Lajoie, hitting at a torrid .403 pace through sixty-four games and 236 at bats. His chief competition—really the only regular within serious striking distance in either league—was Ty Cobb at .379, achieved in 269 at bats. Speaker, despite the attention thrown his way, rested at .330, with serious work ahead if he hoped to land on top.[9] Over in the National League, Fred Snodgrass was unofficially batting .375, but with only thirty-three games and eighty-eight at bats, he still had to increase his playing time significantly to be a factor in the race. Dode Paskert had certainly played in enough games (sixty), but at .335 he trailed Lajoie and Cobb by a ton.[10]

The notion that many baseball observers had harbored for some time, that Napoleon Lajoie at age thirty-five had newfound magic in his batting stick, now seemed a hard fact. Another hard fact: The race for the Chalmers from this time forward would almost certainly be clearly focused on Ty Cobb, the fans' favorite whipping boy, and Nap Lajoie, their darling, the man many consider the American League's first superstar.

Baseball aficionados had been tightly focused on Lajoie for some time now—ever since he stepped onto the top rung of baseball's professional ladder in 1896 with the Philadelphia Phillies of the old National League. At that time the Phillies' infielder was twenty-one years old, and the only question fans had was, how does one pronounce his last name? Most settled on "Laj-way," although, according to the subject of their growing affection, his family name was French and sounded like "La-zhwa" when correctly pronounced.

The Lajoies came by their French name honestly. The family can trace its roots in the late 1700s to Louilly, Auxerres, France, although by 1830 at least a portion of the clan was in Canada, where Napoleon's father, Jean Baptiste Lajoie, was born. When he was in his early twenties, Jean Baptiste married Celina Guertin. The young couple lived near Montreal, and soon after their wedding, they began building a rather large family there. In their thirteenth year of marriage, the Lajoies' offspring numbered four with one on the way. Jean Baptiste to this point knew only farming. He was finding it increasingly difficult to eke out an existence for his growing family. Thus, following the birth of their fifth child, a son, the Lajoies moved south across the border to Rutland, Vermont. A few years and another child later, Jean Baptiste sought work in Woonsocket, Rhode Island, a river town with an abundance of textile mills, attendant job opportunities, and a large population. Jean Baptiste soon secured work as a driver and laborer. Still, given the size of the family, money was scarce. The older Lajoie children, despite their relative youth, went to work in the mills as soon as possible. Another son was born in 1871. Then on September 5, 1874, the last of the couple's children was born. His name was Napoleon (no middle name). His birth certificate indicates that he was the eighth (six boys, two girls) of eleven children born to Jean Baptiste and Celina. The fate of the other three Lajoie children remains unknown.[11]

The financial plight of the Lajoie family only worsened in March 1881, when Jean Baptiste passed away. Napoleon was but six years old at the time of his father's death. By the time young Napoleon was in his early teens, he was already working in the mills, his earnings necessary to help fill the family coffers. Because of his laboring efforts, his education was quite limited. Despite these hardships, Napoleon found time for at least one enjoyable pursuit: he began to play baseball when he was ten years old. His widowed mother, fearing injury to her youngest, did not want him to play. He played anyway. His young teammates called him "Sandy" so that when they shouted his name, his mother would not realize her black-haired son was on the field.[12]

Napoleon's family lived in a number of homes in the Globe Village section of Woonsocket. The first organized baseball team Napoleon played for was the Globe Stars, made up of a group of youngsters from his neighborhood. By the time he was nineteen, Napoleon was playing for the Woonsockets, a semipro team that traveled considerably throughout the region. Napoleon played regularly and primarily as a catcher. Early on one attribute that stood out with regard to Napoleon, or Sandy, as he was called at the time, was his size. He was six foot one and weighed close to two hundred pounds, an unusually big man for the times. Another attribute, one particularly important for a young athlete who liked to play baseball, was his ability to hit a ball. Soon word spread about the young Woonsocket hitter. Nonetheless, Napoleon's chief responsibility was working hard to help support his struggling family. In that regard, he first left the mills to work as a clerk in a local home furnishings store but then opted for a job at a livery stable driving a "hack," or horse-drawn wagon, to deliver wood and coal and even take people to weddings and funerals. Here in the offices of the Consolidated Livery Stable in January 1896, the twenty-year-old Sandy Lajoie began his real journey toward baseball immortality. Lajoie described it thusly: "One day I was sitting in the office when [Charlie] Marston came in and said, 'Can you tell me where I can find that big French kid called Sandy?' 'You must mean me,' I said. And, do you know, he drew up a contract on the back of an envelope for $100 a month for me to play for Fall River the next year. Since I was making $7.50 a week as a hack driver, that $100 looked like all the money in the world."[13]

The complete story is a bit more complicated. In the first place, Fall River was a Massachusetts team that played in the New England League and as such was a professional Minor League team. Second, Charlie Marston was the team's new manager. Marston was standing in front of Lajoie in the livery stable office because he had received a tip from Fred Woodcock, a pitcher who had spent a brief time with Pittsburgh of the old National League. Woodcock had faced Lajoie and his Woonsockets and was impressed with the youngster's skill at the plate. In fact, he was so impressed that he asked Lajoie to play for his own semipro team. Nap replied by postcard, "I am out for the stuff." Woodcock knew then that it would take professional money to snag the Woonsocket slugger. When his friend Marston took over the managerial reins at Fall River and found himself in need of an outfielder for a season fast approaching, Woodcock suggested Lajoie. The offer of a hundred dollars per month for the five months of the baseball season was a veritable beacon for one earning thirty dollars a month. Lajoie signed on—perhaps right on the back of that envelope—and reported that spring to Fall River.[14]

The recent addition to the Fall River roster quickly found New England League pitching to his liking. Marston inserted Lajoie into the starting lineup, and he became a fixture in the Fall River outfield. All told Lajoie played in eighty games for Fall River in 1896. According to Lajoie's biographer, J. M. Murphy, he batted .429.[15] Needless to say, a number of National League teams were showing considerable interest in the Fall River outfielder before the season was up. Although several members of New England's sporting press dropped hints about Lajoie's prowess in hopes of encouraging interest in the rookie from the city's big league entry, the Boston Beaneaters, the team's manager, Frank Selee, apparently did not bite, even though he saw Lajoie play on July 31. Lajoie was not particularly impressive that day, going 1 for 4 at the plate.[16] Also in the stands that day was Billy Nash, manager of the struggling Philadelphia Phillies. This was not the first time Nash had seen Fall River play. Nash liked Lajoie, but apparently he liked Fall River right fielder Phil Geier even better. Geier was hitting .381 at the time and was a year younger than his outfield mate. In early August Nash and manager Charlie Marston began negotiations. Whether Lajoie was part of the initial negotiation is unknown. It is believed that Marston asked for $1,500 for Geier. The Philadelphia manager refused to pay the asking price. To sweeten the deal, Marston apparently offered to add Lajoie. The deal was consummated. The two Fall River outfielders were now big leaguers. Over five seasons in the big leagues, Geier would bat .249 in 349 games. Lajoie's numbers over his Major League career defied comparison, yet Lajoie always felt he was merely a throw-in when it came to his first crack at the big leagues.[17]

Napoleon Lajoie played his first Major League game on August 12, 1896. As the Phillies' first baseman, he batted fifth and singled in five appearances at the plate as his new team defeated Washington 9-0. Lajoie's ability to play first base enabled the Phillies to move their veteran star Ed

Delahanty to the outfield, his natural position. The move allowed Lajoie, unlike Geier, to play regularly, and he responded in kind, batting .326 in thirty-nine games over the remainder of the 1896 season.

His fast start permitted Lajoie to enjoy quick acceptance into the Phillies' team framework. In time Lajoie and Delahanty became good friends and even roomed together—a sharp contrast to the cold reception Ty Cobb received during his early days in Detroit. On the other hand, just as with Cobb, the local sports press fell totally in love with Lajoie. A mere two days after his Phillies debut, the *Philadelphia Evening Reporter* described the new first baseman's "easy, graceful way of playing." Given his size, Lajoie exhibited an ease of movement that defied explanation but left a lasting impression. According to biographer J. M. Murphy, "No adjective has been more commonly attached to any major league ballplayer than 'graceful' has been to Lajoie."[18] He was, in short, a natural both in the field and at the plate, where his smooth batting stroke produced one stinging line drive after another.

The Phillies of 1896 and 1897 suffered through losing seasons. Nonetheless, the team's struggles did little to dampen Lajoie's prospects. Still playing first base, with an occasional foray into the outfield, Lajoie finished among the league leaders in a number of hitting categories. The 1897 season was not without incident, however. In early September *Sporting Life* disclosed that "after several lapses of sobriety this season . . . on Friday last he [Lajoie] capped the climax by appearing on the field in such a condition that he disgraced himself." He was pulled from the game in the first inning "after he had lost the Phillies the game."[19] The remedial action seemed to work. No further incidents related to drinking were reported throughout Lajoie's career.

Because of his second year heroics, Lajoie entered 1898 a star. Along the way, he had earned a new nickname, one that would last him far longer than "Sandy." One of his teammates, a pitcher with the last name Taylor, had a particularly difficult time pronouncing Napoleon's last name. According to Nap, "He tried and tried to say Lajoie, but always settled by calling me Larry, which was as close as he could come."[20] The nickname would stick; many even believed that Larry was part of Lajoie's given name.

Other nicknames would surface over time as well; one in particular that caught many a fancy was "the Big Frenchman."

Midway through the 1898 season, the Phillies made yet another managerial change. They dumped George Stallings—he had replaced Nash in 1897—owing to team unrest and a bucketful of losses. They turned to club secretary Bill Shettsline, but not before Stallings made a position change that figured prominently in the Lajoie saga. In the process of shuffling players in and out of the Phillies lineup, he switched Lajoie to second base. The move proved golden for Lajoie and for the teams he performed with during the course of his career. Stallings refused to take credit, stating, "He'd [Lajoie] have made good no matter where I positioned him."[21] Nonetheless, one could not excel at that position without soft hands, quick reflexes, and enough quickness and speed to cover the ground necessary. Lajoie possessed those skills and performed his second base duties from day one with a fluidity of motion that observers marveled at for years.

Over the next two seasons, the Phillies improved under the steady hand of manager Shettsline. In fact, the Phillies were in first place on May 31, 1900, when Nap and outfield teammate Elmer Flick, the same fellow who figured several years later in the "nontrade" with Ty Cobb, tangled in the clubhouse over who owned a bat. Flick, only a year younger and already a hitting star in his own right, gave up several inches and several pounds to Lajoie. Still, he had engaged in some boxing and wrestling during his earlier days, which gave him an air of confidence in his ability to hold his own with opponents and teammates alike. The previous season he had become angered when Lajoie roamed into the outfield to nab at least two pop flies he thought rightfully belonged to him.[22] Thus, the dynamite was already in place between Lajoie's and Flick's lockers in 1900; the dispute over the bat merely lit the fuse. When the dust settled, Lajoie had a black eye and, much worse, a broken thumb, the result of his left-handed haymaker, which missed Flick and landed against the clubhouse wall. Apparently, Flick's most serious injury was a bruised ego. He left the team in a huff but returned after a three-game absence. The team tried to cover the incident up, but it became impossible with Flick's brief departure and Nap's injury. Lajoie missed all of June and returned in early July to a team no longer in the lead. The Phillies ended the year in third, their record 75-63. Flick played in 131 games and batted .367; Lajoie batted .337 in 102.

The fight with Flick is evidence that Lajoie, like Cobb, would not only not walk away from a spat, he might even start one. When he was still with Fall River, Lajoie had taken exception to an umpire's call. That evening he was with several teammates when they saw the umpire near their team hotel. Nap wanted a piece of the arbiter, and only the firm grasp of his fellow players kept him from striking the man.[23] There would be other flashes of temper through the years, including one affair in which Nap took a wad of chewing tobacco from his mouth and threw it at an umpire, but unlike Cobb, Lajoie confined his fracases to players or umpires. The incidents were all quickly dismissed as part of the game, and none had racist overtones.

Lajoie once said, "When I got mad at an umpire like that, it was a temporary thing and lasted only while I was on the field. I have never had any enemies off the field."[24] He was probably right, although that did not necessarily mean Nap had a particularly outgoing personality. Just the opposite, according to one Cleveland writer who once told his readers that Lajoie would make a bad politician. "They say the limelight has not spoiled Larry, but that it has always been distasteful to him. . . . He's a poor mixer. He doesn't care for the crowd. . . . He's loyal to a few cronies and chums. . . . He is never what they term 'a good fellow,' never 'one of the boys.'"[25]

During the winter of 1900–1901, this reserved man with virtually no enemies might have ruffled a few feathers in baseball's front offices. He became arguably the most important prize in Ban Johnson's effort to establish and, by virtue of securing top National League talent, legitimize his American League as a second Major League circuit. That effort actually began several years earlier, when Johnson, the president of the Western League, the best run of the top Minor Leagues, determined that there was room at the top for a second Major League. By 1900 the National League, which had operated as a twelve-franchise monopoly since 1892, had become an eight-team league.[26] Johnson took advantage of the changed landscape. He convinced National League owners that the American Association, not his Western League, was their real threat and thereby received their blessing to move one of his teams into Chicago. He then subtly changed the name of his league to the "American League." One foot now in the door, the former newspaperman soon announced that he would move teams into Baltimore, Washington, Boston, and Philadelphia, either taking over former territory or placing second teams in direct competition with the National League. Filling those teams with top talent was the next step to equal status. In so doing, this new "Major League" would respect all valid existing contracts, including multiyear contracts, but any player merely "reserved" by his current team was fair game.

Under the National League's "reserve system," a player under contract to a team was essentially bound to that team for the next season if the player and the team had not come to new contract terms by a specific date. If the new league could pluck enough feathers from the peacock's plume, it would take on a colorful new sheen that would attract fans and establish itself as a viable commodity. Napoleon "Larry" Lajoie was certainly one of the establishment's finest and most colorful feathers. By the time Ban Johnson went hunting, it just so happened that Lajoie was ready for the plucking.

It was not that Lajoie was unhappy with the Phillies. His days with the team were "happy ones."[27] The difficulty stemmed from his annual tug-of-war with the man in charge of the team, Col. John L. Rogers, an attorney and an extremely tough hombre when it came to negotiating new contract terms. According to Lajoie, his salary climbed steadily over the years. He earned $1,800 in 1897, $2,100 in 1898, and the league limit of $2,400 in 1899.[28] The fly in the ointment was the common practice of slipping additional money under the table to certain elite players to keep them in line. Lajoie had no problem with the ethics of that practice; he just wanted to be told the truth about what Rogers was paying to other players so that he knew no one was making more. In 1900 the crafty Rogers slipped Nap two hundred dollars extra, assuring him that he and Ed Delahanty, another bona-fide star, were making the same amount of money. In fact, Rogers had paid Delahanty six hundred dollars extra. The additional amount to Delahanty was probably justified. He had batted .410 in 1899. Perhaps the colonel should have told Lajoie the truth. His decision to lie backfired. The colonel had forgotten that Lajoie and Delahanty were not only close friends but also roommates. Lajoie recalled, "I knew what Del got because I saw his checks."[29] As a result, Lajoie, feeling he had been cheated out of four hundred dollars, was angry.

Whether it was merely a matter of good timing or instead a case of a savvy operator picking up smoke signals, over the course of that winter, Lajoie was contacted by Frank Hough, a sports editor for the *Philadelphia Inquirer*. Hough was not just any newspaperman. In contacting Lajoie and other National League players, he was acting as an agent for Connie Mack, the former big league catcher and manager whose last stop had been in Milwaukee, as manager of that franchise in Ban Johnson's Western League. Mack was now in Philadelphia, where he and sporting goods magnate Benjamin Shibe were about to launch the American League's brand new Philadelphia team, the Athletics. Hough and Sam Jones of the Associated Press were also partners in the new business venture. Hough now offered a contract that Lajoie claimed called for him to receive $24,000 over the next four years.[30] Given the amount offered and his bitterness toward Rogers at that point, Lajoie accepted.

At the outset the Athletics' contract with Lajoie remained a secret, but it was not so for long. When Colonel Rogers heard about the signing, he contacted Nap and offered him more. Although he was now under contract with Mack and company, Nap claims he would have considered the offer if Rogers had paid him the four hundred dollars he felt he had been shorted the previous season.[31] Rogers refused, and Lajoie became the American League's prize recruit. Lajoie's league change proved extremely fortuitous for him, the American League, and in the short run at least, the Athletics. In 1901, playing for an Athletics team that finished fourth out of eight, he led his fledgling league in batting, runs batted in (125), and home runs (14)—what is now considered the Triple Crown—and in a number of other hitting categories. His batting average, variously listed as anywhere from .405 (almost certainly incorrect) to .422, and later .426, is at the very least the all-time high in the American League.[32] The figure is tempered by the fact that the American League, unlike the National League, which that year adopted the current rule of counting fouls as strikes until two strikes are accumulated, still played by the old rule whereby a foul ball did not count as a strike.[33] Still, it was an impressive performance that did much to place the American League on an equal footing with its rival. And it was all done with no little controversy swirling around Lajoie and his fellow Phillies converts.

In March 1901 Colonel Rogers, no stranger to courtrooms, entered one in Pennsylvania with a team of lawyers primed to enjoin Lajoie and other former Phillies from performing for the Athletics. Much to their chagrin, Rogers and his litigators lost the first round as a three-judge panel determined that the contracts containing the reserve clause signed by Nap and the others lacked mutuality. They were deemed one-sided owing to the standard ten-day clause, which gave the ball club the sole right to terminate a player's contract on ten days' notice. The case remained in limbo as professional baseball prepared to enter the 1902 season. Then, two days before that season started, the ax fell.

On April 21, 1902, the Pennsylvania Supreme Court decided unanimously to overrule the lower court. A ball club need not prove that it was impossible to replace the services of a player under contract; rather, it need only show that the employee rendered services of a unique character and displayed such expert skills that it made it difficult to find an appropriate substitute. In particular, with regard to Lajoie, the court found that he most certainly possessed those expert skills. In fact, he was "a most attractive drawing card for the public. He may not be the sun in the baseball firmament, but he is certainly a bright particular star."[34]

The bottom line: Lajoie would be prohibited from playing in Pennsylvania for any team but the Phillies. The 1902 season opened for the Athletics on April 23 in Baltimore with Lajoie in the lineup. During the game, a telegram was delivered to Mack advising him that the local court had issued a five-day temporary injunction prohibiting Nap from playing for the Athletics. Mack felt he had no choice but to pull his star from the game and series. Napoleon Lajoie was now in a sort of baseball vortex. He was in fact a free agent with one exception: if he played baseball in Pennsylvania, it must be with the Phillies. Thus, he turned in their direction. At first there was every indication that Lajoie would return to the Phillies, hat in hand.

He met in May with Colonel Rogers, and a deal seemed imminent—that is, until the tenacious legal eagle overplayed his hand, insisting that Nap accept a fine for the time he had missed with the Phillies. The second sacker balked and walked away from the National League forever.

Now Lajoie was really in a state of flux but certainly not unwanted. He could play anywhere but in Pennsylvania, and Johnson wanted to keep him in the league, even if it wasn't with the Athletics. Connie Mack agreed, placing the good of the league before his team's self-interest. The Cleveland Bronchos were a weak link, but their owner, Charles Somers, had deep pockets.[35] Somers, encouraged by Johnson, who sought league balance, offered Lajoie a four-year contract of between $25,000 and $30,000, guaranteed if future legal actions interfered with Lajoie's ability to honor it. Nap signed the contract in May, assured that the Ohio courts would not recognize the Pennsylvania edict. In early June 1902 Napoleon Lajoie and his .250 batting average (1 for 4 in one game) arrived in Cleveland. The Bronchos—some still referred to them by their former name, the Blues— had finished the first-ever American League season in seventh place with eighty-two losses. Now they had a new name, a new manager named Bill Armour, and, along with the arrival of several other fine players such as Lajoie's former Phillies teammates Elmer Flick and pitcher Bill Bernhard, a star second baseman. On June 4 the new Broncho infielder, already designated team captain, debuted before ten thousand adoring fans and doubled to help his new team to victory. The adoption had been neither smooth nor swift, but if you were a long-suffering Cleveland baseball fan, it was oh so sweet. Right from the start, the unusually large crowd loved what they saw. A hero was in their midst. It was a love affair that would last for years.

Switching teams—his third in less than three full seasons—and now cities too did nothing to slow the "Lajoie Express." The player continued to prosper, once again leading the league in batting, this time with an average of .378, two points better than his friend Ed Delahanty, now playing for Washington.[36] Of course, he was not permitted to play in Philadelphia, which limited him to eighty-seven games total in 1902 and created situations in which law enforcement officials met his team's train as it pulled into the Philly station to make sure Lajoie was not a passenger. They found nothing because, as Lajoie recalled, "Whenever Cleveland went to Philadelphia, I'd go over to Atlantic City and live off the fat of the land."[37] Still, even without Lajoie's considerable presence on those many occasions (eleven games over three series), his new team showed marked improvement, finishing in fifth place with a record of 69-67. By the spring of 1903 the baseball war was at an end. Over the winter the National League, recognizing by virtue of attendance figures and roster strength that the new league was here to stay, reached an agreement with Ban Johnson and his league. The National Commission, the body that would eventually approve the Chalmers prize, came into existence at that time as well, giving Ban Johnson a decided upper hand in all the important baseball issues.

For Napoleon Lajoie, the peace treaty meant that he was no longer a tethered man. The Phillies dropped their injunction. He was now free to play a full schedule for his adopted club. If he had harbored misgivings when he first left the City of Brotherly Love for the North Coast of Ohio, that was no longer the case. By now he was part owner of a cigar store in Cleveland. His partner was his manager, Bill Armour. Lajoie was so popular around town that while the team trained in New Orleans, a local newspaper, the *Cleveland Press*, ran a contest for readers to select a new team name. The winner was the Naps, in honor of the Clevelanders' team captain.[38]

After a slow start, the newly dubbed Naps fashioned a respectable season in 1903. They finished in third place with a record of 77-63. Their eponymous slugger once again led the league, batting .344 even though the foul strike rule was now applied to the American League as well as the National by virtue of the formal truce. The team and city looked forward to 1904 with much anticipation. Several preseason polls placed the Clevelanders at the top. In the early going, it seemed they might be correct, as the Naps and Red Sox, league leaders in 1903, tangled for first place, but before long injuries, illness, suspension, and dissension took a serious toll. The suspension—five days—involved Lajoie and derived from the incident in which he became upset at a ruling and threw a wad of chewing tobacco at the arbiter, Frank "Blinky" Dwyer. The tantrum was particularly unwise, given that league president Ban Johnson was in the stands. The dissension, at least as it related to Lajoie, came later in the season, in September. By then the team had fallen on hard times and was mired in fifth place. Hampered by the high expectations and frustrated by his team's indifferent performance, manager Bill Armour told owner Charles Somers that he was resigning from a team that didn't want to be managed. Part of the reason for his departure, he said, was his business partner and star player Lajoie's lack of aggressive play.[39] It was a strange accusation considering that Nap's calling card on offense was his aggressive attitude at the plate; he would essentially draw a line in the sand and swing exceedingly hard at just about any pitch that caught his fancy.

Following his resignation, Armour, who later took over as manager of the Tigers in 1905, remained the nominal manager of the Naps, but captain Lajoie managed the team. Under his guidance, the club moved up a bit, finishing fourth with an 86-65 record. Despite Armour's frustrations with his play, Larry enjoyed another strong season at the plate, hitting .376—more than enough to lead his league once again—and driving in a league best 102 runs. He was the team's star player, and his teammates had responded favorably to his direction as the 1904 season ran its course. Charlie Somers made the logical move, officially offering Lajoie the managerial reins for 1905. At the somewhat tender age—at least for managers—of thirty, Nap accepted. It was a move he would come to regret.[40]

Lajoie's initial reluctance to continue managing his club likely did not stem from concerns about the talent level. In the minds of many, the Naps' roster was loaded with young talent. They shot right out of the gates in the spring of 1905, leading the league as late as August 1, but their fate may have been sealed exactly one month earlier, when Lajoie suffered a spike wound on his left foot in a play at second base. The injury appeared minor and the second baseman stayed in the game, but the wound later became infected from the dye coloring his baseball stockings. He was hospitalized with blood poisoning. Several days later Nap was given chloroform and the wound was lanced. The original prognosis called for the player-manager to miss about three weeks of the season, but soon physicians were warning that amputation was a possibility. Fortunately, the infection subsided, and

Lajoie returned to the field, watching the games from a wheelchair.[41] Nap returned to action on August 28, playing first base. The team, hopes still flickering, was within five games at the time. A few games later, Lajoie hit a foul tip off his injured ankle. He was through for the season. So were the Naps. They finished 76-78 and in fifth place. For the season Lajoie played in only sixty-five games. His batting average dropped almost fifty points to .329. It was a season to forget. The next one was better by degree only. Lajoie played injury-free in 1906—he batted .355, second only to virtual unknown George Stone of St. Louis—but many of his players did not. The team finished third. Shortly after the end of the 1906 season, Nap paused from his pursuit of a pennant to marry Myrtle I. Smith, a divorcée he had reportedly known for some two years.[42] The marriage would last a lifetime.

Before the start of the 1907 season, as Flick sought more money from Naps management and new Tigers manager Hughie Jennings realized his budding superstar Ty Cobb was a hot piece of coal he might not wish to juggle, Lajoie and the Naps turned down a chance to purchase the Tigers' youngster.[43] The pass presented a field day for second-guessers when the 1907 edition of the Naps once again fell short of a pennant, while the Tigers captured the pennant and Cobb won his first batting title.

Once again 1907 found the Naps of Cleveland entering a season with high expectations grounded in logic. Once again they ended a season rife with disappointment. It was not just the fourth-place finish; this time around, the team was becoming more and more dissatisfied with its manager. According to biographer J. M. Murphy, "Nig Clarke [the team's young catcher] wasn't talking to the skipper. George Stovall [first baseman] was suspended once and sent home; he had accused Lajoie of hiring outsiders to spy on the players, and he carried his charges to top front-office officials."[44]

That wasn't the end of it with Stovall. Lajoie recalled, "One day in 1907, one of my players, George Stovall, hit me over the head with a chair during an argument in a Philadelphia hotel. I had moved him down in the batting order because he hadn't been hitting and he'd been brooding over it." On hearing about the incident, many observers thought Lajoie should act with dispatch in ridding himself of the recalcitrant player. Lajoie did not. It just wasn't his style. "He's a good player and we need him," he said.[45]

The controversy, coupled with yet another spiking injury that led to a significant loss of playing time owing to blood poisoning, resulted in a rather stark drop in Lajoie's offensive output. His batting average dropped fifty-six points to .299, his runs-batted-in total shrunk from 91 to 63. For the first time since his arrival in Cleveland, Nap faced criticism from the local sporting press and heard muttering from restless fans. Still, most were able to separate the manager from the player, and Lajoie continued to enjoy unparalleled popularity at home and throughout the league. On September 7 League Park was the scene of Napoleon Lajoie Day. The honoree would have traded the day and accompanying gifts, which included for luck both a floral horseshoe and a small, brown sheep, for a few more victories.[46]

Then came that last frustrating season-ending series with the Browns in 1908, which concluded a ninety-win season with nothing whatsoever to show for it.[47] By now the gloves were off, and the criticism of Lajoie's management technique was a constant in the city's sports pages. Once again Lajoie's performance in the batter's box suffered. His batting average slipped another ten points to .289. His failures at the plate in key moments of the final crucial series only added to his anguish and that of his club. Still, if one stepped back for a moment and took a deep breath, there was much to like about the Naps' chances for a pennant in 1909; the return to Cleveland of Denton "Cy" Young, now a bewhiskered veteran of forty-two, but winner of his age in ballgames during his last two seasons in Boston, bolstered the team's hopes. Young fashioned an impressive season with nineteen wins and a 2.26 ERA, but the 1909 Cleveland Naps started poorly and finished poorly. On August 17 Lajoie, besieged by attacks in the press and facing scorn in the locker room—one local newspaper began calling his team the "Napkins" because of the way they folded up—offered to resign as manager and take a pay cut from his reported $10,000 salary.[48] It appeared later that he had made the same offer twice before.[49] This time, five days later, on August 22, the offer was accepted by Charles Somers, who expressed, at least publicly, his great reluctance and disappointment.

In a formal public statement, Nap thanked the public for its loyalty. He pledged to work as hard as a player as he had as a manager in getting the team to the top.[50]

When the man some Clevelanders once called "King Larry" and others "The Peerless Lajoie" resigned, the Naps were 57-57. Under new manager James "Deacon" McGuire, a former catcher who was initially Lajoie's right-hand man and more recently a scout, the team went 14-25. The two managers' combined record of 71-82 resulted in a sixth-place finish. Lajoie was hurt off and on, answering the call but 128 times. His average improved from the previous two seasons, however. He hit .324, third in the league behind Cobb and Eddie Collins of the Athletics. Still, it was a far cry from Cobb's .377; the Detroiter captured his third-straight title, putting further distance between himself and Lajoie, or anyone else for that matter, as baseball's best player.

The totals for Lajoie's managerial stint in Cleveland, beginning with the 1905 season, when he was officially appointed, were 377 wins, 309 losses, a winning percentage of .550 and one "close but no cigar" finish. At least one contemporary felt that the ease with which Lajoie had mastered almost every aspect of the game, the awesome natural talent that made him such a great player so quickly in his career, was his ultimate downfall as a manager: "The great player-artist [Lajoie] rather disdained the subtleties of the game and responsibility sat heavily upon him. He failed to lift up lesser players to the batting and fielding heights that he had attained so easily. He knew how to do a thing, but to impart to another how it should be done eluded him."[51]

Whatever the cause of his downfall, any loss of popularity in Cleveland stemming from his managerial performance apparently did not affect the admiration for his heroics on the diamond. Shortly after his resignation, the *Cleveland Press* decided it was time to find a more appropriate team name. They ran another contest. The winner and still champion: the "Naps."[52] As the 1909 season closed, Napoleon Lajoie, the player, still enjoyed the enduring love of the folks who paid the bills: the Cleveland fans. The popularity he enjoyed around the league was just as strong as well—perhaps even more so. If nothing else, his failure as a manager made him seem more human. Most fans of opposing teams enjoyed watching him perform in their stadiums, caring not a whit about his trials and tribulations as a manager. As the teams engaged in combat in early 1910, a strong case could be made that Napoleon Lajoie was the most popular player in the American League, rivaled only by Honus Wagner in all of baseball. For example, when the Naps stopped off in Chicago to play a pair of games before heading to Cleveland to face Detroit in their 1910 home opener, the White Sox fans gave the former manager a hand when he came to the plate in the second inning.[53]

However, although Lajoie was likely still the most popular player in the American League, he was no longer its best player. That honor belonged to Ty Cobb. While Lajoie grew older and divided his energies between managing and playing, the younger Cobb had not only caught up with Lajoie as the league's best player but had blown right by him. Entering the 1910 season, Lajoie had every reason to think he could do something to close the gap. The Naps' second baseman was no longer shackled with the unwanted and, for him, disagreeable chore of directing others. He was once again able to focus solely on playing the game he loved, and he was anxious to challenge Cobb for the honor he once felt was his alone. Lajoie, no doubt fully cognizant he had ceded his roost at the top, was confident that he once again could become the best. The chance to win one of Hugh Chalmers's automobiles gave him the perfect opportunity to prove his point.

Chapter Five

Gone were the wooden grandstand and pavilion.
—Franklin Lewis

The home opener for the Cleveland Naps, played against the Detroit Tigers on April 21, was certainly no ordinary event. In the first place, the hometown Naps were still on a high from witnessing and playing behind their ace, thirty-year-old Addie Joss, as he threw a no-hitter in shutting down the White Sox 1–0 in Chicago just one day earlier. Then there was the crowd, 18,832, not a sellout—capacity was listed at 21,400—but an estimated 4,000 more than for any previous baseball home opener in the city's history.[1] Fans looked on as Ban Johnson and Garry Herrmann took their seats and roared when their beloved Cy Young twice fanned an 0-for-4 Ty Cobb. Yet it was neither the game, won by Detroit 5–0, nor Lajoie's single in four tries that caught their fancy. On this date it was a revamped ballpark, the latest version of League Park, that was the object of their affection.

Like most cities favored with baseball performed at the highest level, the story of professional baseball in Cleveland and its ballparks was closely intertwined. Prior to the 1900s that story for the most part involved the old National League. The Cleveland Spiders, later called the Blues, performed in that league from 1879 to 1884. They played their home schedule at Kennard Street Park in what baseball historians generally refer to as League Park I. When that franchise became a victim of a war with the rival

Union Association, the city was without a major team until the Cleveland Blues of the American Association located there and played from 1887 in a new location, American Association Park (League Park II). That park was also the home to the Cleveland Spiders when the National League returned in 1889. By then it was called National League Park. The team moved to a new park, also known as National League Park (League Park III), for the 1891 season. This park was located in downtown Cleveland at the corner of Dunham (later East Sixty-Sixth Street) and Lexington Ave. This park was used by the Spiders until the franchise was eliminated, when the league was reduced to eight teams in 1899. The park became home to the Cleveland Blues in 1900, when Ban Johnson shifted the Grand Rapids franchise of his Minor League, the Western League, to Cleveland. When the league became the American League and the team became the Bronchos and then the Naps, League Park III remained its centerpiece.[2] By the end of the 1909 season, Naps ownership decided it was time for a change. Only the site remained the same.

Now on April 21 League Park IV, or League Park as it was generally known, was unveiled. The main difference between it and League Park III was that it was made of concrete and steel, like many of the new ballparks, including those opened in 1909 in Philadelphia for the Athletics and set to open in June 1910 for the White Sox in Chicago.

According to Franklin Lewis, "Gone were the wooden grandstand and pavilion. In their places were steel and concrete stands, fitted with individual seats. No longer would the average baseball fan sit on a crude bench. Now he was a spectator, a paying guest of the management. The biggest and most startling feature in the new League Park was a wall in right field. It was forty feet high. It started at the juncture of the right-field pavilion and the foul line, two hundred and ninety feet out from home plate, and extended east on Lexington Ave. for more than four hundred feet."[3]

Of course, the high wall made it more difficult to hit home runs, but then the year the new League Park opened, 1910, was smack dab in the middle of the Deadball Era, a period during which home runs were at a premium. Despite the wall and the generous dimensions, at least one expert on ballparks of the era believes that the new park "must be considered the best regular-use hitter's park in the AL during its ten Deadball seasons." The park's wide expanses afforded plenty of room for doubles and permitted more inside-the-park home runs than was typical for ballparks of the day.[4] This was not really so bad, for it was a time when hitters could use all the help they could get.

The Deadball Era is generally considered to cover the years 1901–19. The term "deadball" is somewhat of an overstatement, however. There was a lot more to the brand of baseball played in the early twentieth century than just a dead ball. Nonetheless, it is probably safe to say that the composition of the baseball commonly in use dictated the strategies used by both the batters and the pitchers, particularly in the earlier portion of the era. The baseball in use at least from 1901 to 1909 lacked "resilience," meaning it was not tightly wound, a condition only enhanced by the fact that as a function of cost cutting few balls were put into play.[5] As the game progressed, the ball would soften from use and, when struck, travel even less distance than when new. It would darken both from normal use—or, as it were, overuse—and from intentional darkening, as each infielder did his part to rub it with dirt and many a crafty pitcher applied spit to it to affect its spin and increase its break. The ball and the contrivances manufactured by the players themselves to make it more difficult to hit the ball had a trickledown effect. Because hits were particularly difficult to attain, each run meant that much more. Therefore, the successful manager fashioned strategies designed to get his team that one or two runs. These strategies became commonly known as the "inside game."[6] Batters still strove for extra-base hits, but since it was so important just to get on base, they seldom swung for the fences, choosing instead to choke up and punch or place the ball where it would fall safely for a hit. The bunt was an essential part of the game, and bunting was an art form. Once a runner reached base, the strategy shifted to getting the base runner home. Thus, base stealing, including the double steal, the hit and run, and even the suicide squeeze, in which the runner on third headed for the plate full steam ahead as the batter attempted to lay down a bunt, were major ingredients of the game. Home runs were rare and often inside-the-park, a circumstance magnified by the expansive outfield dimensions in most parks. League and team batting averages were low on the whole, although batters such as Cobb, Wagner, and Lajoie proved the exception.

However, not every fan of the game was enamored with low-hit, low-run defensive struggles. For those who clamored for change, some relief was on the way by virtue of the introduction of a more resilient cork-centered ball. Such a baseball would be just as hard to hit, but since the cork center permitted the yarn to be wound more compactly, it would be more resilient. Once struck, it would travel farther. It would also hold its shape better, allowing it to remain solid and continue to travel longer further into the game.[7] Although the new more tightly wound cork-centered ball was clearly used in 1911 and onward, there is a good deal of confusion as to when this newer, livelier ball was first introduced to the big leagues, particularly whether it was used during the 1910 regular season. The 1911 *Spalding Guide*, an annual review of the previous baseball season, stated, "It is more than probable that nothing during the [baseball] season of 1910, except the playing of the games, attracted closer observation among the students of Base Ball than the introduction of the new cork-centered ball."[8] In fact, the manufacturer of the ball, A. J. Reach & Co., announced publicly on May 6 that the new baseball was being used during the 1910 season in both Major Leagues and a majority of the Minor Leagues.[9] However, years later George Reach, the son of A. J. Reach, told a newspaper, "We used our newly patented cork center ball for the first time in the 1910 World Series."[10]

If the new ball was in use, it made little difference, at least in the American League. The league's overall batting average actually dropped a point to .243 in 1910 and then rose dramatically to .273 in 1911. The National League, which batted .244 in 1909, saw its average rise to .256, but then by only an additional four points in 1911 to .260, perhaps because the new ball was not in use in that league until late in the season.[11] Whatever the state of the baseball in 1910, new or old, as the year progressed, it remained a race between Cobb and Lajoie. These stalwart hitters more than made up for any lack of resiliency in the ball or disparities between the leagues with two very hot bats.

Despite the new season and the added incentive of playing three games in a newly constructed ballpark against the defending league champions, the Naps did not perform well during their opening series at home, losing all three games to the Tigers. It would not get better as the season ran its course. This did not sit well with the team or its fans. The cities of Cleveland and Detroit shared a lot, but a successful baseball team was not one of their commonalities. The Tigers had now won three pennants since the formation of the new league; the Naps none. The Tigers had the goods to capture a fourth-straight pennant in 1910 and fully expected to do so. The Naps could only hope.

Still, the cities were highly competitive in many other ways. At the start of the second decade of the twentieth century, both Cleveland and Detroit were enjoying significant growth in their industrial base and in their population. Although Detroit was becoming the acknowledged automobile center of the universe, Cleveland was an auto center as well, with nine automobile manufacturers within its midst. Furthermore, over the next few years, it would become a leader in the manufacture of auto parts.[12] By 1910 Cleveland was the sixth largest city in the United States with 560,663 citizens.[13] Detroit was in the top ten as well and coming fast with a population of 465,766.[14]

This tale of two growing cities, competing industrially and on the ball diamond, was further enhanced by the availability of passenger steamship service on Lake Erie. Steamers began their lake runs in the early nineteenth century. By the mid-1840s the ships had increased in size and passenger amenities. The 1,136 ton steamer *Empire*, for example, launched with ship-length cabin space and separate saloons for the ladies and the gents. Its 230-foot-long dining room offered fine foods in opulent surroundings.[15] Active service between Cleveland and Detroit began in 1850. By 1878 at least nine steamers were committed to that route.[16] The shipping companies offered day trips and overnight excursions. Travel by ship between Detroit and Cleveland in 1910 was commonplace. The overnight excursions were particularly convenient for baseball teams that played in the afternoon in one or the other of the lake cities, then boarded a steamer for an overnight cruise, and arrived in the other lake city the next day in time for the afternoon game with the local denizen. The practice went on for years. One story has Walter Johnson, for years the American League's dominant pitcher, missing a turn in 1921 when he caught a heavy cold while crossing Lake Erie from Detroit to Cleveland. According to one biographer, "This time he had sat on the deck admiring the stars during a summer night's crossing. . . . The cold lake breezes chilled him, and he spent the Cleveland visit in bed in his hotel room."[17] As late as 1941, Ty Cobb, Babe Ruth, and hundreds of other passengers spent a hot summer evening enjoying cooler lake temperatures as they steamed for Detroit from Cleveland on board the *City of Cleveland*. Author Tom Stanton describes a setting that was probably familiar to baseball teams and others traveling the route in 1910:

> The five-hundred-foot boat—a floating hotel, really—had the ambience of a traveling party. Rows of lights marked each of its decks and shimmered on the rippling water. Fueled by coal-burning boilers, the side-wheeled vessel powered through the great lake, its tall stacks spewing dark, shadowy clouds into a moonless night sky. Although the heyday of the steamer was drawing to a close, the *City of Cleveland* and its sister ship, the *City of Detroit*, promised pleasant journeys and numerous amenities: beautifully appointed public areas, sumptuous meals, musical entertainment, and nicely furnished parlor rooms, some with private verandas. It was a festive, relaxed way to travel.[18]

Smooth sailing aside, the first series in the newest version of League Park had ended for the Naps with that disappointing three-game sweep at the hands of the Tigers. Before they hit the road to St. Louis, they lost two more when the White Sox visited for three. By July 4, the mythical midseason, the Naps were again in Cleveland, but by now they trailed the league leaders by twelve games. They were buried in fifth place. This was no great surprise. What was a surprise was that once again they were playing the Tigers, and the defending league champions were having problems of their own. The Tigers had fared somewhat better than the Naps as the season wore on, but still they trailed the league-leading Athletics by five games. It would not get better as the season progressed, and the gap between the Tigers and Philadelphia widened. If, as now seemed almost certain, these two teams could not excite their fans through a pennant race, then perhaps a two-man race for the batting title and bragging rights as the team with baseball's best batter would suffice. Each team thus supplied its shining star.

Nothing served better to set the Cobb-Lajoie race in high gear than the six-game set between their teams played in the two cities from July 1 through July 5. The first game, won by the Naps in Cleveland 8–3, was particularly instructive, the pot stirred as it often was by the comments of the local press. Whereas Lajoie pounded out three hits in three official trips to the plate, Cobb wore an 0-for-4 collar. The next day in the *Plain Dealer*, Henry P. Edwards, the dean of Cleveland sportswriters and founding member of the Baseball Writers' Association of America, put his pen to whispers of underhanded dealings in the manner of scoring the efforts of the top rivals for baseball's hitting crown:

> There have been charges and counter charges of favoritism in scoring in the cases of Lajoie and Cobb, the two rivals for possession of the championship automobile and it would seem as if Nap Lajoie, himself, yesterday wanted to show the Tigers most convincingly that he earned everyone [*sic*] of his hits. At any rate, he hit the ball more viciously than at any previous time this season and made two three-baggers and a two-sacker. He failed to get any more for [Detroit pitcher] Edgar Willett would not give him the chance, purposefully passing him in the third inning when there were two men on bases and only one out. . . .
>
> As for Lajoie's rival, the famous Ty Cobb—he failed to get a hit—he even failed to reach first base. [Cleveland pitcher Cy] Falkenberg tossed him out twice, he fanned once, while on his other trip to the plate he flied to left field.
>
> So much for the batting giants of the league.[19]

The next day the Clevelanders won again as Lajoie went 2 for 3 and, much to the joy of the hometown rooters, Cobb came up short again with no hits in four at bats. Edwards, not even attempting to conceal his home colors, could not contain his glee:

> Once more did Ty Cobb fail to get a hit. He failed even to approach close making a hit. In fact, he reached first but once and that was when

he forced [Donie] Bush at second in the first inning. And while Cobb's batting average is shrinking, Lajoie's keeps improving and the big Frenchman can all but smell the gasoline.

"You can be Larry's chauffeur," yelled a fan to Cobb when he fanned in the fourth inning. . . . Cobb had a lot of amusement during the game, at that, carrying on a rapid fire conversational sketch with the third base standers whenever the Tigers were at bat. It grew to such proportions, however, that umpire [Billy] Evans was finally forced to inform Ty that his place was on the bench and not leaning over the rail.[20]

Following the contest both teams boarded a boat and steamed for Detroit for a single game, and then they returned to Cleveland for their July 4 doubleheader. Why the mad scramble? The third game fell on a Sunday, and in 1910 Sunday baseball was prohibited in Ohio.

What is today a common occurrence across the panorama of sports, a Sunday ball game, was once a rarity. In the early days of baseball, the idea of men playing the game and men and women watching them play on the seventh day was revolting to many who considered Sunday a day of rest, which people should use to observe the Sabbath. A good deal of that resistance had eroded by 1910—in fact, the first Sunday game in the old National League was played in St. Louis in April 1892—but not in Ohio. That did not mean that the owners of Cleveland's professional teams did not give it the old college try.

Cleveland was one of the westernmost outposts for baseball in the 1890s, and thus baseball owners viewed the city as less restrictive than the eastern bastions of religious conviction, such as Boston and Brooklyn. Banking on this perception, the owners of Cleveland's professional baseball clubs made several unsuccessful attempts to convince state and city authorities to ease the Sunday restriction. The most ardent advocate of the Cleveland owners was Frank Robison, a streetcar magnate who envisioned increased profits for both his baseball and transportation enterprises if he could add Sundays to his home schedule. Since Sunday baseball was already permitted in several other league cities, it was a reasonable aspiration. Robison most famously tested the waters in 1897.

In May of that year, his decision to flaunt the law and play a game at League Park resulted in the arrest of eighteen ballplayers. Arrangements were made to try but one player, Cleveland pitcher Jack Powell. When his conviction was overturned by a lower court judge, the state appealed and eventually won its case in the Ohio Supreme Court, thus sounding the death knell for Sunday baseball in Cleveland for a substantial period. That period extended to 1910, despite the presence of a progressive mayor, Tom Johnson, who fought for many social reforms but ironically stood firm against baseball on the Sabbath until his death in 1911. By that time a new groundswell of support for Sunday baseball had been created by the unveiling of the revamped League Park.[21]

At the earliest stages of American League baseball, all eight teams played Sunday baseball. It was just that some played at home, even in their home parks, while others were forced to take to the road, playing at nearby alternative sites or in the parks of their opponents. According to author Charlie Bevis, in his exhaustive treatise on the history and evolution of Sunday baseball, "Cleveland had been the king of the one-game Sunday road trip."[22] By contrast, the Detroit franchise was able to successfully play Sunday baseball at alternative sites off and on through the years. They began playing on Sundays at home field Bennett Park late in the 1907 season, as the Tigers drove for their first American League pennant.[23]

Thus, the interruption of this early July Detroit-Cleveland series in 1910 was merely a continuation of a practice of long standing, although it was no less frustrating for current owner Charles Somers in particular and Cleveland backers in general. That frustration was driven home when the Tigers won 4–3 in their home park, ending a brief Naps three-game win streak. Detroit then took two of the last three as the teams returned to Cleveland for their July 4 morning-afternoon twin bill split viewed by 24,000 and finished with yet another trip to Detroit, where the Tigers won again. The home cooking seemed to revive Cobb as he went 3 for 5 on Sunday. Lajoie stayed red hot with a pair of hits of his own in three tries, prompting one sports scribe who wrote for the *Detroit Free Press* to declare that the "duel" was on, with it already seemingly conceded that Cobb and Lajoie would be "winner and runner-up in the race for the batting average auto."[24]

The very thought that some reporter in Detroit, or Cleveland for that matter, was already crowing as if the battle for the Chalmers was a two-man race undoubtedly had the fans who rooted for the other fourteen Major League teams and the reporters who covered them seething and spewing unfettered condemnation. Nonetheless, a few days later, when the averages for the first half of the season showed Cobb (.379) and Lajoie (.403) several road miles in front of all the others, they had to concede that the *Free Press* might just have it right. It seemed that only two ballplayers were still batting with a full tank of fuel.

Chapter Six

I was probably the best friend he had on the club.
—Davy Jones

In the first half of the 1910 baseball season, a relative calm surrounded Ty Cobb. To be certain, he played the game with his usual vigor and unyielding manner, but there had been little or no copy for the scribes of the day as it related to Cobb's volatile and sometimes ugly disposition. Perhaps the birth of his first child during the previous off-season had something to do with it, or maybe it was the managerial genius of Hughie Jennings, who determined that Davy Jones would play regularly in left field and shifted Cobb from right to center when Sam Crawford, who formerly patrolled there, complained of a sore leg. This meant Crawford and Cobb were actually in their natural positions, and Cobb's nemesis, Matty McIntyre, was on the bench for the most part. Even when McIntyre played, Cobb stood firm in center. Then again the calm may have related to Ty's status as an acknowledged star who was much more comfortable with his place on the team and his financial station in life. If indeed any one or all of those factors were in place and working to mellow Cobb during the first half of the season, the effect proved of short duration.

Perhaps the first indication that Cobb was simmering just below the boiling point occurred in Cleveland during the July 4 series, presumably during the exchange with fans alluded to by Henry Edwards in his report of the July 2 contest.[1] As it developed, Cobb addressed some "more or less tart remarks" to the fan in the stands who was goading him the most. Said fan filed a complaint with the Naps' front office. They took the complaint to Ban Johnson, who levied a twenty-five-dollar fine without further investigation. Cobb, backed by teammates who claimed the outfielder was unfairly provoked, refused to pay. Johnson suspended him, just before the Tigers July 15 game with Washington. Only when the Tigers paid the fine was Cobb permitted to play.[2]

Shortly after this same Cleveland series, rumors circulated that all was not happy between Cobb and his manager Hughie Jennings. Although the pair denied it, at least one report had Cobb upset in general because the Tigers had just lost four in a row in Philadelphia to the surging Athletics and on a personal note because Jennings had upbraided him for lackadaisical fielding.[3] The Tigers were now a full ten games behind the A's, a team Jennings and Cobb publicly denounced as quitters, and their pennant hopes were encased in exhaust fumes. Perhaps it was time for Ty to turn his attention to winning the batting title, but even there he faced a roadblock: he trailed Lajoie by twenty-four points. If he was going to make headway in that department, he might have to exchange goals. From this point in the season on, it appears Cobb set out to win a car. A late July slump by Lajoie closed the gap unofficially to eight points and served to increase the Tiger's resolve. In the midst of a pennant race, Cobb probably thought no one would notice, but it did not take long before his new tack rubbed his teammates the wrong way. In fact, according to biographer Charles Alexander, who thought the prospect of losing out on a fourth straight batting title was fraying his subject's nerves as the season approached its last months, the problem had started the previous season as Cobb and teammates, in particular Donie Bush and Davy Jones, bickered over missed hit-and-run signs.[4]

The 1910 version of the flap was ignited in the last inning of an August 2 tilt against the Red Sox in Detroit. The problem apparently stemmed from Cobb's insistence that base runners such as Jones, who was batting lead-off to Cobb's number-three slot in the order, look to him and not manager Jennings for base-running signs.[5] The system had already cramped shortstop Bush's playing style to the point that he was no longer batting after Jones and in front of Cobb. He now appeared lower in the order. During the August 2 game, Jones, who stood on first, apparently missed—or just plain ignored—Cobb's sign. The failure of the pair to communicate resulted in an out, ending a rally as the Tigers were beaten 4–3.[6] Later in the clubhouse, Cobb and Jones argued. Jones maintained that Cobb's main concern had become the batting title and not his team.[7] Cobb contended that when Jones ignored his signals, it hurt Cobb's chances at the plate. According to one report, Cobb's language was "forcible if not parliamentary" and included a threat that he would no longer play in the same outfield with Jones.[8] After an off day, the two teams resumed their series. Cobb, reportedly suffering a stomach ailment, was not on the field. Perhaps Cobb had thought Jennings would side with him over Jones. If so, it had not worked as planned, and Jones, not Cobb, remained in the lineup.

Davy Jones, it seemed, was a valuable man to have in a lineup. The thirty-year-old outfielder's law degree and ability to verbally spar with the best of them had little to do with it. His true value lay in his speed. Once on the bases, he proved troublesome for pitchers, and he reached base often enough to deserve a position in the outfield and as the team's lead-off batter, even in the face of demands otherwise from the mighty Cobb. The feud between the two was ironic because Jones once said, "I was probably the best friend he had on the club. I used to stick up for him, sit and talk with him on the long train trips, try to understand the man." Still, Jones found being Cobb's friend "damn hard." He compared playing in the outfield with Cobb and Sam Crawford, whom he deemed a best friend for life, to "being a member of the chorus in a grand opera where there are two prima donnas."[9] Now he was openly at war with one of those divas.

However, a day in the stands watching his team win without him—the Tigers prevailed 4–2 over Boston—and a meeting with club president Frank Navin seemed to convince Cobb that he could put up with Jones if it meant playing ball versus sitting idly by, particularly when unofficial batting statistics compiled through games of July 29, as reported on August 6 by George Moreland's reporting service, revealed that not only had a surging Cobb gained on a badly slumping Lajoie, but he now led him for Major League batting honors.[10] It was said that Cobb told Navin he would return to a playing cast that included Jones.[11] Nonetheless, when the Tigers took the field on the afternoon of August 5 and again beat the Highlanders, Cobb did not play and Jones patrolled left field. According to reports, Cobb presented himself at the last moment, and Jennings, perhaps to underscore who was really in charge, told his star to remain an observer.

Cobb returned to the lineup for the next home game on August 6. In their first times at the plate in a victory over New York, both Jones and Cobb, who two days later would publish a letter denying his refusal to play and his role as the cause of team dissension, received applause from the fans.[12] The argument did little to alter Ty's hitting stroke—he went 2 for 3—but he found another avenue to vent a rage that must have continued to seethe under the surface against at the very least Jones and perhaps now Hughie Jennings as well. Toward the end of the game, a number of fans in the left-field bleachers found an audience with Cobb. At least one report indicated that the fans had been peppering the Georgian with insults since early in the game. Finally, Cobb had enough. He jumped into the stands and attacked "the negro [sic] who had aroused his wrath." A detective and several uniformed police officers stepped in and broke up the scuffle, and Cobb returned to the field.[13] Although the reporter noted "that the offense was magnified in Cobb's eyes by the fact a negro [sic] was party to it," the incident was quickly forgotten, at least by Cobb and the press. A few days later, one writer kidded that Cobb's "recent peevishness" stemmed from worries that pitcher Eddie Summers, who had two hits and almost a third in the next day's game, would sneak in and "beat him to the automobile."[14]

Whereas some complained that Cobb was doing too much to win the batting title at the expense of his team, others thought Lajoie, drawing big crowds and getting big ovations in Washington and New York, was doing too little. Lajoie's recent "light batting streak," as one Cleveland news report termed it, was under analysis in Cleveland and elsewhere.[15] Commenting on how often Nap was asked to execute the hit-and-run play, a trend he had noted over the years when his hometown Nationals played the Naps,

Washington Star sports editor J. Ed Grillo wrote, "Just why a veteran of Lajoie's prowess should be handicapped by playing the hit-and-run game, thus taking a chance of forcing him to hit at a bad ball, when he could wait for what he wanted, is hard to understand."[16] The weekly *Sporting Life* picked up the trend too, albeit in laudatory tone, commenting, "Lajoie is getting to be quite an artistic bunter. Also he is always willing to resort to the hit and run play when necessary. All of which shows that he is losing no sleep over his batting average."[17]

If Lajoie didn't really care about the batting race, others did. On consecutive days in Washington, Cobb was jeered and Lajoie cheered.[18] Meanwhile, the details of Nap's recent batting woes were carried on a daily basis on sports pages around the country in statistical boxes that set off the race and contained interesting titles such as "Auto Chasers." Usually there was no mention that the figures were unofficial. One such box on August 17 showed that Lajoie now trailed Cobb by nineteen points and led Boston's Tris Speaker by just twelve points. Speaker, the Texan who had just turned twenty-two, was making a real name for himself in only his second full season in the Majors, and his best years were still ahead.

The task of scoring a game was an inexact science at best. The concept of offering a coveted prize based on the results of that effort and claiming it as accurate strained all credulity. As Cobb seemed to pull away from the pack, there continued a hue and cry from more than one quarter hinting that sinister forces were at work to boost his fortunes. In an article in the *Sporting News* in early August, St. Louis sportswriter A. J. Flanner discussed how the at-bat qualifiers were excluding a number of players from Chalmers consideration and the prospects of those few players still realistically in the hunt. Thrown in for good measure was the observation that Cobb's speed gained him advantages with scorers. It "enables him to beat out infield drives and bunts that are handled cleanly and scorers are prone to give him the benefit of the doubt when an infielder fumbles, for it is often questionable whether perfect play would have resulted in his retirement. Lajoie's record contains few hits that are not genuine, Wagner is given the shade by scorers oftener than Larry but not as frequently as the Georgia Peach, whose sprinting and spirit are his best assets."[19]

Flanner's assessment that Cobb received the benefit of the doubt from scorers based on his superior speed and base-running skill was just one of many theories on the subject. It was also one of the mildest. At the opposite end of the spectrum was at least one allegation that Cobb curried favor with official scorers by inviting them to his hotel for entertainment.[20] It was left to the reader to conjure up images of just what entertainment it might take to put a single or two in Cobb's hit column when he wasn't in Detroit. Moreover, no evidence was introduced to support the accusation, and in fact, according to Cobb biographer Al Stump, umpire Billy Evans believed that Cobb did his best to upset game officials such as scorekeepers.[21]

The truth about scorekeeper bias probably landed somewhere in between. Statistics maven George Moreland alluded to it in 1908, well before Hugh Chalmers offered one of his autos, when he stated with "certainty" that official scorers were homers when it came to the batting leaders on their local team. He branded such "favoritism" as one of baseball's "greatest evils."[22] In the minds of baseball's conspiracy theorists, this "evil" was alive and spreading its tentacles in 1910 as the battle waged on between Cobb and Lajoie.

By September each individual at bat by the Major League batting leaders became more important, and each hit meant just that much more. Even when the players did not play, thus ensuring the status quo at least for that day, it became big news. When Moreland released his unofficial batting statistics covering games played through September 1, they were quite revealing. Cobb's commanding lead over Lajoie had narrowed to a mere three points. Since Cobb now stood at .362 and Lajoie at .359, it seemed that both men's hitting had tailed off, Cobb's much more so. Speaker stood at .347 and still could not be totally disregarded. In the National League, Fred Snodgrass of the Giants, like Speaker a relative newcomer playing more or less regularly for the first time, was hitting a startling .360. Nonetheless, he had batted only 258 times in eighty-two games and would have to play fairly regularly through the last several weeks of the season to reach the magic 350 credited at bats required to qualify for the prize, let alone to win it with the best average.[23]

In early September it seemed the indomitable Cobb, feeling a growing breeze at his back, had shifted into yet a higher gear. On September 2 he chalked up three hits in a win over the White Sox, adding a pair of safeties the next day for emphasis. Nonetheless, it was noted that a number of his hits were bunts, indicating that the star outfielder was depending on his speed as much as his swift bat and eagle eye to safely reach first base. Then, in a double bill against the St. Louis Browns in Detroit on September 5, he drew a blank in five official plate appearances. Add in two sacrifices and a walk, figure in a lot of unsuccessful bunting—once with the bases loaded—and it added up to one frustrating day for the Detroit slugger. Thus, perhaps it should have come as no surprise when it was revealed on September 7 that Cobb was having problems with his vision and was under the care of an eye doctor. This then was why he did not travel with the team by boat from Detroit to Cleveland as the clubs traded cities in the midst of an eight-game series, interrupted once by a separate Sunday road contest for each club. Yet Cobb played in the first game in Detroit, a 6–2 Tigers win, and not only singled sharply early in the game, but also tripled. When Cobb failed to appear in Cleveland, one local newspaper was quick to point out that he had achieved only a .269 batting average in the seven games played to date in that city.[24] Was there an inference that the un-Cobb-like average, rather than his eye problem, accounted for the absence?

Any inference that Cobb was laying off for that reason certainly seems unfair. Cobb was the ultimate "in your face" competitor. In the previous three seasons, each of which saw him crowned his league's batting champion, he had played in no less than 150 of 154 scheduled games. Any theory that 1910 was different in that regard was debunked on September 8 in a statement issued by Robert W. Gillman, an eye specialist who had examined Cobb. The physician reported that he was treating his famous patient for "cyclitis" of the right eye, an inflammatory condition that "seriously" affects one's "binocular vision." The outlook was good for complete recovery, but only with "complete rest."[25] The statement was not only reassuring but necessary in light of the rampant speculation, including reports of impending blindness, that preceded it. Only slightly less hysteric turns had Cobb nearsighted in the right eye to the point that he closed it and used only the left eye when batting, and run down and suffering from a liver ailment.[26] If there was any truth at all to the latter two reports, it was clear that Dr. Gillman was in charge of the situation and that Cobb would not be playing for a while.

The idea of "complete rest" was apparently repugnant to at least one Detroiter, and an important one at that: Hughie Jennings. The Detroit manager told a reporter that he acknowledged Dr. Gillman's diagnosis of an inflamed right eye. When Cobb came to him requesting time off to rest, he gave him permission, "but I begged him not to worry, for I am satisfied that worry is the biggest part of his trouble."[27]

Since Cobb was already qualified for the Chalmers prize—he had more than 450 at bats through games of September 8—he could lose his grasp on the automobile only if Lajoie got a hot hand. That is exactly what happened, at least early on in September. As 3,008 Clevelanders, clearly disappointed that Cobb was not present to wage war with their hero, looked on and hooted at the Detroit hurler, George Mullin, Lajoie recorded but one official at bat, a single. Mullin passed him on two other occasions. Still, a 1-for-1 day raised Nap's average, as did a 2-for-4 effort the next day. In one seven-game period in early September, Lajoie pounded out fifteen hits. The result was an unofficial eight-point lead on the ailing Cobb through games of September 8.

Nonetheless, in the last three games played by the Naps in Detroit following the Sunday road trips, Lajoie recorded but two hits in thirteen times up against Tigers pitching. In the first of those three games, played on September 12, Nap arrived at Bennett Park in the company of Ty Cobb. Apparently, the batting race wasn't causing disaffection off the field as Cobb gave the Naps' infielder a ride to the ballpark in his automobile and then donned a pair of sunglasses to watch the game—and Lajoie's 0-for-4 struggles—from the grandstand.[28]

Some felt that Lajoie's path to the batting crown would be made that much more difficult by the lack of left-handed batters in the Naps' regular lineup. Lajoie, who batted from the right side, normally terrorized lefties but saw few because the percentages favored right-hand hurlers versus right-hand batters.[29] If, instead of a dearth of lefties, Lajoie was in the midst of a batting slump, he was the last to acknowledge it. The free swinger often said that to his mind, there was no such thing: "It's just the luck of the game—that's all."[30] The assertion made good sense. On the twelfth, while the ailing Cobb watched from the stands, Lajoie batted four times. On three at bats, he made routine outs. On the other he lost a hit when Detroit shortstop Donie Bush ranged far to his left, grabbed a bounding ball off Lajoie's bat, and threw on the dead run to nab him at first in what one reporter branded "as flagrant a case of robbery" as seen at the Detroit ballpark in many years.[31] A lesser shortstop might have watched the ball scoot by as Lajoie took first.

The next day Cobb, who coached a base early in the game, returned to active duty, at least briefly, when he pinch-hit in the eighth inning and promptly struck out on three pitches. If Cobb's turn at the plate was deemed a test, apparently the experiment was termed a failure; this despite one newspaper's assertion that by the time Cobb batted, the light was dim.[32] Over the next six games, Cobb batted just once, striking out quickly once again in a pinch hitter's role. He returned to action on September 20, playing both ends of a doubleheader against visiting Washington. He batted eight times and counted a pair of safeties.

All told, excepting the two brief pinch-hit appearances, Tyrus missed ten games because of his eye problem. Oddly, a report out of Detroit made the length and cause of Cobb's absence even more puzzling. It was said that the outfielder's return to play was occasioned by treatment rendered by an oculist on September 19. The unnamed eye specialist—who, because he was not named, was likely not the original specialist, Dr. Gillman—cured the mighty batter by removing a piece of gravel from his bad eye. Since the condition could and should have been easily treated, a theory was espoused that the real cause of Cobb's absence was his desire to transfer his services to either the Red Sox or the New York Highlanders at a substantially increased rate of pay.[33]

The speculation about the cause of Cobb's eye problems and Lajoie's mild batting slump made for interesting news copy, but how did it play out in their statistical tug-of-war? American League averages from George Moreland compiled through games of September 15, less than a month from season's end, showed the pair in a dead heat. Each was now hitting .361. Speaker was still not conceding defeat at .346. The Giants' Fred Snodgrass at .330 was now facing an uphill battle on all fronts.[34] Of course, these numbers were unofficial, and the closeness of the race only magnified the problem that, as one sportswriter lamented, "there is no way of arriving at the exact official averages of the two sluggers who are fighting it out for the auto gift."[35]

To make matters worse—at least for those baseball magnates hoping for a low-profile, clear-cut result—interest in the batting race, owing to its closeness and the high-profile participants, was picking up around the country, seemingly in direct proportion to the loss of interest in the pennant race. By September 20 the Athletics led the American League by sixteen and a half games. On that same date, the Chicago Cubs had their biggest lead of the entire season, heading the standings by thirteen and a half games. The respective pennant races had little pop and no sizzle. In the meantime the focus was on Lajoie and Cobb. And as the batting race tightened, so did the scrutiny of those who would crown the king: the official scorers. One editorial snippet, appearing in the *Washington Star*, in particular seemed to summarize the dilemmas facing these decision makers—for the most part, built-in frailties—and the difficulties in achieving a just result because of them:

> That the race between Cobb and Lajoie for the automobile has attracted more attention to the struggle for batting honors this year than ever before is true, but whether the offering of special inducements for batting honors is commendable is open to question. The charge is being made that the scorers, through ignorance or favoritism, are handing hits to Lajoie or Cobb in order to help their special pet to win the bubble buggy and the glory. There may be something in this, although most of the howling against the scoring is always unjustified. In case of uncertainty, it is a cinch that the scorer will give the batter the benefit of the doubt. When one of these plays comes up which can be charged either as a hit or an error, one faction among the spectators will accuse the scorer of deliberately throwing a hit to the star if the box score reveals a hit

next day, and another faction will accuse him of maliciously robbing the said star if a hit is not allowed. It would be impossible to satisfy all the fans or players, and when you have special rewards depending upon the scoring, then the difficulties and suspicions are increased, with resulting general dissatisfaction.[36]

The editorial merely put words to the concerns expressed by the members of the National Commission in the first place when they reluctantly agreed to accept the kind offer of Hugh Chalmers and set up rules to determine a winner of his fine automobile. Those concerns were mollified somewhat—enough to gain their assent—by their conviction that it was highly unlikely that one or two hits could mean the difference between victory and defeat. The odds, therefore, were low that any type of controversy would ensue. Nevertheless, here it was, less than a month remaining and two ballplayers were in a dead heat for the lead. A scorer's decision one way or the other could make a significant difference in who eventually finished first. The commission's worst fears were about to be realized. As baseball fans across the country eagerly watched the box scores in ever increasing numbers and rooted for their favorite player in this two-man race, the valuable prize might well be awarded to the one who did not deserve it, and all because a designated pooh-bah in a press box decided to chalk one up for the home team or perhaps even lean toward a favorite player on the opposing team.

Chapter Seven

I'm happy the season is so near over.
—Jack O'Connor

The standard modus operandi for downtown workers who lived in the Cleveland suburbs was their nightly commute on the suburban rail lines. Normally, the operation ran smoothly for train dispatchers, motormen, and conductors alike. Riders tired from a long day of work would board the motor cars, often unfolding their newspaper or taking a brief snooze as they waited for the conductor to place them on alert with the pending arrival at the station closest to home. Not so in the early days of fall 1910. Dispatchers were heard to complain about problems, particularly with those cars leaving downtown after 6 p.m. It was almost impossible to get passengers to their destination on time. The downtowners possessed valuable information. They had better access to the important baseball news of the day. And during the first week of October 1910, only one piece of news was important to Clevelanders: the daily batting results for Messrs. Cobb and Lajoie. How often had they batted in that afternoon's game? How many hits? Those on the motor cars had the scoop. Those in the suburbs wanted it. One dispatcher described a bizarre scene in which suburbanites ran out and flagged down the cars to find out the day's results: "If every person that stopped our cars got on and rode, we would be doing about three times as great a business as we really are. To tell the truth, I guess it would not be a bad idea for us to have streamers painted and nailed to the cars, telling what Lajoie and Cobb did that afternoon. It would save time, all right."[1]

Much had happened since those unofficial batting average tabulations released for games through September 15. While Cobb wrestled with his vision problem, Lajoie, his batting statistics bolstered by several multihit games, had increased his average by several points. Nap picked up his two hundredth hit and one more in five turns at the plate against Colby Jack Coombs of the Athletics in an eleven-inning scoreless tie on September 21. Coombs, a righty, was in the midst of a thirty-one-win season. The tie, which counted in the statistical—if not the win-loss—column, was one of nine involving the Naps that season. Lajoie played and batted in each. The Tigers' only tie occurred while Cobb was out for his eye. Cobb caught a break from the schedule makers when he finally reentered the lineup on September 20. He struggled at the plate that day. Some attributed it to rust, but most felt that a few more days off would serve to ensure a complete recovery. This he got in the way of a three-day hiatus. His Tigers did not return to action again until September 24, splitting a doubleheader with the Red Sox in Detroit. In the first game, Cobb did not bat until the eighth inning and then only in a pinch-hitting role, garnering a hit. Apparently, he was a late arrival; no reason was given for his absence. In the second contest, he went 2 for 3, serving notice that he was quickly getting back in stride. The game account in the *Free Press* relates that for his efforts that day, Ty collected a double and a single in three official trips to the plate. He also sacrificed a base runner to third, which did not count for a time at bat. The game account and box score agree.[2] The next day, September 25, the same two teams would tangle, and once again Cobb went 2 for 3. He was clearly finding his eye. The games of the twenty-fourth and twenty-fifth were apparently properly scored and relayed to the league office without controversy. Later—much, much later—the batting results of those two days would come under a magnifying glass and a brighter light. By then a batting champion had been crowned.

Perhaps it was merely a coincidence, or then again, maybe it was related to Cobb's tardy arrival for the first game of that September 24 doubleheader, but on that same day a news report out of Detroit carried an uncharacteristic outburst from Cobb's teammate and fellow star outfielder Sam Crawford. "Wahoo" Sam, as he came to be known, had been with the Tigers since 1903, arriving from the Cincinnati Reds of the National League already recognized as one of the game's primary sluggers. During his time with Detroit, he did little to tarnish that reputation, often finishing a campaign as one of the American League's batting and home run leaders. He was the acknowledged batting star of the Tigers until he was supplanted by Cobb. He was also considered a gentleman, a player respected by team-mates and foes alike. If he was jealous of Cobb's success, he had kept it to himself as the team enjoyed immense success from 1907 to 1909. Now the team, over fifteen games behind the Athletics, was struggling, about to come up well short in the current pennant race. The native Nebraskan felt he was receiving more than his share of the blame for the Tigers' failures. He went on the attack, claiming he had played his best and should not be "censored." He felt the problem went deeper than "poor playing" and said so publicly. The team lacked "harmony." In terms remarkably similar to those voiced a few weeks earlier by Davy Jones, Crawford branded Cobb the culprit:

I understand that Cobb has complained that with me hitting behind him he has been handicapped on the bases. Maybe it was the same fault that worried Bush to the extent that he was shifted in the line-up. Cobb criticised [sic] Bush unfairly a number of times and on one occasion I remonstrated. Bush is as valuable as anyone to the club.

I have noticed repeatedly that the club caters to Cobb more than to any other player; if he reports late or misses an inning or two little is said. I vouch that if I did the same thing I would be reprimanded right. This is the club's business, however, but I wish to show that others are to be criticised instead of me being singled out as responsible for the club's poor showing this year.

According to the report, Bush and Crawford were no longer speaking to Cobb.[3] Could Jones have been far behind?

No matter the rapport in the Tigers' clubhouse, one thing was clear: Cobb and his bat were communicating nicely and quickly closing ranks with Nap Lajoie. The benefactors of the seesaw battle proved to be the sportswriting set, ever eager for a chance to turn a phrase. A 3-for-4 day for Lajoie meant that he "took a fresh grip on the steering wheel" of the Chalmers. In contrast, a three-pitch strikeout by Cobb meant that he had "spilled a little of the gasoline he is saving for that gift auto."[4] Meanwhile, in New York City a real road race was in the final stages of preparation. On October 1, as throngs of onlookers lined the course, the sixth edition of the Vanderbilt Cup would commence. For at least a few hours, the number of hits Cobb or Lajoie counted that day in their race would be of little mind.[5]

Then, just as the Cobb machinery began to operate smoothly after many bumps in the road, the Lajoie Express struck a pothole, or to be more precise, the pothole struck him. In the first game of a doubleheader played in Boston on September 27, Nap, playing second base and batting cleanup, started off in style, hitting the ball over the head of centerfielder Tris Speaker and all the way to the flagpole for an inside-the-park home run. The four-bagger sent Red Sox rookie starter Ben Hunt to the showers after one inning with his team down three. In the third inning, Lajoie singled over second against Charley Hall, a spot starter and sometime reliever. When he faced off against Hall the next time around, he was struck on the right shoulder by a foul tip.[6] Despite the insult to his shoulder, Lajoie hung in gamely and doubled for his third hit of the day. After that, however, Lajoie completed the two-game set without another hit in four official tries, although he was intentionally walked in the fifth inning of the second game. Furthermore, the next day, September 28, he was unable to answer the bell for the first time all season. According to one Cleveland newspaper, "His shoulder is so sore that he can hardly raise his right arm. He was hit by a foul tip in the first game Tuesday and should not have played in the second. But he stuck it out and was compelled to stay out Wednesday [the twenty-eighth versus Boston]. It is doubtful he will play today [the twenty-ninth]. His whole right shoulder is black, blue and mottled. Whether the bone is hurt or not is not known yet."[7]

It was Lajoie's first absence in this the 152nd game of the season for the Naps. Speculation was that his right shoulder had stiffened as the doubleheader progressed. By game time he could barely raise his arm, despite the efforts of the Naps' trainer to loosen it up. Instead, he was seated in the grandstand, commenting on the unusual view: "It looked mighty queer to me. I saw lots of vacant spaces to hit the ball to up here, but when I am at bat it generally looks as if the other fellows had about forty men out there. I'll be back in the game, though, by Friday, and possibly tomorrow."[8]

Lajoie's absence on September 28 and, as it turned out, on the twenty-ninth as well created a window of opportunity for Cobb that he fully exploited. On the twenty-eighth he went 3 for 3 against the New York Yankees and newly crowned player-manager Hal Chase. Because he had played significantly fewer games than his rival, each Cobb hit—all three of the infield variety—counted just a little bit more toward boosting his average. According to the trackers at no less than two Cleveland newsies, Cobb's perfection boosted his average four points and reduced Lajoie's margin to less than five percentage points.[9] This assessment closely matched that of George Moreland, whose service through games of September 29 had Lajoie at .375 and Cobb at .370.[10]

As Lajoie sat and Cobb sent Yankees players scurrying after his trio of hits, American League Secretary Robert McRoy was in Cleveland announcing the league's plans for a team of All-Stars to play a series of games versus the pennant-winning Athletics should the National League season extend beyond the American League's and delay the start of the World Series from its original date, October 13, until October 17. This would keep the Athletics from going stale in the interim. The games with the All-Stars would begin in Philadelphia on September 10, one day after the official close of the American League season. One of the players named to the All-Star team was Ty Cobb. No members of the Naps, including Lajoie, or the Yankees were selected for play against the Athletics as those two teams were involved in separate postseason series with National League opponents. (The Naps were scheduled for an All-Ohio series with the downstate Reds.) Although the team was in place, the National Commission was still at work in hopes the scheduling squabble could be resolved and such an All-Star series would not be required.[11]

By the end of September, Robert McRoy and the National Commission were in the news for other reasons: McRoy for stating that in Cleveland and Detroit there was more interest in the batting race than in the pennant race and the National Commission for indicating it planned to make sure such a situation did not arise again. According to sports columnist Joe S. Jackson,

> There will be no prize for the leading batsman of the country next year—or, at least, the national commission will sanction the giving of none, though it cannot prevent any one who wishes so to do from offering and handing to the country's chief clubber an appreciation of his performances. But the rows that have arisen, the charges and, countercharges that have been made, and the annoyance that the affair has caused the two league secretaries will result in refusal on the part of the heads of organized ball to take cognizance officially of any prizes of this sort. Secretary Heydler, of the National League, already has refused to attempt to compile the official averages—on which ownership of the auto, of course, must be decided—and the American League, which undoubtedly will get the prize, is refusing to give any information in regard to the race between Lajoie and Cobb.[12]

But that could and perhaps would all be ironed out next year. In the here and now, the games of 1910 had progressed to October. While most everyone in Major League Baseball was merely playing through to the end, the stakes remained high for two of their peers. For each of them, a single at bat could mean victory or defeat. As such, the status of next year's prize was of no concern. The National Commission had accepted Hugh Chalmers's offer of an automobile at the beginning of the 1910 season. It had set the rules. The valuable new vehicle was still very much in play, and at this point, with only a little over one week remaining in the season, neither Cobb nor Lajoie was willing to allow that the other might win it.

That is why Cobb must have winced when a ruling by Billy Evans on a slow roller to second cost him an infield hit in a close win over the Browns. Tigers fans howled their disapproval. On the same day, Lajoie received a gift hit in Chicago, to the delight of White Sox fans, when replacement outfielder Dutch Zwilling lost his fly ball in the late afternoon sun. As a result Cobb went 1 for 3, instead of 2 for 3, and Lajoie went 3 for 4, instead of 2 for 4.[13] However, instead of sulking, the next day Cobb exhibited growing maturity, taking any frustration out on the baseball and not someone in the stands or the locker room. Facing the Browns' Albert "Red" Nelson on October 2, he stroked four singles in five trips to the plate, part of a twenty-hit production off the rookie pitcher. Nelson had pitched particularly well against the White Sox and Athletics, but Cobb and his Tigers owned him this day in St. Louis in a 12–7 victory. Lest one believe every baseball fan in America was in Lajoie's corner wishing Cobb would fail, the *St. Louis Globe-Democrat* reported "a fresh bunch of applause" each time Ty chalked up another hit.[14]

Meanwhile in Chicago, a much more experienced Doc White, winner in 1910 of fifteen of his career 189 victories, was holding Lajoie hitless in three official appearances. The widely divergent performances had a major impact on the batting race. Although no one source could truthfully claim superiority over another when it came to totaling the numbers, the consensus now had Cobb trailing Lajoie by a point or less. Even George Moreland was now caught up in the excitement. On October 3 newspapers reported that the statistics maven had Lajoie hitting .37543, while Cobb stood but a whisper and a sigh behind at .37446.[15]

As if it had been in the game plan all year long, the two aspirants would now face off on the same diamond one last time, the end of their long wooden bats almost close enough to touch one another. On this occasion the confrontation would take the form of a two-game series in Detroit, the home team still vying to edge the Yankees for second place. Following these games, the Tigers would travel to Chicago and face the White Sox in a season-ending four-game series. The Naps would finish their season by heading to St. Louis for a four-game set with the last-place Browns.

Despite the Tigers' prospects for a runner-up spot in the league, the main attraction in Detroit for their games with the Naps was, of course, Cobb versus Lajoie. When rain cancelled the scheduled first game on October 4, H. G. Salsinger, veteran sports scribe for the *Detroit News*, took the opportunity to let each player tell what he saw in the hitting style of the other. Cobb saw in right-handed hitter Lajoie, a player he idolized as a youngster, a wonderful eyesight and physique. . . . One of the few remaining members of the old school—the school of sluggers. . . . Pitchers were not using the spit ball when Larry started out. Today they are and the spit ball demands a "chop" instead of the longer swing. . . . Larry has refused to adopt this method, pursuing the old with as much success as others use the new against the new pitching. . . . Larry is also scientific. . . . He studies carefully every man whom he goes up against. . . . He is a grand batter.[16]

The "scientific" part of Cobb's analysis clashed with an analysis of Lajoie's hitting approach afforded Salsinger earlier by ace Detroit pitcher "Wild" Bill Donovan, who told the writer, "When Lajoie is at bat a pitcher had best put the ball over the plate and trust to luck. If he means to hit it he will go after all kinds, high, low, wide, curve or fastball. He does not sidestep any of them. He just wades in and meets them."[17]

On the other hand, Lajoie told Salsinger he saw the left-hand-hitting Cobb as a "natural hitter." To his way of thinking, "Hitters are like poets—you can't make them. Cobb hit from the start of his career. . . . Then Cobb has good eyesight. . . . He also has speed. He gets many hits because of his speed, beating out grounders." However, even "if he would be slower he would probably still bat at a high figure, for he would hit them out more." And, finally, "he outguesses pitchers. He thinks quickly and he moves fast."[18]

Naturally, Salsinger, who considered Cobb the greatest baseball player he had ever seen, needed to weigh in as well. He decried those writers who said that Cobb would not get as many hits as he did if he had had Larry's slower foot speed. Salsinger cited Cobb's higher number of total bases in far fewer games, as well as his higher number of runs batted in, runs scored, and home runs. In the writer's opinion, this meant Cobb hit the ball harder than Lajoie, an interesting view but of little import in a batting race in which one base counted as much as four and the new automobile was on each player's mind first and foremost, no matter what they said to the contrary.[19]

While Salsinger and others analyzed their strengths and weaknesses,

Cobb and Lajoie watched the weather and waited. The game postponed from October 4 would now be part of a doubleheader set for the next day. That evening following the rainout, both teams were guests at a "baseball night," the final in a series of such events held that summer at the Gayety, a Detroit theater.[20] Although a number of the players from each team attended, it is uncertain whether either Cobb or Lajoie was among them. The night before Lajoie had been spotted at the Cadillac, a downtown hotel that was presumably team headquarters for the Naps while they played in Detroit. The Naps' star had been surrounded by admirers. He had stood his ground for some time, exiting around 9:00, but not before making a few comments about the batting race: "If I can win the automobile, I will be pleased. Whoever gets the machine, I hope it will be secured honestly. I don't know how the figures stand in Mr. Johnson's office, but, however they are, I will be satisfied."[21]

The next day, as the teams warmed up for their double bill, Lajoie resumed his role of shy suitor and agreed to join his equally nonplussed rival Cobb to examine the prize package, sans ribbon and up close and personal, albeit from the back seat. Neither man wanted to appear the least bit interested in his quarry; neither wanted to assume a position behind the wheel. As the players posed patiently and a slew of photographers snapped away, it is safe to say neither was aware of a report about to be published in a Cleveland newspaper later that day. For, according to the *Cleveland News*, reports that the batting averages of the pair stood less than one point apart were erroneous. In what the paper called "practically official dope," discrepancies between several box scores and what was reported by the official scorer to league officials actually gave Cobb a seven and a half point lead (Cobb was at .380 and Lajoie between .372 and .373) as the pair prepared to face off one last time.[22]

The article in the *News*, written by sports editor Ed Bang, the man who succeeded the legendary Grantland Rice, claimed a greater accuracy in reporting based on the use of box scores published in the various cities where the Naps and Tigers had played. The *News* had wired newspapers that limited their reporting to box scores reflecting the decisions of the "official" scorers who reported to league secretary Robert McRoy. These boxes showed Cobb with two fewer at bats and two more hits, while Lajoie had one fewer time at bat and two fewer hits—a significant variation from the "unofficial dope" gleaned from Associated Press (AP) box scores, which showed Lajoie in the lead by less than a point. According to Bang, Cobb's additional hits came from a pair of games in Philadelphia on August 29 and 30. The box scores that appeared in, for example, the *Detroit Free Press* showed Cobb with two hits in four at bats, whereas the Associated Press boxes, trumpeted as the official "unofficial" account of the games, showed Cobb with 1-for-4 efforts on each occasion.[23]

The explanation for the variation from one source to another was not as complicated as it sounds. A Philadelphia journalist named William G. Weart (employed by the Associated Press and not the "official scorer") supplied box scores to morning newspapers throughout the nation. He awarded Cobb one base hit in each contest. Because the games were played in Philadelphia, the scoring system in place called for a local sportswriter appointed by the Philadelphia Athletics baseball organization to act as official scorer. That man was George E. "Stony" McLinn of the *Philadelphia Press*. He ruled that Cobb had achieved not one, but two base hits in each contest.[24]

The errors Bang and his staff found for Lajoie as far as number of at bats stemmed from a similar type of discrepancy in box scores from a game he played on August 20 at Washington. The Associated Press unofficially recorded six at bats and disseminated its results to the newspapers subscribing to its service, whereas other newspaper box scores, for example the one carried by the *Cleveland Plain Dealer*, had five. The lower hit count, according to Bang, could be attributed to a simple error in math, not a discrepancy in reporting, since both the AP and the newspaper accounts added up the same, giving Lajoie 212 hits and not the 214 used by many in reporting a higher average.[25]

When added up, subtracted out, and divided accordingly, the difference in numbers—seven and one-half as reported by Ed Bang—was significant. If true, Napoleon Lajoie's campaign for the Chalmers was in serious trouble. As Bang summed it up, in the remaining six games, Lajoie would "have to hit his head off." Otherwise, he would need to "be content to smell the gasoline of Ty Cobb's new auto."[26] Because the report emanated from a Cleveland paper—and not from Tigertown—it carried an aura of credibility.

It is doubtful, however, whether either Cobb or Lajoie knew about the revised figures as they sat in the rear passenger seats of the Chalmers and bravely nodded and smiled for the horde of photographers. The cameramen completed their handiwork and joined a Bennett Park crowd of just more than four thousand fans who had come to the ballpark to find out which ballplayer would end the day in the driver's seat for the auto. If fans thought one player would leave with a decided advantage, they were wrong. The doubleheader was dead even in almost every way, certainly the most important one, as each player went 3 for 6 for the day, counting an infield hit and a double among his bounty. The teams each won a game. The first went to the Naps in ten innings, and the second ended with a Tigers victory in five because of darkness and rain. Both Cobb and Lajoie were applauded heartily during each plate appearance. Thankfully, there were no controversial scoring decisions. The only partisanship occurred in the tenth inning of game one, when Naps pitcher Willie Mitchell passed Cobb with two out and nobody on base. At the end of the inning, the Tigers' faithful booed Mitchell all the way to the bench.

Now Cobb prepared to travel to Chicago, where he had experienced mixed results in earlier games, encouraged by the fact he would not face White Sox ace Ed Walsh, who had already ended his season and headed home. Doc White, working on a fifteen-win season, was still there, but Cobb had found success with him. Lajoie, clearly aware by this point that he needed some help, headed to friendlier confines in St. Louis, home to the dead-last Browns.

Those Browns, under the direction of first-year manager Jack O'Connor, had won but forty-five games to that point and trailed first-place Philadelphia by more than fifty games. On the eve of their season-ending series with the Naps, there were rumors that O'Connor, "believed" to be working under a two-year contract, planned to step down after just the one year owing to the hopelessness of the situation. If quitting was indeed ever on his mind, the Browns' field general took to the phone with a reporter from the *St. Louis Times* on the morning of the first of four with the Naps and put the matter to rest, saying, "Nothing to it, old boy: nothing to it. ... Mr. Hedges [the Browns' club president] and I have been busy discussing plans for next year for the past several weeks; in fact, we are talking about the 1911 team almost entirely, being thoroughly disgusted over our luck this season."[27]

When it came to St. Louis, Jack O'Connor was a special case. He was born John Joseph O'Connor in that city on June 2, 1869. His early years were spent as an energetic participant in the city's north side baseball scene. He was only one of a number of future baseball stars from the Goose Hill section of town, a neighborhood described by at least one scribe as "run or fight" and where Jack "seldom ran, except when going down to first base."[28] While there he was a catcher for a semipro team known as the Peach Pies, which later earned him the nickname "Peach Pie." One member of that team was Patsy Tebeau. The pair would hook up often over the years.

After beginning his career professionally with a team in Jacksonville, Illinois, he landed a position catching for St. Joseph (Missouri) of the Western League in 1866. He was seventeen and already fully schooled in a game that favored those with a quick temper, always ready and willing to wade into the fray flashing bare fists. O'Connor's build—he was a stocky, square-shouldered man who stood five foot ten and weighed 170 pounds during his playing days—put him in good stead as he developed a reputation as a player who seldom backed down from a fight with players or managers alike. This disposition earned him yet another, perhaps more apt, nickname, "Rowdy Jack."

In 1887, after one successful season with St. Joe's, O'Connor found himself in the Major Leagues at Cincinnati of the American Association. Much to his chagrin, however, his new manager, Gus Schmelz, was a disciplinarian who came down hard on players who liked their drink, fining them five dollars—a substantial sum in those days—each time he caught them with a beer in hand. O'Connor racked up numerous fines. The two were almost instantly at odds. As a result, Rowdy Jack's tires hit the road in his second season in the Queen City. O'Connor recalled, "I finally decided that I couldn't get along with Schmelz and after a big fight, he suspended me and I jumped to the outlaw Denver club, where George Tebeau [Patsy's brother] was manager. I went so well with Denver that Columbus [Solons of the American Association] hired me for 1889 and what do you suppose happened then? Well, sir, my old friend Schmelz moved over there as manager."[29]

This time around O'Connor fared better with his tightfisted boss. He remained in Columbus, Ohio, for most of three years, hitting a career high .324 in 121 games in 1890, while in the words of one baseball historian, "making a fast reputation as the [American] Association's dirtiest player."[30]

He left Columbus midseason 1891, expelled from the league because of "habitual drunkenness, disorderly conduct and insubordination."[31] He finished the year in Denver of the Western Association. However, his success in Columbus had piqued the interest of boyhood friend Patsy Tebeau, now player-manager for the Cleveland Spiders of the old National League. O'Connor, almost twenty-three, joined that club in 1892. He would remain for seven seasons. During that time, he did nothing to shed his reputation as one of Major League Baseball's rowdiest performers, playing for one of its rowdiest teams.

In 1899 O'Connor headed home to St. Louis when the Cleveland and St. Louis franchises, under common ownership, shuffled their rosters. He played for the Perfectos—soon to be known as the Cardinals—that season and part of the next before he was purchased by Barney Dreyfuss's Pittsburgh Pirates. By now O'Connor was no longer a regular, but he was still of value as an experienced catcher. The 1900 Pirates were on the verge of becoming the National League's top team. After a second-place finish in 1900, they led the league in both 1901 and 1902. As such, their roster was stocked with some of baseball's most talented players, a feature that did not elude the keen eye of Ban Johnson as he and his upstart American League went to war with the establishment of which the Pirates were an integral part.

If there is anything to that old saw that politics and war make for strange bedfellows, then Ban Johnson and Jack O'Connor help to prove the point. One of the underpinnings of Johnson's baseball philosophy was the need to clean up the image of the game. Old Rowdy Jack O'Connor fit to a tee the type of player Johnson detested and wished to eliminate from Organized Baseball. Nonetheless, O'Connor possessed several attributes Johnson coveted at this particular moment in the evolution of his dream; he had an insider's access to a number of star players Johnson sought to lure to his new league, as well as the fearlessness and lack of moral fiber to go after them despite his position as a player on a National League team. Under the guise of all is fair in love and war, Johnson secretly hired O'Connor to persuade a bevy of Pirates stalwarts to cast aside the contractual tethers binding them and jump leagues. Because the Pirates were winning big, it would be difficult to convince any of their top players to walk away, but Johnson thought he had just the "inside" man for this task.[32]

According to Ban Johnson, "[Cleveland club president] Charles Somers and myself started from Cleveland for Atlantic City. Prior to this we had had dealings with Jack O'Connor, then a Pirate catcher, and he had agreed to act as our agent in lining up the players we intended to lift from Dreyfuss's team."[33]

Upon their arrival in Pittsburgh in August 1902, Johnson and Somers made contact with O'Connor, who informed them that a number of his team's players remained unsigned for the next season but that Dreyfuss was growing increasingly suspicious and had him under surveillance. He suggested he bring the targeted Pirates players to the Lincoln Hotel, where the American League executives had secured lodging. Later that evening Rowdy Jack arrived with the first of several of their quarry. Johnson and Somers made offers and negotiated through the night. By the next morning, six Pirates players, including O'Connor himself, were under contract with the new American League franchise the New York Highlanders for the 1903 season. Five of the players actually made the jump; one was pitcher Jack Chesbro, who later entered the Hall of Fame. When Dreyfuss learned of the signings, it confirmed what he had suspected: that O'Connor had conspired against him. He suspended him for the remainder of the 1902 season with loss of pay. Johnson claims he picked up the tab, some nine hundred dollars.[34]

In addition to ingratiating O'Connor with Ban Johnson, the move to the

American League resulted in a boost in pay for Rowdy Jack, from $3,500 to $5,000.[35] The backup catcher's true value to the Highlanders was in Jack Chesbro's desire to have him as his catcher. However, O'Connor clashed almost immediately and frequently with his new manager, Clark Griffith. As the season ended, he was pedaled to St. Louis. Rowdy Jack was home again, but this time around he was the property of the American League's St. Louis Browns. Since he spent his off-seasons in St. Louis, the trade seemed quite fortuitous for the aging ballplayer; however, Jack played only a few games in 1904 and left the team owing to a salary dispute. He sat out the entire 1905 season because of a conditioning problem and opened a local saloon with his brother-in-law, Browns pitcher Jack Powell. When the pair decided to get in shape and sign with the Browns in 1906, team manager Jimmy McAleer issued an ultimatum: sell the saloon or give up baseball. The pair opted for the former. O'Connor appeared in fifty-five games but posted a meager .190 average. Still, the veteran's real strength was his ability to handle pitchers and his overall knowledge of the game, traits Browns club president Robert Lee "Colonel Bob" Hedges would remember when he released O'Connor at the end of the 1907 season.

His playing career seemingly at an end, forty-year-old Jack O'Connor resurfaced in Little Rock, Arkansas, in 1909, playing a handful of games for the Travelers, a Southern Association team. By the end of the 1909 season, he was scouting for the Browns amid rumors that after eight frustrating seasons with the Browns and one with the Blues, Jimmy McAleer was on the ropes and O'Connor in line to succeed him as the Browns' field general. Prior to the 1910 season, that is exactly what happened. After all or part of twenty-one seasons of Major League Baseball, many spent giving his managers fits, the rowdy one was now a manager in his own right.

O'Connor's stewardship of the Browns was met with cautious optimism. The caution stemmed from the Browns' seventh-place finishes the previous two years; the optimism because the new skipper had "made a deep study of baseball, and few men in the game have a superior knowledge of the sport. He has a knack of doing the unexpected or outguessing his adversary. . . . O'Connor is assured of a fair trial, and in order to make good as a manager he must, some day round up a first-division team."[36]

Now it was October of a season that saw the Browns sink to a new level. As he approached his team's last series, some thought O'Connor would abandon ship, even if he wasn't given a shove overboard by Browns management. In speaking with the press, he had quickly dismissed any such notion. He planned to remain on board for 1911. Still, apparently forgetting that the regular season ended on Sunday, October 9, Rowdy Jack concluded the interview by telling his caller, "I'm happy the season is so near over. I'm going to fall off the water wagon Saturday night and forget my troubles. But spike that rumor that I'm going to quit."[37]

What did all this mean for Napoleon Lajoie, a hard-hitting second baseman in serious need of a batch of base hits, as he faced a four-game series with O'Connor's all-but-in-the-soup Brownies?

Chapter Eight

It had about the same standing among sportsmen as a
limburger cheese might enjoy at a perfume bazaar.
—John Edward Wray

Only one day separated Ty Cobb from his final face-off with Lajoie when
he and his Tigers arrived in Chicago to begin their season-ending four-
game series with the White Sox. Updated figures following the October 5
doubleheader between the Tigers and Naps had Cobb's average rounded
off at .382 and Lajoie's at .374.[1] By now the Tigers trailed the Athletics by
more then seventeen games, so the focus remained, as it had for the last
month or so, on Cobb as he prepared to put the finishing touches on yet
another league batting title. Nonetheless, the Tigers still had a shot at
second, so there was something else on the line for them to think about.
On the mound for the White Sox, as anticipated, was Doc White. At one
time White's highly effective drop ball had lured Cobb, just like the rest
of them, to his detriment, but not this time around.[2] Although at the end
of the day the Tigers were on the short end of an 11-5 count, they had
battered White and knocked him out in the fourth inning. True to form,
Ty singled and doubled in four tries to hold serve in his match with the
Frenchman, who went 3 for 4 against rookie pitcher Roy Mitchell (4-2
in six games, all starts, 2.60 ERA) before an adoring crowd in St. Louis.
At least one report out of that city, a "Special to the [*Cleveland*] *Plain
Dealer*," claimed that Lajoie's "first safety was a gift from the lenient St.

Louis scorer." Apparently, Mitchell's pitch to Lajoie in the fourth inning was a rolling comebacker, which Mitchell fumbled. It was recovered by the second baseman, who threw wide. In the observer's opinion, the play would have been scored an error "in nine cases out of ten."[3] As it was, Nap gained a little on his rival, yet not nearly enough with but three games to go. Revised unofficial figures in one Detroit paper had Cobb at .382 and Lajoie at .376.[4]

The next afternoon, Friday, October 7, it rained in St. Louis. The Tigers, Cobb in the lineup, took the field in Chicago. On the mound for the White Sox in search of his tenth victory against twelve defeats was Fred Olmstead. The twenty-eight-year-old righty would hand the Tigers a 2–0 defeat and end the season with a sparkling 1.95 ERA. Undaunted, Cobb would double and single off him, ending the day—and, as it turned out, his season—2 for 3 with a walk. By the next morning, Cobb and manager Hughie Jennings were back in Detroit, set to forgo the final pair of games in Chicago. Cobb had asked to be excused, and the request was granted. He would board a ship headed for Buffalo and then wind his way to Philadelphia to join the team of American League All-Stars set to hone the Athletics into a sharp-edged sword for their forthcoming World Series appearance. Jennings was headed to the "wilds" of Scranton, Pennsylvania, or to New York City to watch the city series between the Highlanders and the Giants. It all depended on which newspaper you read. In his absence, the Tigers would be managed by pitcher Bill Donovan.

Although there is little doubt Cobb ended his season on the assumption that he had a safe lead over Lajoie, enough so that playing the two remaining games could only hurt him, there was some attempt to excuse his absence for health reasons. A report in one Cleveland newspaper had him declaring that he was not feeling well.[5] Biographer Al Stump claimed his "eye trouble reappeared."[6] To his credit, Cobb never used either excuse. This did not mean his absence was criticized any less. The Cleveland sporting press was particularly harsh. The prime example appeared in the city's *Plain Dealer* as a caption to a drawing of Cobb, bat in hand, standing atop a pedestal. The paper chided Cobb for "suffering from that peculiar disease, 'congealed condition of the pedal extremities,' known to card players as 'cold feet.' Cobb was similarly stricken a few weeks ago, but recovered as soon as the Cleveland series was ended. His present attack is expected to pass away by Monday. In some sections of the country it is known as chrome streakitis."[7]

The Detroit sports press harbored no illusions. One paper reported simply that Cobb withdrew "after being informed that Larry Lajoie didn't have the slightest chance to land the automobile."[8] The statement raises the question, Who provided Cobb with such definitive information? Just about every newspaper in the country carried different batting average figures at the time. Cobb shied away from any activity that might affect his vision, and thus he probably did not read the newspaper coverage of the race. Would he have sat out the race if he had scanned the October 7 edition of the *Detroit News*? The paper told readers that the latest reports of Cobb's wide lead were incorrect since they had not accorded Cobb with enough at bats. His lead was only four, not seven or more.[9] Or what about that crazy cautionary statement that appeared the same day in "Auto Chasers," the statistical account of the Chalmers race now appearing daily on the sports pages of the *Plain Dealer*? It warned readers that their figures showing Cobb in front by 2.4 points were "a revision of revised figures and contain several corrections. Yet they are unofficial and the actual averages . . . will not be known until announced by the league secretary, Oct. 17."[10] To be sure, it sounded like the caveat was written by a young pup with a keenly nebulous nature fresh out of law school; nevertheless, it was a statement of the truth: no one did have a truly accurate batting count for either Cobb or Lajoie. Thus, despite what Ty may have perceived or been told, Lajoie still had a fighting chance. All Cobb had accomplished was to lock in his totals two games early.

On Saturday Lajoie set about to make up ground, knowing little more than anyone else just how much distance he needed to cover. On the mound for the Browns was their young right-hander, Bill Bailey. At only twenty-two Bailey was already in his fourth season with the Browns, the last two mostly as a starter. On this, the next to the last day of the season, he was in search of only his fourth victory. He entered the contest with a record of 3-17. Lajoie and his supporters could have been excused if they harbored visions of a big day at the plate. As it turned out, however, Bailey pitched one of his better games, surrendering only a pair of runs in suffering his eighteenth loss by a 2–0 count. In the process he quieted Lajoie's bat. In the first and third innings, the Naps' star was thrown out at first on grounders. In the fifth, he swung at the first pitched ball, popping it to Browns third sacker John L. "Red" Corriden for an easy out. In the eighth inning, likely his last at bat, Lajoie lifted what was generally described as a routine fly ball to center fielder Hub Northen. The rookie outfielder camped under the ball, caught it, and then dropped it. It was an error to everybody's eye; everybody that is but the one man who counted, official scorer E. Victor Parrish of the *St. Louis Republic*.[11] Parrish, filling in for the appointed official scorer, Richard J. "Dick" Collins—also of the *Republic*—scored it a double, and Lajoie escaped the afternoon 1 for 4.

The next day newspapers in St. Louis, Detroit, and even Cleveland were almost totally of one mind: Parrish had blown the call. Lajoie's hometown crier, the *Plain Dealer*, painted the best face on the ruling by refusing to call an error an error, choosing instead to simply acknowledge that its fair-haired boy "should have gone hitless" but did not when "first Northen misjudged [the high pop fly], but managed to camp under it, only to drop it. Lajoie was credited with a hit for his effort."[12] The *Detroit News*, with no such reason to turn the other cheek, described it thusly: "The Frenchman [Lajoie] hit an easy fly to Northen. The fielder caught the ball, held it, and then dropped it. There was no chance to give Northen anything but an error. The official scorer, however, chalked it up as a two-base hit." Furthermore, the *News* and at least one St. Louis reporter pointed to irregularities in the first inning, when the Browns failed to chase after a pair of pop fouls before Lajoie grounded out.[13]

The *St. Louis Star* was not nearly as gracious. Although the newspaper had no horse in the Chalmers race, reporter Brice Hoskins might have seen an opportunity to take a swipe at a colleague who wrote for a crosstown rival. Then again, since he tempered his criticism with some praise, he may have been merely telling the truth. After reporting that Lajoie, whose chances for the crown entering the contest were "slight," responded to questions regarding Cobb's decision to quit the race with a shrug of his shoulders and a verbal "I don't care," Hoskins observed that Lajoie played the game that day as if he really didn't care. The reporter then proceeded to light into Parrish's decision to award Lajoie a double:

Official Scorer Parrish, generally conceded to be a splendid authority, credited Lajoie with one two-base hit out of four official times at bat, notwithstanding we fail to understand how he arrived at his decision. Northen ought to have stuck the ball in his pocket, but instead of doing so, he made an obliging muff and the great Larry took two bases on the bobble. We are constrained to believe that Mr. Parrish did not see the play in the same light as almost everyone else saw it, and for at least once during the season made a mistake. Our opinion in the matter is shared by hundreds of others, too, among the number being Walter Morris, former Cardinal, but now owner of the Fort Worth club; Park Superintendent Henry Fabian, who played ball for twenty years; Scout Charlie Barrett of the Browns, a veteran player, and Outfielder Danny Hoffman of the Browns. The opinions of all these gentlemen were volunteered and not solicited. We might add that Brother Lanigan and Brother Lloyd also saw the play our way, and sent in corrections to their papers when they learned how the play had been scored officially.[14]

Billy Evans had umpired a number of Cleveland games during the season. He was the umpire in Saturday's game as well. Afterward, he remarked, "Not until today have I seen anything to make me believe that Lajoie was being helped to win the batting prize." He had heard the rumors but had seen nothing to confirm their credibility. "Not until today [Saturday] have I seen Larry helped out and I'm not even sure he was helped today."[15]

Neither Evans nor any of the newspapers openly questioned Hub Northen's effort in dropping a very catchable ball or Parrish's motivation in scoring the dropped ball a hit. Perhaps one or both were angered at reports that Cobb had laid off in order to protect his lead or moved by the obvious adoration Lajoie received from Browns fans as he gamely struggled to land a hit off the unusual pitching mastery of the Browns' Bill Bailey. Northen never weighed in on the topic. However, Parrish, or at least his newspaper, painted a different scenario of Lajoie's fly ball and

Northen's play for it. Although the *Republic*'s game report did not carry a byline, it is not hard to imagine Victor Parrish pounding the keyboard as he reported—or rather defended—how in his judgment Lajoie had recorded a double under his watch. After acknowledging that "there are those who will contend the big Frenchman is not entitled to a hit," he endeavored to explain why he had awarded him one. Under Parrish's watchful eye the pop fly became "a long fly to right and center. Northen . . . made a try for the ball. After a long run he managed to get both hands on it. He muffed and it went for a two base hit. Some contend that it should have been an easy one. It should, had Northen left it alone and permitted [right fielder Roy] Hartzell to whom it belonged field it. But Northen butted in on the play and messed" it up, giving Lajoie the "luckiest double" he had garnered "in many days."[16]

Was it dumb luck that presented Lajoie with a hit in his last at bat that Saturday afternoon in St. Louis, or was it the underpinning of something much more? Lajoie desperately needed hits, and some combination of Hub Northen and Victor Parrish had just gift wrapped one for him. On Sunday almost the exact same cast of characters would be present for the last two go-rounds of the 1910 season. Could lightning in the form of gift-wrapped opportunity strike twice? It would take less than twenty-four hours to find out.

Normally, when the last day of an early twentieth-century baseball season rolled around and the combatants on the field consisted of a team lost in the middle of the pack and one solidly entrenched at the rear, not many people alive, including the players, cared. Often few fans were in attendance at the game. Those diehards choosing to attend might expect to see crazy combinations of players on the field and sometimes an outfield or infield regular testing the strength of his arm on the pitching mound. However, Sunday, October 9, 1910, in St. Louis presented an entirely different cup of tea. There was still a slim chance that there was something to play for, and a large contingent of fans—at least by Browns standards—paid their way in to see it. The crowd, generally estimated at between nine thousand and ten thousand, was approximately three times the size of the average

1910 crowd.[17] The vast majority of these fans were not there to see Lajoie fail in his quest; they were there to see and in many cases even urge him on to victory.

The fans' interest in the games may have been piqued by articles in local newspapers earlier that day estimating the exact number of hits Lajoie needed to surpass Cobb for the batting title. One in particular, the *Post-Dispatch*, told readers seven hits in eight tries would do the trick, but no less. It was doable but, according to the paper, "will take a tremendous break in luck."[18]

Of course, the figures being bandied around by the newspapers were still only educated guesses, perhaps made easier by the fact that one previously unknown factor, Cobb's batting performance in his remaining two games, was no longer at issue. Further, there is no way of knowing for sure that any of the players, managers, or coaches on either team, including Lajoie, were aware of the numbers that were bouncing around out there. However, someone likely had either read the estimates or heard the buzz before the day's festivities were under way and passed on the news. That someone may well have been Rowdy Jack O'Connor. It is highly likely the Browns' manager, as well as many of his coaches and players, did not take the field that afternoon with a blank slate when it came to knowing how many hits it would take for Napoleon Lajoie to best Ty Cobb and capture the Chalmers.

Jack O'Connor's rooting interest went back a number of years and included his relationship with and admiration for the Big Frenchman, as well as his dislike of Cobb. Lajoie and O'Connor, who himself played ball in Cleveland for seven seasons, had waged battle against each other on the playing field for a number of years when the pair performed in the old National League. During that time Lajoie had earned the respect of the current Browns' manager to the extent that O'Connor named Lajoie the best second baseman he had ever seen play.[19] It seemed that over the years Lajoie had done little to rub O'Connor the wrong way. Apparently, the opposite was true of Cobb. By the time Ty entered the league and started his career, O'Connor was coming to the end of his playing days. As a catcher, however, O'Connor would certainly have butted heads with Cobb.

On the base paths, Cobb was the bane of the catcher, particularly one with rapidly diminishing skills. In his first few years, Cobb's opponents found the player's aggressive base-running tactics particularly galling, because the veterans saw him as a haughty youngster, an upstart who clearly did not know his place. Although there are no reports of major confrontations between Cobb and O'Connor, it does not seem far-fetched that these two men, street fighters that they were, would sometimes pull each other's chain as Cobb challenged O'Connor's throwing arm for that extra base or slid into home bullying Rowdy Jack with spiked shoes held high. Charles Alexander noted that one particular satisfaction Cobb garnered from his 1906 season was that he refused to back down from catchers "like the Browns' Jack O'Connor, who put his hand up behind Cobb's neck and called for his pitcher to throw the ball there."[20]

Then there were the ghosts of 1908. Lajoie had finished in St. Louis that year as well. Back then much more than an automobile was on the line. The Naps had been playing for the pennant. The Browns' contingent, merely playing out the season, had fought them to the wire in keeping with the true meaning of competitive sport and ended the Naps' pennant dream. But the man whose heart was broken in such a way that no one could forget was Napoleon Lajoie, the Naps' manager and star: Mr. Nap himself. There were still thirteen Browns players from the 1908 squad playing in 1910, including star infielder Bobby Wallace. Each of them had to some extent felt Lajoie's pain. Each of them had realized what was now on the line for Nap almost two years to the day later. Would any shed a tear for Ty Cobb should he lose a batting title today? Given a large crowd ready to cheer Lajoie's every hit, a manager who admired Lajoie and more than likely held Cobb in disdain, and a group of ballplayers who had an opportunity to disappoint Lajoie once again yet wished him only the best, was what followed over the next few hours in Sportsman's Park in St. Louis on October 9, 1910, really such a surprise?[21]

Writing for the *Sporting News* some twenty-two years later, Dick Farrington, who does not purport one way or the other to have been in attendance in St. Louis, sets the scene on this last day of the 1910 regular season in terms worth repeating for context, if not for total accuracy: "It was on a graying Indian summer afternoon in St. Louis. . . . Merry Widow hats were quite the thing, '23 skidoo,' was a wise crack, Bull Durham signs made up part of the outfield scenery, the boys were rolling their own and Guggenheimer [whiskey] was selling at a dollar and a quarter."[22]

On the mound for the Browns was young Cleveland native, Red Nelson. Exactly one week before, the twenty-four-year-old right-hander had been touched by Cobb for four singles in five trips to the plate in a 12–7 loss. Today he would be victorious, winning 5–4, but of course that was not the story. The "story" played second base for the Naps and that day batted in the cleanup spot, right behind young center fielder Joe Jackson. In the first inning, behind the approving roar of just about everyone in the ballpark, Lajoie swung hard, lining a ball over center fielder Hub Northen's head. By the time the ball had been retrieved, Lajoie stood on third with a triple. The extra-base hit carried an aura of authenticity, but some were not convinced. H. W. Lanigan had been reporting baseball in St. Louis for various newspapers since 1895. He had a keen eye for the game and its players. Now with the *Times*, he was in attendance that day and wrote that "[Tommy] Leach, [Tris] Speaker, Arthur [Solly] Hofman, Cobb, [Fred] Clarke and that kind would have made the catch. But a catch wasn't on for a Class B workman and Northen failed to make one."[23]

Still, it was the end of the season, the time for noncontending teams to try out young players and prepare for better times. That was the beauty of baseball, was it not? A hard hit ball might be caught; a soft liner might fall. In the hands of one outfielder, a fly ball might become just a "can of corn," while in another, it might become a double or, in this case, a triple. Lajoie had won this battle, but it was only one. Who could argue that it was not fair and square? Yet wasn't this the same young outfielder who had dropped an easy fly ball just the day before, sending writers scurrying to their typewriters pointing fingers at him and the official scorer? Not a few, mostly the sporting press, found the coincidence pushing credibility right up to the outfield fence. And the afternoon was still young.

In the third inning, Lajoie faced Nelson again. This time he grounded one to shortstop Bobby Wallace, arguably the best fielding and throwing shortstop in the game during his era. Now that Wallace was thirty-six, the question was whether this was still his era. Some baseball experts, including Pittsburgh Pirates owner Barney Dreyfuss, certainly thought so. As late as 1911, Dreyfuss called Wallace "the best player in the American League."[24] On Lajoie's bounder, Wallace's effort was variously described. One report described the ball as "badly played. . . . Instead of making a fast throw he [Wallace] 'lobbed' it to first and Lajoie, of course, beat the toss."[25] Another agreed that the ball was "lobbed" and added Wallace's "peg was wide."[26] A third commented that the shortstop's throw "bore about as close a resemblance to a Wallace throw as day to night."[27] Three independent reports arrived at essentially the same conclusion. However, the only opinion that counted was that of the official scorer. In the first game that day, this duty once again fell to Victor Parrish, who, at this stage of the season, more frequently acted as the Browns' official scorer than his boss, Dick Collins, did. Parrish scored Lajoie's third-inning grounder a hit. The Big Frenchman stood 2 for 2 on the day.

By the time Lajoie approached the batter's box in the top of the fifth inning, the crowd was urging him on, sensing something important was playing out in front of them. When Lajoie surveyed the field, he saw Browns third baseman Red Corriden playing well beyond the bag, a position that offered an opportunity to bunt. Like most of the Naps, Lajoie probably knew little of Corriden. That was because the rookie was playing in only his twenty-sixth Major League game and eleventh at third base. His work at shortstop had not impressed; he erred ten times in fourteen games at that spot. He was faring somewhat better at third with only two errors to date, including errorless ball at third in the first two games of this series.

By October 10 Red Corriden had been a St. Louis Brown and a Major Leaguer for just over a month, making his Major League debut playing shortstop for the Browns in both ends of a doubleheader in St. Louis on September 8 against the White Sox. At that time he replaced Bobby Wallace, and Roy Hartzell continued playing third.[28] By now Jack O'Connor was beginning to juggle his lineup quite a bit. The tryouts for 1911 were under way. Corriden, who had just turned twenty-three, played fairly regularly, and until September 19 in St Louis versus the White Sox, he had been a shortstop. On that date, however, he stood at third base, a position that was not all that unfamiliar to the five-foot-nine-inch, 165-pound native of Logansport, Indiana. In 1908 Corriden, who was of German and Irish descent and both batted and threw from the right side, began playing baseball for pay with the Keokuk (Iowa) Indians of the Class D Central Association. During that first season, as well as in 1909, Corriden played third base. A .282 batting mark in his second year boosted his stock. By 1910 he was with the Omaha Rourkes of the Class A Western League. Playing under managers Bill Fox and later William Rourke, Corriden was switched to shortstop, a position he played in 136 games, and batted an impressive .308. The Browns liked what they saw and added him to their roster as their woeful 1910 schedule wound down, but since his arrival in St. Louis, his performance at the plate whether at third or short was disappointing. Heading into these last two games with the Browns, he was batting a paltry .106. Perhaps that was why Corriden did not reach the field at all in the last four Browns contests before this final series with the Naps. Nonetheless, he was at third during the first two games of the series and stationed there once again as Lajoie looked down the third base line in the fifth. In neither of the first two games was there any indication that Corriden was playing Lajoie particularly deep, although in the eighth inning of game one of the four-game series, Nap beat out a slow roller fielded by Corriden at third.[29]

If Red Corriden had been playing deep for Lajoie on that occasion, it would have raised few eyebrows. Many third basemen stood back a respectful distance when the Big Frenchman dug in at the plate. Tales of the bullets that rocketed off Lajoie's bat were legion. It was said a Lajoie drive to left field once killed two sparrows. Another report had a Lajoie drive to center striking the outfield fence with such force that the out-fielder could not dislodge it from the screen in time to make the throw to the infield.[30] Ring Lardner, a writer who could certainly turn a phrase or two, once wrote that "when he [Lajoie] got hold of one, it usually hit the fence on the first bounce, traveling about five feet three inches above the ground most of the way and removing the ears of all infielders who didn't throw themselves flat on their stomachs the instant they saw him swing."[31] Even Ty Cobb once wrote that "Lajoie has a bad habit of 'busting them' down that alley at a rate which is liable to cut a third baseman's 'bean' right loose if he is playing too close."[32]

In game two of the series, Corriden was included among those failing to give sufficient effort on Lajoie's pop fouls. Now his depth at third invited a bunt. Lajoie laid one down, beating it out for his third hit of the afternoon. The crowd continued to crow; their flavor of the day was making hay.

Lajoie's fourth and last at bat of the first game was the same. Whether because of the placement of the bunt, the manner in which Corriden fielded it, his throw, or some combination of the three, Lajoie stood on first with his fourth hit. When the game ended with the Naps on the short end of a 5-4 count, Nap was a perfect 4 for 4. The manner in which he obtained those hits, in particular the last two, raises the question, how did Lajoie become aware of the opportunity Corriden's positioning afforded him? Did he look down the line and see it for himself, or had he been tipped off in advance by his teammates or even someone on the opposing Browns? It seems unlikely that Nap noticed Corriden's position the first time up or he would not have swung away, hitting the ball that many charged was misplayed by Hub Northen. If he noticed Corriden standing far back his second time up, he seemed to ignore it still, swinging and tapping the grounder to Wallace at short. While the grounder to Wallace could have been a swinging bunt, it seems more reasonable to assume that something changed on the field between the third and fifth innings. Either Corriden was positioned differently at that point, or he had been there all afternoon and Lajoie had finally decided to take advantage of it.

After a break in the action, the teams took the field for game two. On the mound for the Browns was Alex Malloy, another rookie right-hander. Malloy, whose Major League career was now one month old, had pitched reasonably well with nothing to show for it. He stood 0 for 5 when he took the mound and 0 for 6 when he left on the short end of a five-hit, 3-0 shutout by the Naps' Cy Falkenberg. For Malloy, it was his last big league game. He would play for a handful of teams on baseball's lower rungs and end his professional career in 1913 with Houston of the Class B Texas League.

As for the main attraction, his sudden love affair with the bunt down the third base line did not dissipate a lick. In his first second-game at bat, Lajoie once again found his new aide-de-camp Corriden camped well behind third on the edge of the outfield grass. The resulting bunt was once again fielded too late to catch Nap at first. There was the usual chorus of cheers, but now there was a smattering of hisses as well. It seems some in the crowd, including Lajoie rooters, only wanted to see the venerable Naps' star win his Chalmers legitimately. Not that anyone doubted Lajoie's skills as a bunter—he often bunted with success, if not frequency—nor that the aging Naps' infielder could still run bases with skill; despite acknowledged slowness afoot, he had stolen twenty-six bases in 1910, the third highest total of his career. Certainly this was not the first time in his career, nor even in 1910, that Lajoie had bunted after observing a third baseman playing him deep. One occasion was earlier that year on May 17, when he did just that to "completely fool the [Washington] Nationals. . . . Before the ball could be recovered and fielded the big Frenchman perched gleefully on first."[33]

When Lajoie batted next against the Browns, in the third inning, there was a runner on first and no outs. Like clockwork, the Frenchman's bunt headed toward third. This time Corriden briefly fumbled the ball before sending it to first, too late to catch Lajoie. Both runners were safe, but there was no immediate clarity as to how the play would be scored. The possibilities included a hit, an error, or a sacrifice. An error meant a time at bat without a hit, ruining Lajoie's as yet perfect day and lowering his batting average. A sacrifice would not count as an at bat. The scorer also could rule that Corriden erred, but because the runner reached second base, Lajoie would be credited with a sacrifice. There were no electronic scoreboards to show fans and players alike the scorer's decision as the game was in progress. The question on everyone's lips: How had the official scorer, in this case Victor Parrish, scored the play? Certainly the Naps, Lajoie in particular, were the most interested, but the Browns posed the question, which was asked and answered more than once with increasing finality by Parrish as the game progressed. In his opinion—the only one that really counted—Lajoie had reached base by error, but because he had bunted and the first base occupant reached second base safely, Lajoie was credited with a sacrifice, meaning his "perfect" day would continue. And that it did, as Lajoie reached base in the fifth and seventh innings and then once again in the ninth, all by virtue of bunts down that by now well-worn third base line. That Nap was able to bat in the ninth inning, and was the third man up at that, is worth an examination all to itself. It took a walk and a hit batsman—Naps manager James "Deacon" McGuire, catching his only game of that season—to ensure Lajoie another time at the plate and an eighth hit, one hit more and one out less than the *St. Louis Post-Dispatch* said he needed to capture the batting title and the Chalmers automobile from Cobb.

As an interesting aside, and probably nothing more, when he learned that his counterpart McGuire was in the lineup, Rowdy Jack O'Connor decided he would catch game two as well. According to the *Cleveland Plain Dealer*, "O'Connor had no intention of catching until [umpire] Billy Evans announced McGuire as the Cleveland receiver. . . . A crack on the bare hand by a foul tip convinced him he had enough in round one."[34] The Browns' manager thereupon replaced himself with part-time catcher Bill Killifer, who finished the game. It was O'Connor's only appearance of the 1910 season, as it was for McGuire. Unlike McGuire, Rowdy Jack did not record an at bat.

As the final out of the season was recorded, it was fairly apparent to everyone that Napoleon "Larry" Lajoie was the newly crowned batting champion of Major League Baseball. A majority of the fans in the large throng filing out of Sportsman's Park were happy; a number reportedly came onto the field to surround their hero. Some later followed him to the train station as he prepared to depart the city.[35] They had come to the park that autumn Sunday hoping to see Lajoie win the batting championship, or at the very least to view some batting fireworks, and that is what they got, even if most of the hits were of the Caspar Milquetoast variety. Although the official figures were not in and would not be for some time, in their minds, Lajoie had won it. Likewise, the players were happy—most of them at least. The vast majority of the reporters were not. Unfortunately for Lajoie, it was the latter group, the so-called Fifth Estate, which would have its say over the next few days and weeks to come. And this group felt there was a whole lot to say. In fact, by the time the average baseball fan in St. Louis and throughout most of the country had finished that first cup of coffee and read the Monday morning edition of the local sports page, the steam that rose in the dining nook could not be accounted for by just the coffee. The words fairly leapt off the pulp; something exceedingly unseemly had occurred the day before at Sportsman's Park, emitting an odor that was not industrial or agricultural in origin.

The media assault on the Browns-Naps doubleheader of October 10 was spearheaded by members of the St. Louis sports press, many of whom—unlike the majority of Detroit and Cleveland reporters—were in attendance at the games. They had no oars in the Cobb-Lajoie race but believed that their local team had besmirched the honor of the game by not providing the Naps with fair competition. Because the stories out of St. Louis were flashed over the sports wires to all parts of the country, the tenor of these reports carried great weight. Perhaps the most blunt and vociferous report-age was penned by H. W. Lanigan of the *St. Louis Times*: "I have been on the baseball assignment in St. Louis since 1895. A member of the *Sporting News*' staff for one year, I have worked on the dailies through every year from 1896. It was the first time in all the half innings and full innings, short games and long games, good games and bad games, that I have seen the honesty of the national pastime questioned. What happened goes under the name of burlesque, state some, and should not be taken seriously nor have any afterclap. Maybe so."

Lanigan went on to describe what he saw, conceding that Parrish was correct in his scoring and "wouldn't have been very far out of line if he had given Lajoie nine out of nine, instead of only eight out of eight." Then he offered this description of Lajoie's last seven times at the plate:

> Larry would show by his stand at the plate that he was going to bunt the ball up the third base line. The catcher would hold the big mitt forward on a line with Larry's chest. The pitcher would make sure of his aim and if Larry was served even one curve all day those in line with the plate missed it. The third baseman, Corriden, would start to back up. He would go practically to the end of the dirt. In reality he looked more like an assistant left fielder than the regular third baseman.

All seven times Larry bunted up the third base line. Only once did his tap go foul. That proves that his batting eye was either remarkably good, or that Pitchers Nelson and Malloy failed to put any "stuff" on the balls they dished up. He couldn't miss his bunt. That's all there was to it.[36]

In a separate column, Lanigan noted that Red Corriden's dead bat had suddenly come alive during the doubleheader; he had five hits in the two games to go with the eight from the previous twenty-four. Now in full conspiracy mode, Lanigan charged that on the field that afternoon "little Corriden was probably acting under instructions and in return for services rendered got helped out himself."[37]

Like Lanigan, John Edward "Eddie" Wray of the *Post-Dispatch* was a veteran of the St. Louis baseball wars; his Wray's Column was a hodgepodge of diamond "dope" that drew readers to his paper like syrup to pancakes. In its report of the games, his paper charged that the previous afternoon's events were nothing but a "hippodrome," and an unconvincing one at that: "There were few of the 10,000 fans present who could be convinced that the Browns were not trying to aid Lajoie." Still, the paper was unwilling to throw Lajoie under the bus: "The great Cleveland second baseman cannot be blamed for taking advantage."

In his column, Wray minced few words, characterizing the Browns as "party to a little baseball crime," before turning up the rhetoric one more notch: "This closing incident is the sort of episode that causes sport to be sent to the cleaners, every now and then. In merry-go-round horse racing, it was known as a 'shoo-in' and it had about the same standing among sportsmen as a limburger cheese might enjoy at a perfume bazaar."[38]

Over at the *Star*, another St. Louis scribe, Billy Murphy, even alluded and compared the previous day's happenings at Sportsman's Park to the scandal that occurred with the Louisville ball club in 1877. That particular blemish on the sport involved allegations that several players took money to throw ball games. The players involved were banished from the game.[39]

Naturally, the Detroit and Cleveland press took a more parochial view of the proceedings. There was general agreement that Lajoie's perfect day would push him to the top by the narrowest of margins, but at that juncture reaction to the manner in which the batting race ended diverged. Newspapers in Detroit tended to carry the negative allegations streaming off the typewriters of their St. Louis brethren. One Detroit writer, Harry Neily of the *Times*, however, took the middle road, charging that Cobb "quit cold." When the Browns laid down, presenting Lajoie with an opportunity, "he took it." As such, "Cobb simply was beat at his own game"—and all in an effort to win a prize "which gave to the donors a lot of free advertising and to baseball a wallop in the face of honesty and a kick on the seat of integrity." In the end sadly "are two popular idols discovered on this pleasant autumnal day with considerable mud on their respective coat tails."[40]

In Cleveland, the *Plain Dealer* mentioned that the game had been branded by St. Louis writers as "hippodrome" and "tinged with a charge of illegitimacy," but chose to concentrate more on Lajoie's perfect day, "an accomplishment believed unparalleled in baseball history."[41] Lajoie's hometown papers proudly pointed out that the St. Louis fans had lustily urged Nap on during the games and swarmed the field at the finish, almost intimating that somehow this justified what had in fact occurred. In this vein the *Leader* reluctantly conceded that "the Browns did not make any superhuman effort to stop Larry." Nonetheless, "Lajoie is the most popular man in St. Louis, for all the fans were with him heart and soul. A big mob followed him to the station when the Naps left for Cincinnati [to play an exhibition series.] They howled for a speech, but Larry gave them an exhibition of his 'auto' smile and ducked."[42]

Although the St. Louis press contingent led the parade with the Detroit sportswriters close behind, it did not take long for team officials to get into the fray. In the early 1900s Frank Navin had arrived on the Detroit Tigers' management scene as the club's chief bookkeeper. In less than a decade, he had parlayed the position into that of business manager and then survived ownership changes to become team president and a part owner himself. Now, as chief team spokesman, the thirty-nine-year-old executive took serious offense to the shenanigans in St. Louis, eschewing the automobile contest itself, because as he well knew, "these prizes only serve to create dissension on a team." In fact, this might be the last anyone would see of prizes and bonuses for players. He then defended his star player: "It [the doubleheader] looked like a raw deal, all right, but I don't know whether or not the league will take action. The league can throw out games for justifiable reasons." Nonetheless, it was his opinion and fervent hope that when the official tally was complete, Cobb would win the batting title anyway.[43]

Across the lake the Naps' spokesman was a "jubilant" E. S. Barnard, the team's vice president. The former college football coach and newspaper editor insisted that he "didn't see how anyone can protest with good grace. Lajoie played right up to the minute and Cobb quit when he thought his average was heavy enough to insure his winning the auto."[44]

The team official in the middle was Bob Hedges, a Browns owner and club executive since the club's arrival in St. Louis in 1902, following an initial American League season in Milwaukee. Hedges had been a spectator at the October 9 doubleheader, yet had little to say—at least immediately after the games—about his team's play. The *St. Louis Times*, however, reported that during the afternoon "the genial [Browns] boss paced up and down the promenade, his famous smile replaced by a frown." It was further reported that at one point Hedges proclaimed, "I wish I had two cabbages, I'd send one to O'Connor and the other to McGuire." This was all that was heard from the owner, if indeed he even said that much, before he supposedly left town later that day, traveling first to northern Indiana and then to Chicago, reportedly to watch the Cubs play the A's in Game Three of the World Series.[45]

What about the men who would be king, Cobb and Lajoie? Within a few hours, just about anyone with an opinion had offered it; certainly these two could not be far behind. Upon his delayed arrival in Philadelphia to join the All-Stars, Cobb spoke briefly, taking the high road—a smart move that could only win him fans. Expressing surprise at the results of the doubleheader, he regretted that "either Lajoie or myself did not win the prize for the highest average without anything occurring which could cause unfavorable comment. I am not prepared to make any charges against either Lajoie or members of the St. Louis team."[46]

Lajoie took the opposite tack, initially stating he would have no comment. He then spoke to reporters in Cincinnati, offering several:

Every hit I made in the double-header played in St. Louis Sunday was made on the square.

I did not speak to a St. Louis player about my batting average. I asked no favors from anyone, and worked my head off to make the safe drives I collected.

After my first hit, a clean drive to center for three bases, the St. Louis players played deep, expecting me to pound the ball out every time. I fooled them the next time up by beating out a bunt, and knowing that a bunt would be the unexpected every time up, continued to "lay" the ball down and beat it out.

I read an account of the two St. Louis games this morning in which it was stated that the St. Louis players had aided me to secure enough hits to nose out Ty Cobb in the fight for the batting championship of the major leagues and the automobile which goes with the honor this season. That is absolutely untrue. Not only was every hit I made a clean drive, but the St. Louis scorers cheated me out of one hit in the third inning of the second game. With a man on third, I bunted the ball down the left field line. Corriden, nor any other player, could have handled the ball in time to get either of us. Instead of crediting me with a hit as should have been done, the official scorer gave the fielder an error and me a sacrifice hit. Instead of eight hits in eight times at bat, I should have nine safe drives to my credit. . . .

You can take it from me that they don't hand you anything in base ball. Two years ago we could have won the American league pennant by taking both games of a double-header from St. Louis. Members of the St. Louis team were pulling for us to win the flag. But did they hand us both games and the flag? Not on your life. They buckled down, worked their heads off, won one of the games, and beat us out of the [pennant] bunting in one of the hardest races in the history of the game.[47]

Lajoie had taken the offensive. Not only had he done nothing wrong, a position most observers also held, but the Browns had done nothing wrong either. By referring to the painful season-ending series with the Browns in 1908, using it as an illustration of the honesty of the sport, Lajoie ignored the possibility that the previous day's chicanery was but a payback, albeit a bittersweet one at that. The real villain in all this, according to a straight-faced Lajoie, was the dastardly official scorer, the same one roasted by the local press for already gifting him on at least two occasions that week. This was not the response from Lajoie many expected, certainly not St. Louis writer Brice Hoskins of the *Star*, who said, "We wonder if when spinning along in his [Lajoie's] newly acquired prize, each puff of the motor will not carry with it an echo of something closely akin to shame and regret."[48]

Lajoie had to be kidding, right? After all, this was the same player who seemingly cared little about the auto race and who required prompting from Naps owner Charles Somers to show a little selfishness and hit away as the season waned, rather than constantly sacrificing his at bats for the team.[49] Any thoughts that the Naps' infielder spoke tongue in cheek about the scoring of the twin bill vanished when the comments of official scorer Victor Parrish hit the sports sheets.

Neither the fact that Parrish, who wrote for the *Republic*, made his initial comments regarding his scoring to his own paper nor the reasons he gave for his scoring of the doubleheader were surprising. Two other elements aside from the rulings themselves were of particular interest and decidedly out of the ordinary. The first happened during the second game; the next well after both games were complete and the dust had supposedly settled.

According to Parrish, the first game "was attended without incident, save that there was a continual procession to the press box for information regarding the scoring." But after Lajoie's second at bat in game two, the one Parrish scored an error on Corriden and a sacrifice for Lajoie, events took a bizarre turn. At once questions arose as to how the play had been scored. Parrish explained the ruling, and this information was imparted to the St. Louis bench.

A few moments later Harry Howell, a former pitcher of the Browns and now scout for the ball club came to the press box.

"How did you score that play?" Asked he.

"A sacrifice hit and an error," I replied.

"Can't you stretch it a point and make it a hit?" he asked.

"I could, but I won't," was my reply.

Howell remained around the press box for a few moments attempting to argue the correctness of the scoring.

A few minutes after he left the bat boy of the St. Louis Browns came to the press box and told me he wanted to see me behind the stand. My reply was that anything he had to say to say it then and there.

He then handed me this unsigned note [a facsimile accompanied the article], written in lead pencil:

"Mr. Parrish: If you can see where Lajoie gets a B. H. [base hit] instead of a sacrifice I will give you an order for a $40 suit of clothes——sure. Answer by Boy [sic]

In behalf of —— I ask it of you."[50]

According to Parrish, the second eyebrow-raising exchange took place several hours later:

After I arrived home from the ball game that evening my telephone rang.

"You don't know who this is?" Was the greeting.

I replied that I did not.

"This is Mr. Lajoie," was the reply.

"Who?" said I.

"Mr. Lajoie," again came the reply.

"I understand that you are having some trouble regarding my hits in today's games." said he.

I replied that I was having no trouble. That it was other parties who are having trouble.

"How many hits did you give me?" said he.

"Eight hits in eight trips to the plate," I replied.

"Don't you think I should have had [illegible] in nine times at bat?" was the answer.

My reply to this was that had I thought so I would have scored them as such.

"There is no chance for you to see nine hits?" came over the phone.

"Absolutely, no." I retorted.

After refusing an invitation to go to the hotel the conversation was cut off.[51]

Nowhere in his statement did Parrish claim that the caller was Napoleon Lajoie, only that the caller identified himself as such. The allegation that it was "the people's choice," however, hung over the baseball world like the center-field flag at the stadium on a windy day. There for all to see.

One who had yet to be heard was Jack O'Connor, a figure in the eye of the storm as much as anyone else. If he thought the weekend's events would fade away as quickly as the memories of the Browns' season just past, he had another think coming. When contacted by reporters, he was ready with his version of Sunday's activities, telling them, "Lajoie outguessed us. We figured he did not have the nerve to bunt every time. He beat us at our own game. I will not send any of my players in to play up close to Lajoie when he tries to bunt."[52]

And then amid all the consternation and gnashing of teeth, Lajoie picked up support from foreign quarters. One day after Lajoie's hitting or, if you would prefer, bunting spree, he received a telegram: "The grandest congratulations from Bill Donovan, George Mullin, Edgar Willett, Eddie Summers, Oscar Stanage, Davey [sic] Jones, Tom Jones and George Moriarty."[53] Given the mounting controversy placing the legitimacy of Lajoie's accomplishment in serious question, it can be argued that this brief cryptic message from eight of Ty Cobb's Tigers teammates, four regular position players and four starting pitchers, said a great deal more about Cobb's standing with his teammates than it did their admiration for Napoleon Lajoie. Now in Philadelphia, Cobb reportedly admitted he had not telegrammed congratulations, intending to await a final tabulation of season averages.[54]

Cobb fared much better in other quarters. After hearing testimony from a woman called before his Detroit court to answer complaints from neighbors about keeping two goats and twenty-five geese behind her house, one Judge Phelan promised to let the woman go if she sent one of the goats to Cobb. In the words of Judge Phelan, "Mr. Cobb was cheated out of his automobile, but we'll see that he is accorded some honor, anyway."[55] The Hamilton-Brown Shoe Company of St. Louis felt Cobb was wronged as well and donated $250 to start a fund to purchase a car for the Tigers' star.[56]

And maybe, just maybe, help for Cobb was on the way from on high, in this case the Chicago offices occupied by the large figure cut in more ways than one by the president of the American League, Byron Bancroft Johnson. If so, the possibility had escaped Jack O'Connor. During an interview with a St. Louis reporter, O'Connor had struck a defiant pose, stating that all the discontent with his team's performance and his managing tactics meant nothing to him: "So far as I am concerned, the season is over." When told there were rumors of a pending investigation, he responded, "Investigation be damned. It doesn't make a bit of difference to me, because, as far as I know, there is nothing to investigate."[57] Perhaps Rowdy Jack was emboldened by reports out of Cincinnati from Chairman Garry Herrmann that the National Commission would not allow prizes to be offered again in the future but was taking a wait-and-see attitude with regard to this season's affair.[58] Or maybe he took solace from the remarks of Hugh Chalmers, the man in current possession of the keys to the car, who said he planned to abide by the decision of the National Commission as to a winner, rather than enter a protest. While expressing regrets that an offer to help promote the game had turned sour, Chalmers said that his company "probably will not ask that the alleged quitting of the St. Louis club be investigated."[59] And then there was Ty Cobb, continuing to take the high road, voicing sentiments such as "I do not propose to get mixed up in any controversy" and "I hardly think there will be an investigation if the commission waits for me to demand one."[60]

But O'Connor was wrong. Almost as soon as he claimed the commission he chaired would sit back and wait, Garry Herrmann changed direction, telegraphing the *Detroit Free Press* that the St. Louis "affair" was not before his commission: "The matter you refer to is an American league [*sic*] affair."[61] It would henceforth be addressed, if at all, by Ban Johnson.

However, Herrmann had hardly needed to come forward; his statement was a mere matter of protocol. When it came to the American League, and just about anything else having to do with Major League Baseball in 1910, Ban Johnson did not take his orders from either Garry Herrmann or the National Commission. He was a power unto himself.

Chapter Nine

Never again.
—Ban Johnson

The last thing Ban Johnson wanted or needed was for a controversy over
a batting title to overshadow the World Series. By 1910, on the eve of its
seventh edition, it was not only baseball's showpiece, but also America's
top sporting attraction. Even the notion that there might be a distraction
was particularly galling to Johnson. It was his mastery in maneuvering his
upstart American League into a position of equal footing with the established National League that furnished the fodder for the championship
playoff in the first place. He therefore began to lay the foundation for an
investigation that would promptly bring the Chalmers matter to a close.
He was confident that the other two members of the National Commission
would eventually agree that this was solely an American League matter.

That Johnson in a few short years had become the most powerful man
in baseball was no more remarkable than how he had arrived there in the
first place. Now forty-six years of age, the Ohio native was the son of a
school administrator who had settled in the Cincinnati area. After bouncing
around several Ohio colleges, including the University of Cincinnati Law
School for a brief stint, the young man took a job in 1886 as a sportswriter
at a Cincinnati newspaper. Although his baseball-playing career was limited by injury and did not advance beyond a few games as a college and
semipro catcher, his knowledge of sports and his opinionated nature soon

advanced him to an editorial job, from which he took a number of controversial positions. In the early 1890s his advocacy for the aptly named Players League offended some but won over at least one player, Charles Comiskey, a first baseman with a huge future in the game. Eventually, that friendship helped secure Johnson the presidency of the Western League, an upper-level Minor League circuit. Under his tutelage, which included establishment of a number of tightfisted rules, the league prospered. When the National League pared its ranks from twelve to eight teams just prior to the 1900 season, he saw a window of opportunity and marched his renamed American League to war with the baseball establishment in order to institute a second but equal league. By 1903 there was peace in what could now be properly called Organized Baseball, mostly obtained on Johnson's terms. Since then his power within the game as a whole had increased tenfold. By 1910 he was at, or very close to, his zenith.[1]

Ban Johnson's stature—he was a heavy man with a fleshy face—and his stern demeanor—just try to find a photograph of him smiling—only added to his dictatorial air and the facility with which he achieved his goals. Writer-commentator Bob Considine once described the president of the American League as a "ruthless dreamer who lived and died believing that baseball was perfected in order to serve him as a gigantic chess board on which to move his living pieces."[2] In 1901 Jack O'Connor and Napoleon Lajoie had both been pieces on that chessboard. Now almost a decade later the integrity of Johnson's league was under attack at an inopportune time, and these two pawns were among those primarily involved in causing the mess.

At the outset, Johnson and the other members of the National Commission had reacted to news of Lajoie's hit largesse and the Browns' alleged complicity by stating they would ban similar prize contests in the future. But Johnson soon came to realize that this would not be enough. Baseball's heretofore fine reputation as a game played by true sportsmen was getting a good tar and feathering. He needed to look no further than the editorials and columns of newspapers across the country to realize it, and this fed his rising anger. In that regard the editorial staff of the *St. Louis Star* was quick to point out that the popularity of the game in its town, saddled as it was with two subpar franchises, was dependent on fan perception that the game was played "on the square." The staff members called on Browns management to investigate immediately.[3] The *Detroit Free Press*, while defending Cobb's decision to leave early for All-Star service as an act of "general good" for the American League, warned that "no worse fate can come to the national game than a reputation for crookedness."[4] Similarly, its crosstown competition, the *News*, stated that "when base ball suffers a loss of integrity; it loses that which it will find exceedingly difficult to recover."[5]

The critiques were not limited to the three cities most involved. In Philadelphia, for example, the *Inquirer* editorialized against further prizes, arguing such a stance was "for the good of the game." Its comments were carried by wire service to other papers.[6] And the *Washington Post* published the column of Detroit's Joe S. Jackson, who noted that Lajoie had probably fallen into the scheme and that now Cobb was gaining support as an underdog. At the same time, Jackson cautioned that "unless some way can be found to deal with the St. Louis affair, a new cause for questioning the honesty of the game—and this, once doubted, will start the structure to toppling—will be offered."[7]

Ban Johnson had heard enough. He hinted at his intentions within twenty-four hours of the offending twin bill when he remarked that "even if the assertions prove unfounded, the merest suspicion of crookedness works irreparable injury to the game."[8] In his mind, the game was afoot—Johnson's game, that is—the sort in which all roads lead to and from his office in downtown Chicago, and no decisions other than his were final. On October 10, even though only one day had passed since season's end and the official score sheets for the final contests had yet to be turned in to Secretary McRoy, he issued the following statement to reporters:

Those reports [out of St. Louis] may not be altogether true, but I intend to find out, and have started an investigation of them to learn the facts regarding those hits credited to Lajoie. Until I have learned the truth, I will not decide what course to pursue. It may be that the collusion charged was only apparent, and the reports were colored.

From the reports, I gathered that the hits, if irregular, were the fault of Northen, an outfielder, and Corriden, a shortstop, who was playing third base. Both are minor leaguers just breaking in. It is not natural to suspect them of favoring Lajoie at the expense of their own reputations, which they have yet to make. It would be much more natural to suspect them of ignorance of how to play for Lajoie in the field, and of being tricked by a batsman of his well-known resource. But I can tell better about that after I receive the authentic information I am after.[9]

The league president had spoken with authority, and yet he had given himself an ocean of space in which to swim. After all, like most folks, he had undoubtedly gained the bulk of his information to date from newspaper reports and, given limitations of the era relative to long-distance communication, perhaps a telephone conversation or two with Browns owner Hedges, umpire Evans, or even scorer Parrish. In addition, Johnson was fully aware that although most observers felt Lajoie's eight hits would push him past Cobb to a batting title, it was his office that would make the final tally. At this point the official score sheets from neither Cobb's two weekend games nor Lajoie's four had reached the league office. Most of the newspaper box scores had been taken from score sheets that were the work of reporters at the game. Only one score sheet—the one prepared by the official scorer assigned by the home team to that particular game—would carry the imprimatur of the league and be rendered official. Even the official scorer's act of certifying and mailing a game sheet and the subsequent receipt at league headquarters did not render the inquiry final. Because each score sheet carried the risk of typographical error, the normal procedure was for an accountant to perform an audit. This typically took several weeks. Given the unusual circumstances surrounding the batting race, perhaps normal procedure would be altered. Robert McRoy alluded to this when he stated that customarily he would not give out the final league batting averages until after Thanksgiving; however, he then went on to say that if his boss, Johnson, requested the averages earlier in order to award the automobile, he would furnish them.[10] At any rate, that decision too rested totally within Johnson's control.

While he and his secretary waited for the official score sheets from St. Louis, Johnson set forth his investigative shopping list. He wanted reports from the official scorer and umpire assigned to the October 9 doubleheader at Sportsman's, in this case Victor Parrish and Billy Evans, respectively. He wanted personal interviews in Chicago with Jack O'Connor, the Browns' manager, and his third baseman, Red Corriden. He also wanted to hear from Harry Howell, the Browns' scout who had allegedly visited the press box and approached Parrish during the game. In passing, he wanted to speak with Bob Hedges, owner of the Browns. In sum, he wanted to cover a lot of ground, and he wanted to do it quickly. He needed to smother this growing brushfire before the flames and smoke fanned out and cast a cloudy shroud over baseball's fall showcase, the 1910 World Series.

When it came to the direction the investigation would take, some thought that O'Connor entered the fray down in the count concerning his standing with Ban Johnson. The *St. Louis Times* printed a report out of Chicago claiming that the American League president had done his best to dissuade the Browns from hiring O'Connor to manage in 1910. Reportedly, Rowdy Jack's aggressiveness—a trait that seemed to perturb Ban little in 1901, when he persuaded O'Connor to recruit National Leaguers for his fledgling American League—bothered Johnson.[11] The *Times* went further, telling readers that after Sunday's affair, Bob Hedges dropped his son off at Culver (a military academy in Indiana) and then headed to Chicago to confer with Johnson:

> Hedges is a silent man. He acts. He hurried to Chicago that night without waiting for a conference with his manager, although it was the final game of the season. Next day he was in secret conference with Ban Johnson, president of the league.
>
> Hedges returned to St. Louis [three days later on] Wednesday. As usual he is silent. He makes no charge against anyone. He defends no one. But it is known that Hedges and Johnson have an understanding, and that the result of the investigation [O'Connor's dismissal] will be felt, if not announced in due time.[12]

Hedges had a different version of his meeting with Johnson. He told the press that he and the league chief "hardly touched upon the Lajoie matter." In his mind, an owner should not deign to "discuss the work of an official scorer." He should not do so even if he disagreed with the scorer's decision, "which is not saying that I do in this case." At the most, he agreed that he was happy that there would be a thorough investigation "of an unfortunate affair."[13]

That "thorough" investigation would certainly involve Harry Howell, one of Hedges's favorite Browns players. Howell, like O'Connor, was an interesting study. Although he was working for the Browns as a scout on the afternoon in question, his baseball résumé wielded far more heft. Born in New Jersey in 1876, Howell was a plumber in 1898 when he was grabbed by the Meriden Bulldogs of the Connecticut League as a pitcher and utility outfielder. He was so impressive that before the season was over, he was purchased by Brooklyn of the old National League. Over the next several seasons, he bounced back and forth between the National League clubs in Brooklyn and Baltimore. He was owned by the latter franchise in 1901, when the Orioles became one of the original teams in the American League. In 1903 he became one of the original New York Highlanders, later the Yankees, when Ban Johnson invaded the country's largest city and installed the Orioles there. While in New York, the young Howell, who also played multiple positions in a utility role, began developing a spitball. In 1904 he was sold to the St. Louis Browns and became a mainstay on the pitching staff of the perennially losing club. Owing much to a spitball that was said to be the wettest in the game, Howell often lost more than he won, but he gave up few runs, finishing among the league leaders in earned run average from 1904 through 1908.[14] In 1905 he led the league in complete games. He was also one of the most popular Browns players. Nicknamed "Handsome Harry," the right-hander was admired alike by players, fans, media, and of course, the ladies. He also, at least before October 9, 1910, had done little to annoy Ban Johnson. That he was scouting that day for the Browns, rather than serving the club in his usual player's role, is deserving of special mention.

Only two seasons before, Handsome Harry had won eighteen games for the Browns' team that ended the Naps', and thereby Nap Lajoie's, pennant hopes. He had lost the same number of games that season, but his 1.89 ERA and complete game total again were among the top in the league. At thirty-one he was far from washed up. That all changed in 1909, when he injured the shoulder on his pitching arm while throwing during infield practice. He appeared in but ten games in 1909 and unsuccessfully tried rehabilitation. In March 1910 he had what turned out to be unsuccessful surgery and spent the early portion of the year as his club's pitching coach. He tried to pitch one time in relief, was roughed up, and was removed after just more than three innings. It was his last appearance. He became a scout for the Browns, known to all in attendance, including the Naps, and available for tasks at hand when Lajoie took his last shot at the Chalmers on that fateful Sunday.

It did not take long after Ban Johnson announced his investigation for O'Connor and Corriden to incur the president's wrath. The pair, particularly O'Connor, had been on a short leash to begin with, and Johnson began drumming his fingers on his desk and bellowing to reporters almost immediately. By Thursday, October 13, when neither the Browns' manager nor his rookie third baseman had graced his doorstep, Johnson was hopping mad and said so: "O'Connor has failed to report according to instructions, and I propose to drive him out of organized baseball if he does not comply with my request within 24 hours. Third baseman John L. Corriden, who is said to have favored Lajoie, thus enabling the latter to secure eight hits in the two games last Sunday, has failed to report at this office for a hearing. If he is not here by noon tomorrow I'll suspended him indefinitely."[15]

Earlier that day Hugh Chalmers, bemused but not discouraged, had offered baseball his solution. He left a message at Johnson's office advising that he was willing to offer automobiles to both Cobb and Lajoie. After all, the automobile baron sold his wares in both Cleveland and Detroit. He did not wish to offend either constituency. Johnson wired thanks, but he preferred deferring any decisions pending completion of his investigation.[16] Meanwhile, his primary target, O'Connor, was making his case, as well as Red Corriden's, in a St. Louis newspaper. The *St. Louis Post-Dispatch*, seemingly ignorant of the fact that O'Connor was on call for a Chicago confrontation with the big boss, reported that the St. Louis manager was headed to Chicago to take in the third and fourth games of the World Series and planning to wager $1,000 on his league's Athletics to boot.

According to that daily, O'Connor's job was safe. After all, not only was his name inked to a contract with the Browns that ran through 1911, but the debt incurred by O'Connor's "yeoman service" to the Johnson war machine during his battle with the National League in the early 1900s would be repaid when his case rested on Johnson's desk. But just to make sure, Rowdy Jack made his case out in the open, saying that he had not conferred with owner Hedges and was not aware that Red Corriden had been ordered to Chicago to confer with Johnson:

> The kid [Corriden] is innocent of any wrongdoing, so far as I know. He is a game kid. As far as favoring Lajoie or Cobb, it sounds foolish to me.
>
> Off the field, I'll wager that Corriden doesn't know Lajoie or Cobb, and as far as forming a friendship or dislike for either one, I will say that he hasn't seen enough or been in the big league long enough to do anything like that.
>
> As far as I am concerned it wouldn't make the slightest difference who won the automobile. It's true that Lajoie is well liked. But don't get the impression that Cobb isn't a friend of mine. I regard him as one of my best acquaintances and friends in the baseball business.
>
> The games Sunday were a farce. I believe everybody realized that when Jim Maguire and I put on the masks and big [catcher's] gloves. I had intended pitching Dudley [sic] Criss and letting everybody have a good time. The crowd was out to get its money's worth and I planned to let them have it.
>
> But take it from me, there was no "lay-down." Corriden had no instructions to "pull" to Larry from me, and I think he played for the Frenchman on the last day of the season as he would in July. Yes, I am signed up to manage the Browns next year and expect to be on the job.[17]

Harry Howell was talking to the *Post-Dispatch* too, reminding readers that he was not in uniform or on the bench that day and sought only information:

> I was merely asked by one of the Cleveland men in [sic] the bench to find out how the scorer had construed a play. I was in the stand and

of course, went up to the press box and inquired about the play, as I myself was interested, too.

After I had found out Mr. Parrish intended to score the play as a sacrifice and an error, I talked with him a few seconds, as I thought the play should have been scored a hit.

After taking back the information to the Cleveland players [*sic*], who had asked me to find out for him, my connection with this affair ceased. I have no knowledge of any note sent to the press box.[18]

The remarks of both O'Connor and Howell are interesting and, perhaps unwittingly, shed significant light on this incident. O'Connor had now admitted that he saw Sunday's season-ending double bill as a "farce" and played it as such. This increases the likelihood that if he had not planned to manage his team to maximize Lajoie's enjoyment at the plate, he was open to suggestion. Emboldened by a crowd cheering Lajoie's every turn at the plate, he may well have become caught up in the spirit of the enterprise early in game one, if not before. This is bolstered by Harry Howell's comments. If indeed Handsome Harry was urged by someone on the Cleveland bench to visit the press box to inquire about scoring, it reinforces the idea of an engaged Naps bunch, ready to pull out all the stops to win a batting title for brother Lajoie and even to entrap a fun-loving, anything-goes manager like O'Connor in a web of conspiracy. Harry's statements do little to detract from the notion that the Browns were willing participants in a plan hatched by the Naps that probably was not premeditated but rather developed as the pair of games proceeded. What was left out of Howell's statement was who on the Cleveland bench conscripted him to do the bidding. It is difficult to tab Lajoie, given his first swinging at bat. He undoubtedly became caught up in the moment, but it is hard to weigh him down with more culpability. A better choice is Cleveland manager Jim McGuire, acting alone or in combination with one or more of his veteran Naps players. It seems unlikely that Howell would undertake his quest for just anyone on the Naps' bench, but no one will probably ever know.

The idea that the players' conspiracy to aid Lajoie evolved as the October 9 games progressed is bolstered by the comments of Roger Peckinpaugh, the Naps' shortstop in both games. Talking about the doubleheader years later, at age eighty-three, Peckinpaugh, who at the time was nineteen, recalled that the idea germinated after Lajoie started the day with three hits: "It then occurred to somebody that if Larry could get four or five hits he might win the batting championship from Cobb." After the one Lajoie bunt was called a sacrifice, "they arranged to walk a flock of Cleveland hitters so Larry could come to bat again, which he did, and he bunted for another hit." As to the player's psyche, "there was nothing at stake in all of this, and it wasn't like throwing a game, so no one seemed to think any harm would be done if Larry got all those hits."[19]

The delay in the arrival of O'Connor and Corriden did afford Ban Johnson one luxury. By the time they arrived, if they ever did, he would have in hand the reports of his official scorer, Richard J. Collins, and acting scorer, Victor Parrish, as well as that of umpire Billy Evans. According to many, Evans is one of baseball's all-time great umpires. By 1910 he was in his fifth year as an American League arbiter. Born in Chicago in 1884 and raised in Youngstown, Ohio, the onetime newspaper reporter fit Ban Johnson's criteria perfectly: umpires must be men of integrity with a reputation for fairness. Evans's credibility was his calling card, enhanced by a willingness to admit the occasional mistake, a trait he shared with few of his brethren. There was no question that he held the respect of the baseball community. In 1907, while he was umpiring in St. Louis, one of his calls enraged a young fan, who tossed a bottle in his direction, fracturing his skull. He was unable to finish the season but returned the next.[20] Here he was in St. Louis, the focal point once again, having been assigned to work a normally meaningless year-end series, one suddenly bathed in controversy. His valued opinion became an important piece of the puzzle that Ban Johnson sought to solve. In this regard Evans was already on record as saying that up until the Saturday game in St. Louis, he had seen nothing that season to make him believe that Lajoie was being helped by opponents to win the batting title.[21] Obviously, Parrish's decision to score a hit for Lajoie on Northen's handling of his fly ball during Saturday's contest raised Evans's eyebrow or he would not have mentioned it.

Even then he was equivocal at best. Nonetheless, Evans's official report on Sunday's games would be anxiously awaited by many.

As anticipated, the umpire's report indeed arrived in Chicago before O'Connor and Corriden. On Wednesday evening, October 12, Ban Johnson announced that in a detailed four-page report, the umpire had deemed each play scored a hit by Lajoie in Sunday's games legitimate and Red Corriden's positioning within the bounds of propriety.[22] Johnson, however, refused to release the report itself or disclose additional details, pending completion of his investigation. He also didn't disclose whether or not Evans had raised questions about the scoring of Saturday's game. And, most decidedly, he failed to mention whether or not he and Evans had entered into a frank discussion that included arm-twisting before Evans wrote and finalized a report totally approving of the actions of all involved in Sunday's doubleheader.

Although Evans's report was now in hand, Johnson had not yet received either the official score sheets or the official scorer's report on the games. Asked how he planned to handle awarding the automobile in view of the issues surrounding the race, Johnson said he was presently inclined to recommend to the National Commission that it ask Hugh Chalmers to withdraw his offer. The American League would then present both Cobb and Lajoie with prizes of equivalent value.

As Johnson saw it, "It has been a remarkable contest between Lajoie and Cobb, and I believe both men have worked manfully and honestly for the prize. They are not under suspicion in this investigation. The race between them has been so close, and the indications are the official figures will make their final averages so nearly tied that I would prefer giving them equal prizes for what they have done. It is not up to the automobile people to do that, but I think the American league [sic] should."[23]

It seemed Johnson was taking the position most seasoned observers expected, as expressed quite succinctly by H. G. Salsinger of the *Detroit News*: "Someone will feel the ax fall later on. Johnson has more diplomacy than do anything at the present time; action on his part would stamp the charges of crookedness with truth, and it is Ban's play to show them exaggerated." In the Detroit sportswriter's view, Johnson had already tipped his hand. Tongue-in-cheek Salsinger told faithful readers that they should "leave it to big Ban to master such a situation." Then the scribe went on the attack, explaining that he was

> not trying to dispute Ban's word, but Billy Evans said last Sunday that the hits were questionable. Ban saw Billy and Ban says Billy said the hits were O. K. All of this being in the course of whitewashing which Ban is pursuing.
>
> Both teams and their managers will naturally say the hits were O. K. Why shouldn't they? The members of the St. Louis and Cleveland clubs are only human.
>
> The official scorer was also called upon to explain. He said the hits were O. K. Why shouldn't he say that? Did he score them hits, and would he if he should have marked down errors?
>
> Probably the official scorer is the only man in the whole mess who is right without a doubt. The scorer couldn't have credited Lajoie with anything but eight hits, try as he might.[24]

While Johnson talked and Salsinger pounded the keys, Red Corriden scurried, his baseball future on the line, arriving in Chicago on October 13, undoubtedly dreading his sit-down the next day with baseball's reigning czar.

As Johnson prepared to interrogate Corriden and hopefully O'Connor, the scribes wrote and the cartoonists drew. A few writing types even penned some poetry, a popular method of the day for contributors to air grievances and offer other sentiments. Edgar A. Guest, a Detroiter and syndicated poet whose verse often appeared in newspapers and magazines, penned his rhymes in the Cobb-friendly *Detroit Free Press*. A glance at the first stanza confirms the general theme:

> I'd like to be as popular as Larry Lajoie;
> I'd like to have a lot of friends to ease my weary way;
> I'd like to have them do for me what they have done for him;
> 'Twould make this life of mine, I'm sure less burdensome and grim.
> How nice 'twould be for me if I were entered in a race,

To have them trip the other man and kick him in the face;
My cheeks would flood with manly pride as in I walked to get
The prize I had so barely won, and yet, and yet—and yet—[25]

This ditty was mild compared to one that appeared in a column written for the *Chicago Tribune* by HEK, the initials of its veteran sportswriter Hugh Keough. It read in part,

When Larry faced the St. Louis' fire
He'd 8 to go to be secure,
And what they thought he might require
They slipped it to him, that's pretty sure. . . .
But hully, gee!
What must a meek outsider think
When tricks like that they put across?
When at one frameup they will wink
How do we know what games they toss?[26]

Criticism of Lajoie mounted as Cobb continued to take the high road, stating publicly that he had no problem with Lajoie winning the title if it was fairly obtained, while implying that he doubted such was the case. J. Ed Grillo wrote in the *Washington Star*, admitting that he could not brand Lajoie a conspirator, but charging that his actions in taking advantage of the situation were "unsportsmanlike."[27] William Peet of the *Washington Herald* agreed that Lajoie was honest and not part of a conspiracy. But as for Lajoie the man, Peet had a different view, a writer's view of a man who fiercely guarded his privacy: "The fans in every American league [*sic*] circuit are strong for Lajoie, with whom he is a great favorite. The baseball writers do not, and probably never will, like him. He was never known to hand out an item of news, and when it came to an interview he was tighter than the proverbial clam."[28]

Heywood Broun of the *New York Morning Telegraph* defended Cobb by taking on his detractors and calling him "the best [player] of any time." He told readers that the Detroit star had become "perhaps . . . the least-popular player who ever lived" because "pistareen ball players whom he

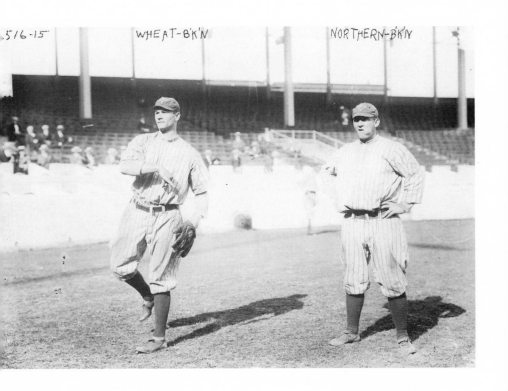

1. Browns outfielder Hub Northen (*right*), shown with Hall of Famer Zach Wheat while with Brooklyn in 1912, was accused of misplaying Lajoie fly balls on both October 8 and game one of October 9, 1910. (George Grantham Bain Collection, Library of Congress, Prints and Photographs Division LC-B2-2516-15)

2. Members of the 1908 Detroit Tigers stop for a photograph before leaving for spring training in San Antonio, Texas. Players of note include outfielders Matty McIntyre (*third from the left*), Davy Jones (*fifth*), Sam Crawford (*seventh*), and manager Hugh Jennings (*far right*). (George Grantham Bain Collection, Library of Congress, Prints and Photographs Division LC-USZ62-135394)

3. Outfielder Sherry Magee of the Philadelphia Phillies expressed displeasure when his National League–leading batting average of .331 in 1910 did not earn him a Chalmers automobile, which was presented to the leading batter in baseball as opposed to the leader in each league. (George Grantham Bain Collection, Library of Congress, Prints and Photographs Division, LC-DIG-ggbain-09136)

4. Fred Snodgrass, shown here in 1910, made a strong early run for the Chalmers in his first full season in the New York Giants' outfield. He tailed off, ending the year batting .321. (George Grantham Bain Collection, Library of Congress, Prints and Photographs Division, LC-DIG-ggbain-09008)

5. St. Louis Browns owner Robert Lee Hedges, photographed in December 1910, not long after he dismissed manager Jack O'Connor for allegedly easing up on Napoleon Lajoie on October 9 in order to help him win the Chalmers automobile over Ty Cobb. (George Grantham Bain Collection, Library of Congress, Prints and Photographs Division LC-USZ62-133647)

6. (*above*) Although quotes by Hall of Fame umpire Billy Evans (shown here in 1914) raised doubts about the Browns' efforts to retire Nap Lajoie, his report to Ban Johnson following the October 9 doubleheader not only claimed Lajoie achieved his 8 for 8 legitimately, it said he should have been credited with a 9-for-9 day. (George Grantham Bain Collection, Library of Congress, Prints and Photographs Division, LC-DIG-ggbain-17207)

7. (*right*) St. Louis rookie right-hander Albert "Red" Nelson, shown here in 1912, was on the mound for the Browns in game one of the October 9, 1910, doubleheader. He was "victimized" for four hits by Lajoie on the way to eight hits on the day. (George Grantham Bain Collection, Library of Congress, Prints and Photographs Division, LC-DIG-ggbain-50297)

8. (*left*) In 1911 Hall of Fame shortstop Bobby Wallace (*left*, with fellow manager Hal Chase of the New York Highlanders) succeeded Jack O'Connor as manager of the St. Louis Browns. (George Grantham Bain Collection, Library of Congress, Prints and Photographs Division, LC-DIG-ggbain-09306)

9. (*below*) The 1910 St. Louis Browns finished 47-107 in their only season under manager Jack O'Connor. He stands ten players in from the right in this team photo. Hall of Famer and future Browns manager Bobby Wallace is to O'Connor's immediate right. (Bell & Palfrey, Library of Congress, Prints and Photographs Division, Pan Subject-Sports No. 162)

10. (*above*) Ty Cobb received his Chalmers in Philadelphia on October 18, prior to Game Two of the 1910 World Series, as members of the American League pennant-winning Philadelphia Athletics looked on. Lajoie was unable to attend to accept his vehicle owing to a postseason series with the Cincinnati Reds. (National Baseball Hall of Fame Library, Cooperstown NY)

11. (*right*) Red Corriden was a rookie shortstop/third baseman with the Browns in 1910 when thrust into the middle of the controversy over the legitimacy of Napoleon Lajoie's "hits" during the October 9 doubleheader in St. Louis. He managed the Chicago White Sox for most of 1950. (National Baseball Hall of Fame Library, Cooperstown NY)

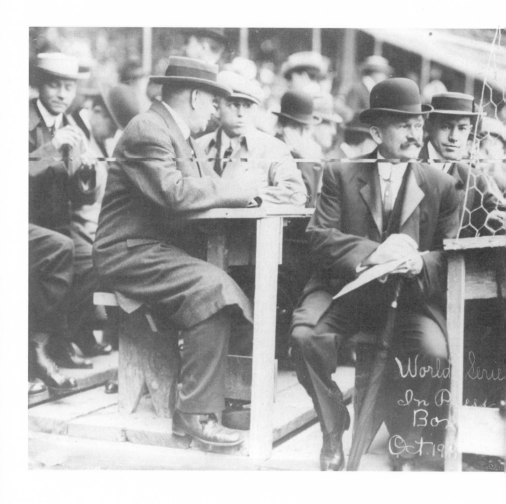

12. (*above*) Official scorers in 1910 were selected by the home team from the local press corps. The scorers (shown here in place during the 1911 World Series) sat in the press box with their reporting brethren. (National Baseball Hall of Fame Library, Cooperstown NY)

13. (*right*) In 1910 Ban Johnson was the president of the American League and the most powerful figure in the game. He did not take kindly to anything that interfered with public interest in the forthcoming World Series and so acted quickly to resolve the Chalmers controversy. (Boston Public Library, Ned McGreevey Collection)

14. (*above*) When this photograph was taken in 1904, Napoleon Lajoie of Cleveland (*left*) and Honus Wagner of the National League's Pittsburgh Pirates were generally acknowledged as the best hitters in their respective leagues. By 1910 Wagner's star still shone bright, Lajoie's somewhat less so. (Boston Public Library, Ned McGreevey Collection)

15. (*right*) Although he reached star status primarily as a hitter, Napoleon Lajoie, shown here circa 1906, was also a smooth-fielding second baseman. (Boston Public Library, Ned McGreevey Collection)

16. In thirteen Major League seasons, seven with the St. Louis Browns, Harry Howell (shown here circa 1905) compiled a record of 131-146. He was scouting by October 9, when he was accused of complicity in helping Napoleon Lajoie in his quest for the 1910 batting title. Howell's involvement cost him a chance to umpire in the American League. (SDN-003801, *Chicago Daily News* negatives collection, Chicago History Museum)

17. By most reports, "Rowdy" Jack O'Connor earned his nickname early in a twenty-one-year playing career. At the end of the 1910 season, his first as manager of his hometown St. Louis Browns, he was fired for allegedly directing his team to "lay down" for Napoleon Lajoie in the latter's run for a Chalmers automobile. (SDN-053751, *Chicago Daily News* negatives collection, Chicago History Museum)

18. (*above*) A combination of his love for baseball and marketing genius led Hugh Chalmers to offer one of his company's automobiles to Major League Baseball's top batter for the 1910 season. When the batting race ended in controversy, the additional publicity was a bonus. (Courtesy of Detroit Athletic Club)

19. (*right*) By 1910 standards, Napoleon Lajoie, who stood six foot one and weighed 195 pounds, was an imposing figure at the plate with bat in hand. (Burton Historical Collection, Ernie Harwell Sports Collection, Detroit Public Library)

20. (*above*) Boston Red Sox center fielder Tris Speaker, shown here taking a break with Ty Cobb, was only twenty-two when he finished the 1910 season in third place in the race for the Chalmers with a .340 batting average. (Burton Historical Collection, Ernie Harwell Sports Collection, Detroit Public Library)

21. (*right*) Ty Cobb liked to swing multiple bats, usually three as here, in the on-deck circle. Early in his career, many, including his teammates, thought he was just showing off. However, shedding two bats as he stepped to the plate made his single war club seem light by comparison. (Burton Historical Collection, Ernie Harwell Sports Collection, Detroit Public Library)

22. (*above*) Following the 1909 World Series, Ty Cobb left for his home in Augusta, Georgia, driving a Chalmers-Detroit vehicle on a promotional tour. The trip attracted many onlookers such as this crowd, which turned out as Cobb arrived in Gaffney, South Carolina. (Burton Historical Collection, Ernie Harwell Sports Collection, Detroit Public Library)

23. (*top right*) In 1910 twenty-two-year-old Naps outfielder Joe Jackson (*left*), shown here with Cobb (*center*) and Lajoie had a higher batting average (.387) than either hitting star; however, he fell far short of qualifying for the Chalmers with only seventy-five at bats. (Private collection of the author.)

24. (*bottom right*) Prior to the final 1910 meeting between their teams, a doubleheader in Detroit on October 5, the press asked Ty Cobb and Nap Lajoie to pose in a Chalmers vehicle. Each refused to sit behind the wheel, so this photograph was taken of the pair (Lajoie on the *left*) seated in the rear seat. (Burton Historical Collection, Ernie Harwell Sports Collection, Detroit Public Library)

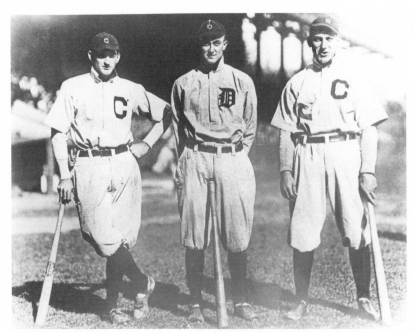

SHOELESS JOE JACKSON   TY COBB   NAPOLEON LAJOIE

25. The Chalmers Motor Company factory was located on East Jefferson Avenue in Detroit. In 1910 sales of Chalmers motor vehicles ran in excess of six thousand. (Walter P. Reuther Library, Wayne State University)

has shown up dislike him, third basemen with bum arms, second basemen with tender skins, catchers who cannot throw out a talented slider—all despise Cobb. And their attitude has infected the stands."[29]

Perhaps Lajoie read or heard about the comments, for all at once he was back in the news, volunteering information about Victor Parrish's startling claim that he had received a phone call on the evening after the doubleheader from someone purporting to be Nap. In a report out of Cleveland, datelined October 13, the Naps' infielder admitted that he indeed had placed the phone call to the official scorer, pleading his case for nine hits rather than the eight he had been awarded. He surprisingly explained that he would not have called but for the urging of umpire Billy Evans, as well as members of the Cleveland ball club, who felt him entitled to the additional hit. At the same time, Lajoie strongly denied offering a suit or any other prize if Parrish would change his ruling.[30]

In this regard Nap Lajoie had a strong supporter in Ban Johnson. Johnson told reporters, "I do not believe for a minute" that Lajoie would offer the scorer a bribe. Nonetheless, on one point involving the official scoring that day, Johnson was clear: henceforth, the individual appointed as the official scorer would be the one who scored the game. In the future, Johnson would himself name the scorer, or at least be more involved in approving the scorer, and there would be no delegations of that assignment.[31]

Johnson's comments about scorers were timely. In the days that followed the doubleheader, several reports mentioning favoritism bestowed by scorers on hometown heroes during the 1910 season surfaced. One report reminded readers of Lajoie's claim that he had been robbed of a hit by a Boston scorer, an allegation Red Sox owner John I. Taylor now flatly repudiated. According to Taylor, both Cobb and Lajoie had received equal and fair treatment in his ballpark.[32] Over in Chicago, knowledgeable sports writer Sy Sanborn recalled two plays in the recent White Sox–Tigers series in which it seemed that Cobb benefitted from some questionable fielding by a Sox outfielder.[33] Sanborn did not take issue with the scoring of the plays as hits, but merely bringing them to public attention raised questions marks. In Cleveland it was said that at least a dozen American League players stood ready to offer affidavits to the effect that Cobb was shown favor in scoring in games played in Detroit; three players were even ready to state that there were overt efforts to boost the Georgian's batting numbers.[34] In reality an issue could be made over almost any scoring decision made with respect to Cobb or Lajoie throughout the season.[35] The matter was becoming overblown with endless speculation, charges, and countercharges. As soon as Johnson completed his meeting with Red Corriden, he endeavored to end it.

By the time Corriden crossed Johnson's threshold on Friday, October 14, the American League president had one additional piece of evidence resting in his in-box. Sometime the day before, Johnson had received the report he had requested from the official scorer. The score sheets themselves were already in Johnson's possession, but now he had the written explanation to boot. Of course, in an exclusive to his newspaper employer the *Republic*, Victor Parrish had already told everyone his version of events and his reasoning in reaching his rulings relative to Lajoie.[36] Presumably, nothing changed in this official version. Since Parrish was acting for Richard Collins in scoring the games in St. Louis on October 9, Collins prepared and forwarded to Johnson a signed statement of his own. In his statement Collins reported that he sat near Parrish during the games and agreed with Parrish's ruling as to each hit credited to Lajoie. Collins added that after the game several reporters compared their own scoring and discussed their opinions. All save H. W. Lanigan of the *St. Louis Times* were in concert.[37] (Lanigan, albeit seriously doubting their legitimacy, firmly believed that Lajoie should have been credited with nine hits and so scored it for his newspaper.) The reporters referred to by Collins undoubtedly included the three men, "the integrity of whom cannot be questioned," Parrish had mentioned in the statement released by his newspaper.[38]

Bolstered by Evans's report and by the recent addition of reports by Collins and Parrish, Johnson met with Corriden and then almost broke his office door down sharing his findings with the local press, mindful that the reporters in turn would share it with the rest of the nation. Although careful to remind his audience that a final verdict awaited the arrival and debriefing of O'Connor, Johnson did nothing to dissuade those who believed that he intended, as he had from the beginning, to clear all involved in the St. Louis hippodrome of any wrongdoing:

I found Corriden an intelligent and ambitious young player, and that he comes of a good and reputable family. After questioning him closely and going over the hits one by one I was convinced that Lajoie did not get them through any connivance on Corriden's part. The reports sent out from St. Louis do not seem to have been absolutely true. Corriden told me one of the hits which were called bunts was not a bunt at all, but a hard poke which he was just able to reach close to third base and which he could not possibly have reached at all if he had been playing in or had started in for a bunt. It was not a hard hit, as he explained it, neither was it an ordinary bunt, but a ball which Lajoie reached out and poked as hard as he could without taking a full swing at it.

I have found no evidence as yet of connivance among the players, but will not form my opinion until I have had a talk with O'Connor. Then I expect to communicate with the automobile people and give out a statement in detail which will include all the facts I have been able to get and the actual official averages of Cobb and Lajoie, compiled from the official scores in our possession.[39]

An additional statement by Johnson, carried in a St. Louis paper, had the league chief excusing Corriden as a neophyte infielder up against the highly skillful, wily Lajoie, a batter who "can turn the trick against the most experienced veterans of the game time and again." Once again O'Connor was the turnkey: "I have insisted that he report in order that the whole affair be sifted to the bottom. From all the testimony I have been able to secure, all of which agrees with that of Corriden, I think that O'Connor can give explanations which should satisfy the most prejudiced fan that there was no intentional wrongdoing."[40]

In at least one regard, Johnson and O'Connor were not on the same page. While Ban claimed that Rowdy Jack's physical presence was a requirement, the Browns' manager claimed that his trip to the league boss's lair was purely optional: "I'd rather go to Chicago to see Johnson, although it was made optional to report by mail or in person. The affair has gone beyond the laughing stage and the sooner the heads of the League understand the folly of thinking there was any conspiracy in the matter, the better for baseball."[41]

If nothing else could be gleaned from O'Connor's remarks, it certainly appeared that the manager had finally come to the realization that his job was on the line. On the other hand, O'Connor, claiming that he had not felt well over the last few days, had yet to visit with his immediate boss, Bob Hedges. Perhaps he wanted to head to Chicago first, cash in any chips he still had with Johnson, and gain the executive's backing before a face-to-face with Hedges. Reports circulated, however, that Harry Howell had visited Hedges on Friday, October 14. The topic of conversation of the meeting held in Hedges's office was unknown, as was the result, but when confronted by reporters in Hedges's outer office prior to the meeting, Howell added to his original version of events, claiming that he had visited the press box at the behest of two Browns players and two Naps. When asked about the facsimile of the note that had been released to the public, Harry stated firmly that the handwriting was not his, nor did he recognize the handwriting as that of someone he knew. When he stepped out of his office, Hedges, as well as club secretary Lloyd Rickart, were asked the same question. Neither claimed to recognize the handwriting, and Hedges claimed that the Browns' batboy did not meet the description he had received from Parrish. Later in the day, despite lavishing praise on Howell, Hedges left reporters with an ominous message. Asked if he thought that Howell had made a "grievous" error in going to the press box, Hedges replied, "People who make mistakes generally pay for them."[42]

If O'Connor thought that a meeting with Johnson might save his job, the *St. Louis Times* continued to disagree. Its editors believed that the manager's delaying tactics in heading to Chicago, plus his wager on the World Series, given Hedges's battle against open gambling at his ballpark, would sink his ship. That notion apparently justified the following headline in the October 14 edition: "O'Connor Will Not Manage Hedges' Club Next Season."[43]

Across the St. Louis landscape, the ever-skeptical Eddie Wray delivered his verdict. He too saw difficulties ahead for O'Connor. He had been one of the first to label the proceedings of October 9 a "hippodrome." Wray was not about to let up now. According to the *Post-Dispatch* columnist, after interviewing one man (Corriden), Ban Johnson had decided "that he [Johnson] is right about this scandal thing and all St. Louis is wrong." Maybe, Wray mused, it was best to sentence the incident to a quick death. After all, "the memory is not pleasant to anyone." Nonetheless, "Ban B. [Johnson] never forgets; neither is he ever misguided in matters pertaining to baseball. Probably, despite the whitewash, in his own mind he has the correct idea of the St. Louis happening; and, although he may now be compelled to still the cries of the outraged 'for the good of the game,' he'll have his little inning with the ax ere the next season starts."[44]

By the time Wray's verbiage was in print, Johnson and the object of the columnist's predictions of doom and gloom, Jack O'Connor, had met. According to reports, the meeting began around noon on the fifteenth and lasted approximately two hours. On that same Saturday afternoon, Hugh Chalmers arrived from Detroit and went into conference with Johnson, his offer of an automobile for both Cobb and Lajoie most likely still on the table. And while Johnson conferred, his secretary, Robert McRoy, pored over the score sheets, culling them for only the at bats and hits of Cobb and Lajoie, ready to help Johnson put an end to this embarrassment, now going on one week old. Then, once again, Johnson made a beeline for the press, wasting absolutely no time in issuing a signed statement that touched on all the bases, to coin a weak pun, and awarded the batting title to Ty Cobb, thereby—at least in Ban Johnson's mind—bringing the aggravating affair to a firm and final end. The statement of the American League president reads in its entirety as follows:

A thorough investigation has satisfied me that there is no substantial ground for questioning the accuracy of any of the eight base hits credited to Player [*sic*] Lajoie of the Cleveland club by the official scorer in the double header on Sunday, October 9, at St. Louis, and all of them have been admitted to the 1910 batting records of the American league [*sic*].

Before reaching this conclusion I considered a detailed statement from Umpire Evans, who officiated in these games, as well as a special report from Mr. Collins, the official scorer at St. Louis, who saw the games and endorsed the correctness of the scoring of Mr. Parrish, his assistant. I also personally discussed with Manager O'Connor and Third Baseman Corriden of the Browns the incidents of these games which were the foundation of newspaper charges of collusion between members of the St. Louis team and Player Lajoie.

Their individual explanations were supplemented by an indignant denial that the third baseman misplayed his position at his own instance or through instructions from any one connected with the St. Louis club, and Manager O'Connor attributed Lajoie's success in making infield hits to his shrewdness in switching from the driving system he usually employs to bunting, thereby springing the unexpected on Corriden, whose major league experience is limited and whose regular position is at shortstop.

I accept this explanation as a vindication of Player Corriden. It is a matter of comment that Lajoie frequently resorted to the bunt in the later stages of the pennant race. I desire to call attention to a declaration by Mr. Evans in his report that in his judgment Lajoie was entitled to nine hits instead of eight. This is corroborated by the fact that in his report of the games in the St. Louis Times Mr. Lanagan [sic] gave nine hits to Lajoie.

When the National league's [sic] candidates for the Chalmers trophy had been eliminated by the phenomenal records of Cobb and Lajoie the attention of the baseball world was focused on the daily performances of these grand batsmen, each representing a distinct type. As interest increased the partisans of each became more pronounced, and feats of these popular favorites were played up by the press to the neglect of other features, including the position of teams. Newspaper writers, ball players, and patrons took sides and became zealous in their support of their favorite.

Neither Cobb nor Lajoie asked for or received favors from the pitchers or players of opposing teams, and each attained his average on merit, but each has been criticized more or less, Lajoie on the St. Louis incident and Cobb for leaving his team before the close of the race.

The records of the American League for 1910 show that their respective batting averages are as follows: Cobb, 509 times at bat, 196 base hits; percentage, .384944. Lajoie 591 times at bat, 227 base hits; percentage, .384084.

This margin is meager, and each of the contestants has during his connection with the American league contributed much to its prestige by his magnificent batting and all around work. I will certify to the national commission that Cobb has a clear title to the leadership of the American league batsmen for 1910 and is therefore entitled to the Chalmers trophy, as none of the National league batters approached his record.

An offer from me to purchase a duplicate of the Chalmers trophy for presentation to Lajoie in recognition of his services to the American league throughout his connection with it and as a reward for his grand batting record during the season just closed was met by Mr. Chalmers with an urgent plea that his company be permitted to donate a similar machine of its make, and I have acceded to his request.

I have requested President Hedges of the St. Louis club to further probe the charge that some one connected with his club attempted to influence the official scorer, and will insist that, if developments warrant it, adequate punishment be meted out to the guilty party or parties.

[signed] B. B. Johnson[45]

Along with issuance of his signed statement, Johnson appeared outside his office to make a brief oral statement. In fact it was but two words. Raising his right hand he swore, "Never again."[46]

In an interesting aside, the article in the *Chicago Tribune* that carried Ban Johnson's complete statement noted that the batting statistics listed in the article for Cobb and Lajoie were "announced as official, although apparently a slight error has been made in figuring if the times at bat and hits are correct." Indeed, if the at bats and hits for each player were correct, then Cobb's average was .385068 (not .384944) and Lajoie's .384094 (not .384084). The errors did not change the result or the fact Cobb had won by the scantiest of margins; one hit less and Cobb would have finished second at .383104. The errors, however, also did little to convince one of the accuracy of McRoy's calculations. To the contrary, the errors were clear indications of calculations made in haste. They underscored why normal policy called for an independent audit of final league batting and pitching figures, a procedure presumably not yet undertaken when Johnson announced the winner of the batting title.

At least one reporter took Johnson and his office to task. According to Harry Neily of the *Detroit Times*, "If the people who divided 196 by 509 and got .384944 cannot add any better than they can divide it might not be a bad plan for the president of the American league [*sic*] to cause to be published the dates, times and base hits of both Cobb and Lajoie so the public may do its own addition and be satisfied with the answer."[47]

Nonetheless, the results stood as announced. According to Johnson, his findings and decision regarding the award were made pending final approval from the National Commission, but no one doubted for a minute that all the decisions that would be made by Major League leadership had now been made. Ban was a reporter by trade. He fully understood the power of the press and how to use it to best advantage. He had done so in this case, taking pains to ensure all that his maneuvering and the results of his interview process were fully aired in newspapers across the country. In addition, by wrapping up the Chalmers controversy seven days after it had occurred, he had put the matter to rest, at least as much as he could, almost two full days before the start of the 1910 World Series. That event, scheduled to begin at Shibe Park in Philadelphia on the afternoon of October 17, now hopefully would not be played in the shadow of controversy.

Reaction by the press was swift and, for the most part, in keeping with earlier editorials analyzing the fracas. According to Detroit's *Free Press*, all that "very smooth article as a league executive [Johnson]" had done the day before was release "his prepared-in-advance verdict."[48] Its pulp rival, the *Times*, affirmed its position that the incident demanded an investigation, "but the future of the game DID NOT [*sic*] demand the whitewashing of the guilty parties nor the marking of any ONE man as the scapegoat."[49] And Johnson's verdict did nothing to change the skepticism etched across Eddie Wray's forehead from the start. "It's a soiled page—," he concluded.[50] A

Clevelander, writing tongue in cheek as "John Doe," found it "fortunate for Ban Johnson that the figures came out just so, making Cobb winner by an eyelash. How lucky the auto company came forward with a machine for Larry."[51] The writer would have readily agreed with the suggestion that Johnson could put the entire matter of scoring errors to rest by providing the public with the official box scores of all games involving Cobb or Lajoie.

One St. Louis paper ventured that Johnson had done his best to protect Corriden after he opened up and told him the truth about what happened during the final two games of his season. The piece opined, "To acute observers there was more under than over the surface of this [Corriden's] interview." In a particularly sage moment, the author of the unattributed article summarized overall reaction to the incident by writing that "everyone thinks that it was simply a case of perverted good-fellowship" and that "when O'Connor did not prevent the foolishness he wrote his own removal as manager of the Browns."[52]

The vast majority of media criticism was directed at the leniency Johnson accorded the Browns. The press did not seem upset that Ban had limited his inquiry to the Browns. After all, he had interviewed only players from that club, and his directive to Hedges asked the Browns' executive to investigate whether any of his boys had tried to influence the scorer. Meanwhile, no arrows were aimed at the Naps, or more pointedly at Napoleon Lajoie, although Harry Howell had certainly implicated at least some team members in connection with his visits to the press box.

Not everyone was dissatisfied with Johnson's call. Ty Cobb, the chief beneficiary of the league executive's ruling, was "simply delighted," although he could "scarcely believe it." He even had room in his heart for Lajoie. When told a Chalmers was headed Nap's way as well, Tyrus considered it "bully news." Although he was happy that his hard work had earned him the batting title of both leagues, he considered his battle with Lajoie "of a most friendly character." It was "pleasing" that his rival would receive a reward for his efforts. He thought the games in St. Louis were "on the square." On the other hand, before the dust completely settled, Cobb felt it was time to clear the air on his early exit from Chicago: "So far as my leaving the team before the end of the season is concerned, I can say this: I asked Manager Jennings ten days before the season closed to give me permission to leave the team, as I wanted to pack up and take an automobile trip to Philadelphia and play with the All Stars. I had planned not to go to Chicago, but the race for the prize was close, and so I went to Chicago and played two games."[53]

At the very least, Cobb's explanation was honest, even though it probably did little to change the minds of those, including his teammates, who thought he played the game for his own purposes. If he intended to leave the impression that he answered the call to defend his lead in the batting race by carrying his season forward in the Windy City, it did just the opposite. It was a frank admission that had the Chalmers prize been his, he would have bagged out even sooner. He might have been better off silently accepting his booty, rather than raising such a flimsy defense.

For his part Lajoie continued to play on both sides of the fence. A day or so before, Lajoie had talked to a reporter by phone from his farm, where he was "too busy" to care who was awarded the car. He wanted all to know, "I'm as happy as a lark." At the same time, he continued to "insist" that he was entitled to nine hits on that last day.[54] Now that he had received the official results, he once again talked with reporters. "I am quite satisfied," he maintained, "that I was treated fairly in every way by President Johnson." He had nothing but respect as well for the batting prowess of Ty Cobb and was "glad for his success." Nevertheless, there was that dratted official scorer. Nap thought he had made an "error."[55] Despite receiving the keys to a new car, Nap was having a rough time letting that one go. Still, he immediately wired Cobb his "heartiest congratulations."[56]

Lest one look at the results of Johnson's investigation and brand Lajoie as someone who was merely looking a gift horse—or, in this case, horseless carriage—in the mouth, it is worth taking the time to analyze what that ninth hit, though certainly obtained under dubious circumstances, would have done for Lajoie in the batting race. If Lajoie had been credited with an additional time at bat and hit instead of a sacrifice, which did not count as either, his final average would have been .385135. This is based on 228 hits in 592 at bats. When compared to either .384944 (Cobb's figure erroneously released by Ban Johnson to the press as "official") or the correct figure of .385068, Lajoie wins the crown. Since Johnson took pains in his statement to point out that both umpire Billy Evans and veteran reporter H. W. Lanigan supported nine hits for Lajoie, the idea subsists that the Frenchman had a point.

Another who tried to make a point but to no avail was Philadelphia Phillies outfielder Sherry Magee, by all accounts the leading batsman in the National League, an honor that brought with it no Chalmers. Magee might have taken the slight better had Lajoie not received a car. "There is," he told reporters in Philadelphia for the World Series, "no reason why a beaten contender in the American [League] should be treated better than a champion in the National."[57] Perhaps Sherry's batting average of .331, more than fifty points below that of either Cobb or Lajoie, had something to do with it.

At least Magee still had his job. That was no longer the case for Jack O'Connor and Harry Howell. In a statement released within twenty-four hours of Ban Johnson's statement of October 15 clearing all involved from wrongdoing—save those Hedges might find had attempted to influence the official scorer—Hedges dismissed his manager and his scout. A St. Louis newspaper termed the dismissal an action that "will dumbfound the local sporting world," one only recently convinced of a total whitewash.[58] In Hedges's own words, after a "careful and exhaustive analysis and investigation," he had "not found the slightest evidence of crookedness in last Sunday's games"—this despite branding the games as "attended by deplorable incidents." In addition, the Browns' owner was satisfied "that there is no misconduct on the part of Manager O'Connor or player Corriden and that scout Howell did nothing wrong in asking the questions of the official scorer." Nonetheless, O'Connor received an unconditional release, sans flowery good-byes. Hedges had praise on the other hand for Howell, who pitched so well for his team and for so long: "He threw his arm out in the services of this club two years ago, and for that reason I have kept him in my employ and might have so continued him had it not been for the unfortunate notoriety given him."

And there it was in a nutshell: the alleged basis for the Browns' president's decision. It was all about the "notoriety." According to Hedges, it was "up to every club owner to keep the game clean and free from any taint of suspicion or scandal. . . . Suspicion, gambling, crookedness, hippodroming or faking of any sort would be its downfall."

It does not take a vibrant imagination to believe that when Ban Johnson and Bob Hedges met in Chicago to discuss the handling of the participants thought primarily responsible for the dubious play in Hedges's bailiwick on October 9, Johnson orchestrated the plan. He had determined that minus any proof of wrongdoing, the best path would be to find no wrong. The mess could then become a team problem. As such, Hedges as the club owner, rather than Johnson as league official, could act in the name of that wonderful catchall, "the good of the game." Although he never said it once in a ten-paragraph signed statement released to the public on the evening of October 15, it was there when Hedges said he acted "because there has been so much public talk and so much criticism in the papers." That was enough for him, "irrespective of any other reasons before last Sunday's games," to dismiss O'Connor and Howell.[59] It was enough for Ban Johnson too. He had gritted his teeth the day before in Chicago as he pronounced all innocent and his league and its games fine and dandy. He did so knowing full well that he had already given Hedges the proverbial "blank check." Thus, Hedges had the complete blessing of—if not an outright edict from—baseball's reigning pope to fire his manager and his scout before the start of the World Series.

Just how sure was Ban Johnson that O'Connor and Howell would be history? He was sure to a certainty, at least as to O'Connor. When Johnson issued his statement clearing everyone involved, he already had a letter in his possession from Hedges informing Ban that as Browns president, he was going to dismiss O'Connor. Sometime during the evening of October 15, Johnson announced O'Connor's pending dismissal to the press:

I [Johnson] am in receipt of a letter from Mr. Hedges in which the owner of the St. Louis club discusses the recent Lajoie affair. Mr. Hedges notified me that he had decided to sign a new manager in place of Mr. O'Connor, but he did not intimate that he suspected his former manager of being implicated in any irregular scoring deal. Under the circumstances he feels that he cannot afford to take any chances of placing his club under a cloud, and therefore he decided to start next season with a new slate. As far as I know there are absolutely no charges of unfairness to be made against Mr. O'Connor, and no official action on my part will be taken. The matter was entirely up to Mr. Hedges, and he appears to have disposed of it by severing his connection with his manager.[60]

As can be seen from the tight wording of this latest statement from Johnson, the league's head honcho continued to perform a high-wire act, taking great pains to make it clear to one and all that he had nothing whatsoever to do with Hedges's decision to dump his manager. More than two decades later, Jack O'Connor would talk freely about his meeting with Johnson preceding Hedges's announcement and the manner of his dismissal, summing up his actions on the bench during the October 9 doubleheader by telling his interviewer, "I wish I had it to do over again." As to his trip to Chicago and its aftermath,

I'll never forget my conference with Johnson. He, of course, put the blame on me for permitting the players to be out of position, but as much as admitted to me that the evidence showed that I had not directed my men to help Lajoie. It was their own doing. So it was that I left the conference feeling pretty certain that no drastic punishment would be handed out to me. In fact, I had been led to believe that a fine or reprimand would be all there was to it.

I got on the train for St. Louis at night. Remember, I was under contract for 1911 as manager. When the train reached Springfield, Ill., the Pullman porter came to me and asked me if I had seen the morning newspaper. I told him I hadn't. "Well," said the porter, "there's bad news for you. You've been fired." And sure enough, there was the story of my dismissal in big type.[61]

Harry Howell was in St. Louis when news of his dismissal was announced. He reacted to it thusly:

It is true that I did ask the official scorer what he had given Lajoie. I did so at the request of the Cleveland players, who asked me to ascertain. I was not on the grounds in uniform nor on the bench.

I have no word to say. I never was a quitter or a "squealer" and I am not going to quit or to squeal now. I am still young, have two good hands and average intelligence. I think that my friends and the public believe in my integrity and honesty. I always have made it a point to be civil and obliging to everyone. I was merely civil and obliging in this case. But as I say, I'll take my medicine and saw wood.[62]

By the afternoon of Sunday, October 16, Ban Johnson was observed hopping on board a swift train to Philadelphia, ready to watch the World Series. Attempts to prompt further comment on the Cobb-Lajoie affair came to naught. However, the president of the American League was ready to expound on the Athletics' superior pitching prowess, and he did, predicting Philadelphia would capture the crown.[63]

The opening game of the 1910 World Series was played in Shibe Park on Monday, October 17. The Athletics won 4–1 over Chicago's Cubs. Just as Ban Johnson predicted, the Athletics' pitching, under the command of Connie Mack's ace Chief Bender in this one, was the difference. Game Two was set for the next day, also at Shibe. Prior to the contest, also won by the Philadelphians, the Cubs took the diamond for fielding practice. As they went through their routines, a pair of Chalmers automobiles were driven into the ballpark and positioned in front of the grandstand. Ty Cobb, present and seated at the time in the press area, was called to the field and presented with his prize for winning the Major League batting title for 1910. Lajoie was not present. His vehicle would be shipped to him. Following the presentation, Cobb stood in front of his new auto. As a number of the Athletics stood behind him and the vehicle, the cameramen photographed the scene. Cobb then took the driver's seat, while former teammate and baseball showman Germany Schaefer and current teammate Bill Donovan, one of those who wired his congratulations to Lajoie, hopped in the back. John E. Bruce, secretary of the National Commission, took the driver's seat of Lajoie's "consolation" prize. A couple of unidentified men climbed in the back. Photographs were taken of these men and their machines, and then Ty took off on a motorized trip around the outfield, the Lajoie vehicle in hot pursuit and the Shibe Park faithful roaring. Moments later Game Two began, and the World Series replaced the Cobb-Lajoie affair as baseball's rightful October feature story.

Over the next few days, as the Athletics captured their first world title, talk about the Chalmers race was essentially limited to the need to reform the system of scoring. In this case, as in most cases of cries for reform after the fact, the horse was already out of the barn. Still, some thought that the Chalmers affair had exposed a flaw in baseball's peripheral apparatus that should and could be repaired going forward. One suggestion was to organize the official scorers into a system similar to the one in place for umpires. In such a system, the scorers would be appointed by the league and travel from city to city. They would not travel with the players or stay in the player's hotels. They would not be beholden to the players for story quotes or material for their stories. Over time they would achieve an independence not currently enjoyed or even sought by the sportswriters chosen by the individual teams.[64]

At least one central figure in this most recent affair, Napoleon Lajoie, agreed with the reformists:

I believe all this talk [about the batting controversy] will hurry one reform that is needed badly. They ought to have traveling scorers, just like umpires. The official figures as kept now are jokes. . . . [T]hey should change the system of scoring if so much importance is going to be placed on the figures. When I first broke into the big leagues batting and fielding averages attracted little attention. Nobody bothered with them. Now they seem to be of as much interest as the box scores. If the public wants the dope it ought to get it straight.[65]

None of this talk aided Harry Howell. He needed a job, and baseball was about all he knew. October 21 was an off day in a World Series that had now returned to Chicago, where the day before the Athletics won again to forge a 3–0 lead. Howell traveled to Chicago and went to the office of Ban Johnson to discuss his dismissal. Although he had no appointment, Harry thought perhaps he had banked enough goodwill over the years to gain an audience, but alas, Johnson would not see him. In the president's defense, it was the middle of the World Series, and it is almost certain that the executive had returned from Philadelphia to face a busy schedule. There were reports that while Howell waited to see Johnson, he fielded a number of job offers, including a scouting position from Clark Griffith, manager of the National League's Cincinnati Reds. Other potential offers included managerial positions in the Minor Leagues, work Harry supposedly preferred.[66] At some point Howell had even entertained ideas of becoming an umpire and had the support of at least one St. Louis columnist, who stated that Johnson had at one time made the former Brown just such an offer.[67] Howell remained in Chicago and tried to see Johnson again the next day. It was, however, obvious by now that Johnson had no intention of seeing him, so he returned to St. Louis hoping to meet to discuss a managerial position with owners of a team in the upper-level American Association.[68] Nothing came of it, at least in 1910. By the end of the year, Howell was still jobless; Ban Johnson was on record saying that Harry Howell would never umpire in the American League.[69]

Over the next month, as the baseball world reflected on a World Series won by the Athletics over the Cubs in five games, there was the occasional mention of the Cobb-Lajoie affair. One item mentioned that as late as mid-November, Lajoie still awaited delivery of his Chalmers. It seemed "friends" were trying to secure Ohio license plate number "384" for the vehicle to signify Lajoie's 1910 batting average. That number was already in use. Eventually, Lajoie secured the license number by writing to the current holder, who agreed to give it up.[70] Once Lajoie was in possession of the vehicle, he planned to motor south in it to the 1911 spring training. He would do so with the best wishes of Ty Cobb, who graciously penned a congratulatory note to the Naps' infielder, wishing him a happy driving experience.[71] Cobb, in fact, was feeling downright charitable. Former teammate Germany Schaefer, who owned nary a vehicle, reportedly joked that he would have won the Chalmers given more at bats. Cobb, whose garage was already overflowing, offered him his old one. Schaefer, a comedian but no fool, took Ty up on the offer.[72] Of course, unlike Lajoie, Cobb was already in possession of his Chalmers, having picked his up at the World Series. One report had him accepting an invitation for a three-heat match driving race with Nap Rucker, a pitcher for the Brooklyn Dodgers. The event would take place in Atlanta in early November.[73] After earning a fee for providing his observations on the first two games of the World Series to readers of the *Detroit Free Press*, Ty, his wife, and his baby climbed on board his prize auto and headed south, ultimate destination, Augusta.[74]

There was even talk that Cobb, Lajoie, Wagner, and Magee, all at one point or another seriously involved in pursuit of the Chalmers, were being pursued by a theatrical entrepreneur for a tour with his vaudeville company. The skit, titled "A Batting Rally," would see the introduction of an early version of a batting machine. The pay—$250 to $300 per week for fifteen weeks—sounded too good to be true and even then would likely not be enough to lure the bashful Honus Wagner onto the stage.[75]

At long last, in late November, the American League released its official batting statistics for 1910. (The official National League season records were released a week later.) By now ideally the figures had been subjected to an independent audit. At the very least, the totals were arrived at through a careful review of the records by league secretary Robert McRoy. The batting average leader was Ty Cobb. His average was rounded off to .385, based on 196 hits in 509 at bats, the same at-bat and hit totals announced by the league office back in mid-October. Lajoie's average was rounded off to .384, based upon 227 hits in 591 at bats, also the same batting totals as previously announced. Lajoie's appearances in 159 games, a figure he reached because his team played in nine tie games, led the league. The tie games did not count in the standings—the Naps' final record was 71-81 in 1910—but they counted statistically for the individual player.[76] Cobb had established his numbers by playing in 140 games. The closest American Leaguer was Boston's Tris Speaker, who hit .340. The National League statistics confirmed that Sherry Magee at .331 was on top among those with sufficient times at the plate.

Release of the official American League numbers also confirmed what was already known. Cobb and Lajoie had enjoyed remarkable years in 1910 almost across the board when it came to hitting. Lajoie led the league in number of hits, with Cobb second. Cobb led the league with 106 runs scored; Lajoie and Speaker tied for second, each with ninety-two.[77] Cobb with sixty-five stolen bases finished second to the Athletics' Eddie Collins, who had eighty-one. Lajoie was far behind, but his total of twenty-six steals was certainly not shameful. Larry led the league in doubles with fifty-one; Cobb was second with thirty-five. Even in a power category such as home runs Cobb's eight tied for second, two behind league leader Jake Stahl of Boston, while Lajoie's four tied for fourth. Figures were not then kept in such categories as runs batted in (Cobb second, Lajoie fifth) and total bases (Lajoie first, Cobb second) or for on-base percentage, slugging percentage, or OPS (the combination of the two), but Cobb was first and Lajoie second in all three categories. As usual, the numbers would become grist for the mill in hot-stove discussions throughout the winter months.

As the year drew to a close, in addition to the ongoing discussions about the need for changes in the official scoring system, including a suggestion by National League president Thomas J. Lynch that scorers be appointed by the Baseball Writers' Association, there was at least one other unsettled matter.[78] The St. Louis Browns were still without a manager. In late October it was reported that Bob Hedges conferred with Charley Carr, the recently resigned manager of Indianapolis of the American Association.[79] After his club had finished seventh in 1910, Carr claimed that he was retiring to work full-time at his sporting goods store. By the end of the year, by all accounts Carr remained out of baseball. In mid-December *Sporting Life* reported that shortstop Bobby Wallace was a top candidate for the job, although the club had completed its annual meeting without making a decision. There was some speculation that the club was waiting until after the first of the year. Jack O'Connor was being paid through the end of the year but claiming he was under valid contract through 1911. He had indicated his intent to ask for reinstatement or compensation as of January 1. If neither was forthcoming, he planned to sue. The thought was that the Browns were waiting until January 1 to hire a manager as part of their own litigation strategy.[80] That may not have been it at all. It soon became apparent that bigger things were going on with the St. Louis Browns.

On December 20 a meeting was held at the St. Louis Racquet Club and attended by Ban Johnson; Charles Comiskey, owner of the Chicago White Sox; and a group of St. Louis businessmen intent on winning approval to buy the controlling interest in the Browns. Johnson and Comiskey represented the American League committee. Frank Farrell, owner of New York's American League entry and a committee member, did not attend. Apparently, the American Leaguers were favorably impressed, because the St. Louis "syndicate" received the pair's blessing for the purchase pending formal passage by the league's owners, a mere formality at that point. The sale became public on December 21.[81] Along with the announcement was the news that current president and major stockholder Bob Hedges would remain as president until a January 1911 meeting to elect new officers. According to Ben Adkins, a spokesman for the new owners, "Hedges sold out and is no longer a director." Hedges, fighting back tears, confirmed the sale. "It's just like breaking up a family," he said.

As to a new Browns manager, the picture was still blurred. Indications, however, were that Bobby Wallace was reluctant to accept the job. The leading candidate was now Fred Lake, who had managed the Boston Red Sox during part of 1908 and all of 1909. Regarding the recently deposed Jack O'Connor, syndicate spokesman Adkins issued some markedly pointed remarks: "Jack O'Connor will be paid in full. I believe O'Connor has too large a following in North St. Louis not to have him on our side. I think O'Connor was dealt with too severely. President Ban Johnson said he thought it would be best for us to settle O'Connor's claim as best we could. We intend to pay O'Connor in full and Jack will be in our employ next year. What position he will hold I do not know at the present time."[82]

It now appeared that the last dangling shoelace would be tied in what had started out as a rather simple affair designed to reward baseball's best batsman. For all intents and purposes, the Cobb-Lajoie affair was all set to become just another footnote in baseball history. But it was not over, not by a long shot.

Chapter Ten

*President Hedge's [sic] attitude on the stand
created an unfavorable impression.*
—newspaper clipping, National
Baseball Hall of Fame Library

One year and three days after Jack O'Connor and his Browns completed their 1910 season with that controversial doubleheader against the Cleveland Naps, his legal representative entered the clerk's office of the Circuit Court, City of St. Louis, and filed a petition on his behalf against his former employer, officially known as the St. Louis American League Baseball Company. The legal paperwork, signed by attorney Horace L. Dyer and filed by him on O'Connor's behalf on October 12, 1911, in what was the court of general jurisdiction in Missouri, initiated a lawsuit in which O'Connor claimed the Browns were in breach of contract when they dismissed him after only one year of a two-year contract to manage the team for an annual salary of $5,000. The lawsuit claimed damages of $5,000 plus legal costs, the losses O'Connor claimed he sustained as a result of his unjust firing. In addition to a copy of the alleged contract, the court files contain a letter dated November 29, 1910, from R. L. Hedges, written in his capacity as Browns president, to John O'Connor confirming "what you have understood for more than a month past," that the baseball club had decided to "terminate its contract with you as a member of the St. Louis American League Base Ball club for the season of 1911, and that you have been tendered an unconditional release." Hedges offered to provide his former manager with "the reasons for the termination" if O'Connor requested them within the next five days.[1]

The initiation of court proceedings by Rowdy Jack followed a period of relative calm after the storm of controversy the previous fall, but the silence of the litigants apparently belied a rising tension, at least on the part of O'Connor. In the early months of 1911, the need for changes in the system used to appoint official scorers had been mentioned frequently. In addition, consideration was given to continuing the Chalmers prize, seemingly a dead horse, albeit under a radically altered format.

At his league's meetings in mid-February 1911, Ban Johnson attempted to address the problems encountered in 1910 with undue pressures brought to bear on official scorers by the public, as well as by players and managers. He did not intend to propose that scorers should be screened for competency, nor that there be a slate of scorers appointed by each league to travel the circuit in like manner to the cadre of umpires. He planned only to suggest that their identity be concealed to all except league officials, club owners, and of course, the scorers themselves. Given Johnson's position of authority, it seemed doubtful there would be much resistance to his idea. National League secretary John Heydler would propose a similar plan for his league.[2] The National League had actually used such a system until it was dropped by the league in 1891. However, the proposal, at least in the senior circuit, was not met with favor by all. Barney Dreyfuss, the president of the Pittsburgh Pirates, told *Baseball Magazine* in July that he was "opposed to having any mystery about the scoring. Every player and patron should know who is doing the official work. If the scorer is in the limelight he will exercise more care."[3] Later, when Thomas Lynch, the National League's president, proposed that the Baseball Writers' Association appoint official scorers, he too met resistance; the chief worry was that the plan would involve the group in baseball politics.[4] In the end, the system for appointing official scorers went forward essentially unaltered.

There was greater unanimity with regard to accepting Hugh Chalmers's offer to continue to present his motorized creations to baseball's top annual performers, but not without a few fits and starts of its own. In early October 1910, several days before the Naps and Browns faced off in their season finale, H. W. Ford, the corporate secretary for the Chalmers Motor Company, wrote Garry Herrmann, the chairman of the National Commission. In addition to asking when the National Commission wished to schedule the presentation of the 1910 Chalmers automobile, Ford advised Herrmann that Chalmers wished to offer another automobile for the 1911 season. Hugh Chalmers knew he had a good thing going. His company was getting an enormous amount of publicity through the closeness of the race and the name recognition of the final combatants, Cobb and Lajoie. Perhaps already sensing some resistance on the part of baseball's ruling body with regard to approving future awards of this type, Ford added the following to his letter: "He [Chalmers] is quite willing to present this car to the National Commission and allow that body to offer it for any competition which it sees fit; either for the champion batsman, the champion run getter, the champion base stealer or for the championship in some other connection, although it is our feeling that the contest among batsmen probably arouses more interest among fans than any other would."[5]

Less than a week later, Lajoie accumulated eight hits, a controversy flared, and the National Commission's resistance turned into downright implacability. As the two leagues entered their winter meetings in early 1911, it seemed highly improbable that the National Commission would endorse any system of player awards, certainly none which left the contest in the hands of official scorers. Of course, if someone wanted to offer prizes to players for batting contests, there was no legal way to prohibit them, but baseball would not sanction it. Hugh Chalmers was aware of the situation he had innocently created. He wanted the publicity he derived from offering his motor vehicles as prizes, yet he respected the professional game and wanted its imprimatur. His letter of October 1910 had suggested possible alternatives to a batting race; now he set about offering alternatives that would keep his advertising bonanza alive for years to come.

By May 1911 the perseverance of Hugh Chalmers and his associates had paid off. A new system for awarding Chalmers automobiles to high-achieving baseball players was in place. Under the new system, a new

Chalmers motor vehicle would be awarded at the end of the year to one player in each league who, in the words of Chalmers, had "done the most to help his team in its League pennant race." The decision makers under the new plan would be a panel of baseball writers, one from each Major League city. They would be known as the Chalmers Trophy Commission. The writers' selections would be confined to the league in which their city's team (or teams in the case of New York, Boston, Philadelphia, Chicago, and St. Louis) played. Each writer would rank eight players, with a first-place vote counting as eight points and an eighth-place ranking counting as one point. The player with the highest total of points in each league would secure the automobile. In addition to game performance, Chalmers suggested the writers consider various aspects of a player's comportment, including "conduct on and off the field, loyalty, integrity, attention to training rules, [and] time of reporting to his club," when making and ranking their selections.[6]

The revised system offered a number of advantages over the old one. It was now in essence a "most valuable player" award, based upon a selection process that was much less open to the abuses of the batting race of the previous season. There was still the risk of favoritism, but it was much more spread out since the writers had to select and rank eight players, not just one or two from their city. Chalmers suggested that the new system would reduce "partisan influence" by producing a result based on "a concensus [sic] of opinion." As in 1910 Chalmers sought and received the permission of the National Commission to offer the awards. On the other hand, Garry Herrmann and his cohorts on the commission sought to distance themselves from the awards to avoid an embarrassment, should one occur. Chalmers, presumably at Herrmann's suggestion, or at the very least, with his approval, asked and received the assent of Herrmann's old friend Ren Mulford Jr., a well-respected correspondent for Herrmann's hometown *Cincinnati Post* and the national weekly *Sporting Life*, to appoint the reporters who would cast the votes for the eventual winners.[7]

Any list of the American League's top candidates for the restructured Chalmers prize in 1911 would include, of course, Cobb and Lajoie. Although the pair met often across the diamond, the setting offered scant opportunity for in-depth discussion. On April 26, following an afternoon contest in Detroit won by the Tigers, last year's dynamic batting duo found themselves on the same train to Cleveland for a rematch the next day in the Ohio city. Apparently, the two found plenty of time to talk. A friendly discussion of their torrid race ensued.[8] It is hard to believe, however, that either man really spoke his mind when it came to that subject. They also most certainly avoided any discussion of the continuing animosity between Cobb and teammate Sam Crawford, who, like many other Tigers, thought that in 1910 Cobb was all about himself. Cobb and Crawford stopped speaking and then entered an uneasy truce on the eve of the new season.[9] Perhaps one reason for Crawford's reluctance to engage was a remark Cobb supposedly made that spring to a Detroit writer seeking his reaction to the congratulatory telegram sent to Lajoie by eight of Cobb's Tigers teammates: "Oh, when I pass some of them on the street, I just honk the horn of my new [Chalmers] car at them."[10]

Problems with teammates notwithstanding, Cobb had another banner year at the plate in 1911. From a personal standpoint, it might well have been the greatest season of his career. In 146 games he batted .420, leading the league in that category as well as in runs scored (147), hits (248, then an American League record), singles (169), doubles (47), triples (24), stolen bases (83), and RBIs (127). He even finished second in home runs with eight. The effort earned him a second Chalmers automobile. He received first-place votes from all eight panel members, making him the unanimous choice with sixty-four points. Lajoie, who was burdened in April by the death of teammate Addie Joss and in August by the death of his oldest and closest brother, Jeremie, batted a solid .365, but he played in only ninety games. As a result, he received but five points from the writers and finished well down on the list of vote-getters. The National League vote and that circuit's Chalmers went to Frank Schulte of the Chicago Cubs. Cobb received his vehicle in a brief ceremony at the Polo Grounds in New York City prior to the third game of the 1911 World Series, played that year by the Giants and the defending world champion Athletics. That evening Hugh Chalmers held a lavish banquet feting the scribes who made up his trophy commission. Hugh announced the he would continue to hand out his annual prizes. In attendance were the three members of the National Commission.[11] The scene was a far cry from that at the end of the previous season, when Herrmann and company tried their best to distance themselves from the ugly scenario that had developed in connection with Hugh Chalmers's promotional scheme.

Rowdy Jack O'Connor watched the 1911 season unfold and stewed. Following Ban Johnson's investigation, Red Corriden and Harry Howell had each fared better than O'Connor, making his situation seem all that much worse. This is not to say that all was rosy for the pair. Before the 1911 season, the Browns placed Corriden on waivers. He was picked up by the Pittsburgh Pirates, but during spring training, the Pirates released him. He ended up playing most of the season for Kansas City of the American Association. Then, in August, his contract was purchased by the Detroit Tigers. Nevertheless, he did not play Major League Baseball in 1911. Howell, his career as a pitcher definitely on the rocks, focused his efforts on landing a Major League umpiring position. Turned away in that regard by Ban Johnson the previous October in the wake of his dismissal, Harry returned to Chicago and gave it another try in February. This time, according to at least one newspaper source, Johnson was more receptive. Howell was allegedly told that were he to accept either the Minor League umpiring or managerial spots presently open to him, he would be given an umpiring position in the American League in 1912.[12] It does not appear that Howell did either. Instead, some evidence suggests that in 1911 Harry Howell played eighty-nine games at second base for Louisville and St. Paul of the American Association.[13]

Thus, by August 1911 the baseball careers of Corriden and Howell were moving forward albeit in altered fashion, while that of Jack O'Connor seemed at an end. In response, by mid-August O'Connor authorized his attorney, Horace Dyer, to file suit: "I [O'Connor] have called on Hedges, but because he refused to pay me $5,000 we did not come to any understanding and I told him I would file suit."[14]

That O'Connor was even dealing with Bob Hedges at that point is a mystery of some sorts. As 1910 drew to a close, all indications were that in short order the Browns would be under new ownership and Bob Hedges would no longer be a part of the club. Of more particular import to Jack O'Connor, a spokesman for the new ownership group not only indicated a strong interest in reaching a quick and amicable settlement with O'Connor, but he also spoke publicly of finding employment with the Browns for their former manager.[15] As late as mid-January, it appeared the deal was still on. The interested buyers had shown their goodwill by paying Hedges $30,000 for the option to buy the club. The money would act as a down payment if the deal was consummated but was to be forfeited in the event the deal fell through. Somewhere along the way, the purchasers backed off, perhaps owing to internal disagreements or maybe nothing more than cold feet. Hedges eventually pocketed the deposit money and kept his interest in the ball club.[16] Since he had been reluctant to sell his interest anyway, he was not that unhappy. Bobby Wallace became the new manager. O'Connor not only didn't receive a job with the organization, but he did not have a monetary settlement for his disputed contract either. He saw litigation as his only viable recourse.

Unlike criminal cases, in which the accused is accorded a constitutional right to a speedy trial, civil litigation tends to unravel like a fine wine, given to ripen, if not always improve, with time. The defense often seeks delay in the hope that a frustrated plaintiff will either dismiss the case or be willing to settle for less than he or she wants in order to move beyond the matter. In addition, as time passes, the memories of witnesses fade; perhaps a key witness or even the plaintiff might pass away. Judges, their dockets overflowing, do little to move along the civil cases assigned to them. Any or all of these circumstances work in the favor of the civil defendant. Often little significant activity occurs in the case until a serious trial date is set and it appears settlement is unlikely. Such was the case in the fall of 1911 with Jack O'Connor's lawsuit. All of nineteen months passed before the lawsuit went to a jury trial before the Honorable Judge George C. Hitchcock in Circuit Courtroom #3 in downtown St. Louis on May 12, 1913. By then, although Bob Hedges and Ban Johnson were still in place with the baseball establishment, several of the other key witnesses, as well as the plaintiff himself, were differently situated.

By the time the O'Connor case reached trial, Red Corriden was back in the Major Leagues, playing as a part-time infielder with the Chicago Cubs. In 1912 he spent most of the playing season in Kansas City, although he played thirty-eight games with the Detroit Tigers. He crossed into the National League in December of that year, when the Cincinnati Reds purchased his contract from the Tigers for $7,500. Four days later, on December 15, Corriden went to the Cubs in a multiplayer deal with the Reds.[17] By then, Harry Howell had turned to umpiring baseball games rather than playing in them. Much to his chagrin, his work was confined to the Minor Leagues. In 1912 he worked games for the International League, and in 1913 he was employed by the Texas League. Even Jack O'Connor was back in the "game" in a manner of speaking. In 1913 a new league, the Federal League, opened play in six cities. Since it did not operate under the National Agreement, which governed teams in the two Major Leagues and the Minor Leagues, the Federal League was a so-called outlaw league. One of the cities that fielded a team was St. Louis. O'Connor was signed as the team's manager. Although the league initially did not go after players currently under contract to American and National League teams, it soon became clear that it aspired to compete with those leagues and become a third Major League. Rowdy Jack must have gleefully rubbed his hands together at the mere thought that he might enter the back door of the very establishment that only two seasons before had barred his entry through the front.

As O'Connor's lawsuit against his former employer, the Browns, neared trial, there was the usual flurry of activity. Shortly after receiving the paperwork initiating the lawsuit against them, Hedges and his Browns had retained attorney George H. Williams, a former judge who was now a partner in private practice with the St. Louis firm of Stewart, Bryant and Williams, to represent them. "Judge" Williams, as he was still addressed, had served on the bench of this same circuit court from 1906 to 1911. Since presiding judge George Hitchcock had served on the bench since 1909, the judicial careers of Williams and Hitchcock had overlapped. It remained to be seen whether the fact that the judge and the lead defense counsel had been judicial colleagues gave Judge Williams a leg up in the case.

Early in the legal proceedings, the Browns' lawyers filed an "answer," that is, a formal response to O'Connor's claims by which the Browns generally denied each allegation in O'Connor's petition. On May 8, 1913, four days before the trial, Judge Williams filed an amended answer, this time carefully delineating just what the Browns found objectionable with their former manager's claims. In the amended pleading, the Browns claimed that their contract with O'Connor "expired" on October 15, 1910, at which time he was terminated. O'Connor had claimed that he was under a two-year contract with the Browns when he was wrongfully terminated. One of the key issues of the case was, therefore, the length of the contract. The remainder of the Browns' amended answer specifically referred to the last two games of the 1910 season and the batting race between Napoleon Lajoie and Ty Cobb. It specified that O'Connor violated his contract with the Browns by favoring Lajoie in his batting race and characterized managing the Browns' ball club to achieve that end as "unmindfull [sic] and in disregard and violation of his [managerial] duties." The amended answer went on to say that "the said plaintiff instructed one Corriden, who played the position of third baseman for the defendant club, to play so far back of his regular and ordinary position as third baseman as to allow the said Lajoie to make what are known as 'base hits,' which the said Lajoie could not and would not have made had it not been for said instructions." The Browns were arguing that on October 15, 1910, they terminated O'Connor for just cause and that even if there were a contract for O'Connor's services for the 1911 season—a fact they denied—he had violated that contract by his "unfaithful" actions on October 9, 1910.[18]

That the Browns intended to fully air the events of October 9, 1910, as a key to their defense was clear on April 19, 1913, when Judge Williams took the sworn oral deposition of Red Corriden in St. Louis. Horace Dyer, O'Connor's attorney, was present by right and had the opportunity to cross-examine. Dyer was a bit of an athlete himself, having played fullback for the Michigan Wolverines' football squad in the early 1890s, while in Ann Arbor studying for his law degree. Before going into private practice, he had served as an assistant city attorney in St. Louis and later as an assistant in the U.S. attorney's St. Louis office.

The deposition of Corriden was presumably taken for a number of reasons. By that time the trial date was scheduled and appeared firm. Since Corridén was playing baseball, his team's schedule may have interfered with his ability to appear at the trial in person. Obviously, he was a key witness that either side might want to call as part of its case in chief. O'Connor would wish to establish that if Corriden played back at all at third base, it was not on orders of his manager to favor Lajoie. The Browns hoped to establish just the opposite. By deposing this witness before trial, not only could they discover what he planned to say and tailor their trial presentation accordingly, but his testimony under oath could be preserved and presented in his absence as if he were present at trial. The only drawback—a major one at a jury trial—was that the jurors, the ultimate triers of fact, would not get the opportunity to see the witness testify live and, thereby, judge his demeanor as they attempted to sift through the testimony of each witness for the truth. Still, Corriden's testimony by deposition was better than no testimony at all.

Ban Johnson was presumably deposed for a different reason. The American League president still presided over league affairs from his office in Chicago. He might well have huffed and puffed if called upon to travel to St. Louis to testify, but he would have done it if he thought it served the purposes of his league. In view of the potential impact of his testimony, plaintiff's counsel wanted to learn in advance what he might say in court. The attorneys for each party agreed to travel to Chicago on May 8, just four days prior to trial, in order to take Johnson's deposition. By then the Browns had filed their amended answer and the gauntlet was fully thrown down.

On the morning of May 12, the trial began with the selection and paneling of a twelve-person all-male jury. This portion of the trial is known as voir dire. The attorney for each party is permitted to question the entire jury panel, in this case eighteen men, to determine whether the jurors can render a fair and impartial verdict. The questions seek to cull out jurors who might carry a bias that would influence their decision to the detriment of one party or the other. Of course, the unspoken goal of each attorney is to select jurors who will ultimately rule in his or her client's favor. During his questioning on behalf of deposed manager Jack O'Connor, Horace

Dyer sought to determine whether any of the jurors had attended Browns games. None of the eighteen answered in the affirmative. Perhaps this was not so unusual, given the Browns' dismal showing in 1910. During his turn Dyer's courtroom opponent, George Williams, revealed that eight of the eighteen panelists had played baseball at one time, either as amateurs or professionally. One in particular admitted he favored the Browns, whereas two others had already formed an opinion of the case; yet another said that O'Connor was his friend and that they had discussed the case. The answers probably kept these forthright jurors from further service. Finally, after all this information was filtered by the parties and their attorney, a jury was seated and opening statements were made by each attorney on behalf of his client.

In his opening Dyer claimed he would prove that his client, O'Connor, had been hired for both 1910 and 1911. He had been faithfully performing his duties when the defendant baseball club breached his contract by firing him. Furthermore, from that time until he was hired to manage a club in the Federal League, he had been unable to earn a living. During his time at the podium, Judge Williams countered by telling the newly impaneled jurors that the issue before them "resolves itself as to whether O'Connor faithfully gave his services to the club and the game. We [the Browns] will show O'Connor made a hippodrome of the game."[19]

Now the trial, conducted—much like a baseball game—under certain ground rules, could begin. The burden of proof was on the plaintiff, O'Connor, who needed to corroborate his claims with a preponderance (greater weight) of the evidence. The first witness his attorney called was Rowdy Jack himself. After initial questioning to establish his client's baseball career, Horace Dyer read the contract terms into the record and asked his client whether he performed his duties under the contract. With that assertion in the record, Dyer then turned back to the contract of employment between O'Connor and the Browns. An early issue arose over who had the original contract. Rowdy Jack claimed that when he entered into the contract with Bob Hedges in St. Louis, it was presented in duplicate. According to O'Connor, he was told by Hedges that one copy was to be sent to the American League president and the other would be kept by the ball club. In that regard Hedges told him that no player ever received a copy of his contract. Thus, neither O'Connor nor his lawyer had an exact copy of the contract. As it turned out, neither did the Browns. When questioned by Judge Hitchcock, Browns attorney George Williams admitted that the ball club could not find the original. Instead, after considerable argument and with certain limitations imposed by the court, they relied on a form contract produced by the Browns, but with the blanks filled out in ink as they would have been in O'Connor's contract. The contract seemed much more applicable to a player than a manager. However, O'Connor examined it and acknowledged—probably at the urging of his attorney, who needed the evidence as part of his case even more than did the Browns—that it represented the contract he signed; it was admitted into evidence. Thereupon, Dyer read it to the jury.

Two portions of the contract were of particular import. In paragraph 1 of the eight-paragraph document, the Browns agreed to pay O'Connor "**Five Thousand Dollars** per season, **for 1910 and 1911**," to manage their team. In paragraph 2, the managerial services of O'Connor were engaged "beginning on or about the **1st** day of **April, 1910**, and ending on or about the **15th** day of October 1910, which period of time shall constitute the life of this contract." (A note by the court reporter was entered into the transcript after the words of the contract were read into the record by Dyer. It said that, except for the boldface words in paragraph 1, words in boldface were written in ink in the otherwise form contract. The boldface words in paragraph 1 were written in ink between the lines.)[20]

It is clear from a first reading that paragraphs 1 and 2 of the contract were in opposition as they related to Jack O'Connor's term of service. In clause 1, it appears certain he was hired by Hedges for two seasons, but in paragraph 2, it appears equally clear that October 15, 1910, was designated the end of the contract term. Clearly, this issue went to the heart of the case and might well have required a primer on Missouri contract law to sort out. If O'Connor had been hired to manage for just one season, the question of whether he had been wrongfully terminated was moot. If he had indeed been hired to manage for two seasons and failed to faithfully perform his duties during the first season, he could have been terminated as per paragraph 1. After reading the contract into the record, Horace Dyer introduced the letter of dismissal sent by President Hedges to O'Connor in late November 1910. He then turned his client over to Judge Williams for cross-examination.[21]

The cross-examination of a witness by opposing counsel is an art. A skillful cross-examiner seldom asks a question for which he doesn't already know the answer. Since, unlike the party calling the witness, the cross-examiner can lead the witness by asking questions that attempt to elicit the answer he or she seeks, cross-examination is a key component of any trial. In this case the witness under the heat lamp was the plaintiff, and this only heightened the import and impact of the testimony. Judge Williams spent little time with O'Connor before he delved into the events of October 9. The first skirmish occurred when the Browns' counsel attempted to show that heading into the last day of the season, O'Connor was well aware that Cobb and Lajoie were locked in a tight battle for the batting title:

> Q. [by Williams] Those two men [Cobb and Lajoie] headed the league, did they, in batting?
>
> A. [by O'Connor] I don't know. [Joe] Jackson at that time was right up among them.[22]

O'Connor was technically correct. In 1910 a youthful Joe Jackson, playing with the Naps, finished the season with a .387 batting average. However, he recorded only seventy-five official times at bat, well under the number needed to qualify for the Chalmers prize. Nonetheless, Rowdy Jack's answer to this and any number of other questions reflected his feistiness on the witness stand; he was ready and willing to cut a fine point whenever the opportunity presented. For example, when he was asked if he knew about the automobile that would be awarded the batting winner, O'Connor testified that "he didn't know it personally" but had seen it in the newspapers.[23]

Of much more import were Rowdy Jack's responses to questions about his instructions regarding field position given to his players on the day of the doubleheader. O'Connor, forgetting or omitting that he played briefly at the start of game two, testified that during both games he coached his team from the first base line:

Q. [by Williams] I asked you what instructions you gave Corriden that day?

A. [by O'Connor] I gave them all instructions to play back for Lajoie; my whole infield and outfield. . . .

Q. Had you given Corriden any special instructions that day?

A. No, Sir; I hadn't given Corriden any special instructions that day.

Q. Except that you told him, with others, to play back?

A. Always to play back for Lajoie. The outfielders just the same.

Q. Where did you give those instructions to Corriden?

A. Out on the ball field.

Q. That day?

A. Yes, Sir.[24]

O'Connor testified that the instructions were delivered to his players on Sunday afternoon prior to the first game and were the instructions he gave his players whenever they played against Lajoie. His memory was more clouded when it came to Lajoie's big day at the Browns' expense; he was unable to recall that an issue arose over whether one of Lajoie's at bats had resulted in a hit or a sacrifice.

Q. [by Williams] Don't you remember the question arose as to whether that was a sacrifice hit or a hit—the ninth one?

A. [by O'Connor] Indeed, I don't.[25]

Then Judge Williams asked the witness about Harry Howell's note. O'Connor, never bothering to deny that the note was Howell's, replied that he was unaware of the note "until two or three innings afterwards." At that point, O'Connor claimed, he told Howell he had made a mistake and he should retrieve the note.[26] Making little inroads with this line of questioning, Judge Williams then commenced what certainly must be one of the longest examinations of baseball infield positioning ever conducted. The questioning naturally was directed at O'Connor's positioning of third baseman Red Corriden on the day in question. After establishing that his third baseman would normally be stationed "between the grass from the infield and the grass from the outfield," Williams asked O'Connor to tell him how far back from normal Corriden was directed to play during the Sunday doubleheader with Lajoie's Naps.[27]

> Q. [by Williams] I want you to testify now, as an expert who has been playing baseball for twenty-six years, as to what [is] the ordinary and regular position for a third-baseman, in the field, to play?
>
> A. [by O'Connor] Probably about from five to eight feet back of third base.[28]

After establishing how far from the third base bag Corriden should have been positioned, Williams sought to compare how Corriden's positioning differed on October 9:

> Q. And Corriden played back for Lajoie?
>
> A. Yes, Sir.
>
> Q. How far back?
>
> A. About eight feet.
>
> Q. You mean eight feet further back than the ordinary and regular position?
>
> A. Yes.[29]

Judge Williams must have been nonplussed at O'Connor's response to his next series of questions. He asked the former manager if Ban Johnson had asked him about whether he had Corriden play back for Lajoie. O'Connor replied that the league president never asked him. Perhaps because he had Johnson's deposition testimony in that regard in hand, he let Rowdy Jack's responses stand unchallenged, instead preferring to delve into whether the manager had instructed his pitchers to get Lajoie to bat as many times as possible during the doubleheader. This too was denied, but once again it fed into the defense's overall strategy.

> Q. [by Williams] It was as square a game as you ever played in your life?
>
> A. [by O'Connor] Yes, Sir.[30]

Some twenty years later, in his interview with sportswriter Dick

Farrington, with the spotlights now off, O'Connor essentially stood by his courtroom testimony but did give a little ground:

I got the rap for that Lajoie affair, but it wasn't all my fault. I suppose as manager I might have directed my infielders differently. Still, it was the last day of the season and I let the players run things pretty much to themselves. Sure, I knew Lajoie was due to get whatever breaks could be passed his way. All of the players wanted him to beat out Cobb. In fact, there was nothing basically crooked about it and it so happened that the hits credited to Larry had no bearing on the result.

We won the first game and in the second game there was no chance for the Browns, because they were shut out. The truth is that the games, having no bearing on the pennant race, were more genuinely contested than usually are the wind-up games of a schedule, when it used to be the custom to do a lot of horse-play, clowning and switching about of the players. I do not present this as a defense for what happened, but these are things that occur to me now, nearly 23 years later. Mind you, not a nickel was wagered on the games.[31]

One of the tactics of a good trial lawyer is to anticipate what evidence you will be able to elicit from a witness you plan to use in your case and set the stage for that witness's testimony through another earlier witness, even an uncooperative one such as O'Connor. Given the perspective of hindsight, Judge Williams's question about O'Connor's meeting with Johnson and Johnson's failure to ask O'Connor about the positioning of the Browns' players was part of his strategy. The Browns' attorney felt that even if O'Connor denied it, Ban Johnson might offer a different and more credible version of the meeting. In much the same manner, Williams now questioned O'Connor about whether during the doubleheader he criticized Corriden for getting to one of Lajoie's bunts (presumably the one deemed a sacrifice), knowing that no matter O'Connor's response, he would later elicit testimony from one or more witnesses to the contrary:

Q. [by Williams] Did you criticise [sic] him for getting one of those balls that he got?

A. [by O'Connor] No, Sir. . . .

Q. And you didn't tell him that he ought not to have gotten the balls that he really got?

A. No, Sir.[32]

Williams now jumped to a new topic, asking O'Connor whether he knew if Lajoie was going to bunt. O'Connor said he did not know it. What about when Lajoie, normally a "free hitter," choked up? That maneuver, to O'Connor, signified hit and run, not a bunt.[33] After considerable go-round on this point, Judge Williams turned to Rowdy Jack's efforts in 1911 to find employment. The former manager testified that other than being in the saloon business for a time, baseball was all he knew. He had tried for a baseball job as a manager or scout in 1911 to no avail. The intrepid Williams then made another unsuccessful attempt to get O'Connor to admit that he had instructed his pitchers to walk batters in order to give Lajoie more plate appearances and sat down.

Dyer's questioning of O'Connor on redirect was not particularly lengthy. He elicited testimony from his client that both Lajoie and Cobb were his friends, even though he had never played with them. As to whether he spoke with Lajoie on the day of the doubleheader, the answer was no. Further, Lajoie had not entered an understanding with anyone else on the Browns regarding facilitating his batting results. Dyer established that Corriden was quite inexperienced, particularly at third, and that Lajoie had a reputation as baseball's hardest hitter. During cross-examination O'Connor had stated that he also wanted his players to play back for Joe Jackson. On redirect Dyer brought out that not only did O'Connor also consider Jackson a hard hitter, but whenever his teams had played against Lajoie and Jackson, he had instructed his men to play back when they were at bat.[34]

On re-cross-examination Judge Williams attempted to show that O'Connor's concerns for his third baseman were overstated. After all, the pitcher had to stay in the area around the pitching rubber and was thus unable to back up to protect himself from Lajoie's ferocity. This opened the door for one last punch by Dyer:

Q. [by Dyer] Now, by playing back for a hard-hitting man, can you field the ball better, or have you more of a chance to get the hit than if a man was playing in front?

A. [by O'Connor] That is why they play back.

On that rather positive note, Dyer rested his case; his client was his only witness. Judge Williams had punched hard but failed to land any knockout blows. He would now have to counterpunch with his own witnesses. The court took a noon recess and reconvened at 2:00.

The first witness for the defense, Bob Hedges, offered a sharp contrast to his former manager, Jack O'Connor. The head of the Browns was a businessman and a genteel sort. This, however, did not mean he would run from a fight. Early in his testimony, he described the games of October 9 as a sham:

A. [by Hedges] The game looked, from a spectator's standpoint, as if it was a hippodrome pure and simple.[35]

Dyer's objection was sustained and the testimony stricken from the record, but the jury still heard it.

At the conclusion of the doubleheader, Hedges told the jury, he left St. Louis immediately: "I was compelled to go away. Before I returned I went to Chicago. I told Mr. [Ban] Johnson how the game appeared to me." Williams asked Hedges if he received any instructions from the league's president.

A. [by Hedges] Yes; he told me to get rid of O'Connor; he wasn't good for baseball. [Colloquy between counsel omitted.] That he wasn't a manager.[36]

Hedges was careful to testify that he had asked for waivers on O'Connor before he issued a formal letter of notification of release. Rowdy Jack had been saying that he had been blackballed from the league. The testimony by Hedges would serve to show that not only had he followed proper procedure but that no other American League team had an interest in hiring the fired manager in that capacity or as a player. This was underscored by Horace Dyer when it was his opportunity to cross-examine. Early on he tried unsuccessfully to get Hedges to admit that Johnson had written to him that O'Connor could no longer play ball in the American League.

As his cross-examination of Hedges played out, O'Connor's attorney spent a good deal of time exploring the negotiations between the parties prior to the execution of the signed contract. Judge Williams's attempts on behalf of the Browns to limit such testimony were overruled by the court, which permitted Dyer to question Hedges about the ambiguity in the contract between one clause that referred only to 1910 and another that included both 1910 and 1911. Hedges admitted that he wrote "1910 and 1911" into the contract in ink in the one paragraph, as well as "1910" in the other. He attempted to explain away the ambiguity by saying, "We [baseball clubs] have a right for holding the players over for the next year on a reservation list." He was referring to the controversial "reserve clause" that permitted a club to hold on to a player from year to year if it wanted to do so. The only way a player could avoid the restriction and eventually sign with another club was to sit out a year without pay, a risky proposition. In making this argument, the Browns were taking the position that O'Connor was a player and as such governed by baseball's curious indenture system. The argument ignored the fact that O'Connor was a manager first and foremost, a fact Hedges later reluctantly admitted. It also failed to adequately explain away the ambiguity between the two paragraphs.

As his cross-examination of Hedges continued, Horace Dyer tried his best to get the Browns' executive to admit that O'Connor had refused to sign the contract unless it called for him to manage the Browns for at least two seasons. Hedges agreed that this is what Rowdy Jack initially wanted, but said that he was eventually willing to sign and indeed had signed the contract for one year. Dyer pressed harder. Over strenuous objection from Williams, he asked why, if O'Connor had agreed to only the one year, Hedges had then written "1910 and 1911" into the early portion of the contract. Cornered, Hedges attempted to explain away this obvious glitch in the Browns' case by telling the court and jury that "it was a mistake."[37]

Before he let Bob Hedges go, Horace Dyer returned to the events of

October 9 and their aftermath. Hedges agreed that during the double-header, he never went to the field to express his disapproval of the manner in which O'Connor was directing the club. Nonetheless, he dismissed O'Connor "because I didn't like the way he handled that ball club out there that afternoon"—not because Ban Johnson had told him to do so. Hedges claimed that although he had never talked to O'Connor at any time on October 9 or thereafter, he had told several people ("the chances are it was newspaper men") that O'Connor should come see him. He believed he had also written O'Connor to this effect. Although he couldn't produce the letters in the courtroom, he believed he had them.[38]

It is extremely difficult to assess the effect that a witness's testimony has on a jury without being present to gauge the manner in which the witness responds to questioning. However, with regard to Bob Hedges's testimony, at least one news report commented that owing to evasive replies, "President Hedge's [sic] attitude on the stand created an unfavorable impression."[39]

Attorney Dyer steered clear of one subject during his cross-examination of Hedges. The latter's letter of November 29, 1910, to Jack O'Connor dismissing him advised the manager that the Browns had "elected to terminate its contract . . . for the season of 1911." This raises the question, Why would Hedges mention a contract for 1911 if he knew there was none? Perhaps Mr. Dyer was saving that argument for his final summation to the jury, for it well might have been his strongest as to the length of the contract.

Next up for the defendant was Richard J. Collins, the veteran reporter for the *St. Louis Republic* and paid official scorer for the Browns' home games. According to Collins, he missed the first game of the October 9 doubleheader but scored the second one. He testified that he was in the scorer's box when a note was received. He did not know who sent the note, which was delivered to his "associate" Parrish, but when Parrish passed the note to Collins, he "told him [Parrish] to tear it up."[40] On cross-examination Dyer was brief; however, he did labor to bring out, as he did with a number of witnesses, that Napoleon Lajoie was one of the hardest hitters in the league.[41] Later on re-cross, after Judge Williams had established that witness Collins considered eight hits in nine times at bat unusual, Dyer was able to establish that Collins saw nothing unusual in the play that day.[42]

In what may have been a surprise to some, the next witness summoned to the stand by Judge Williams was Clarence F. Lloyd, a baseball writer for the *St. Louis Post-Dispatch*. Lloyd testified that he reported on both games for his newspaper. In his opinion Red Corriden "played pretty deep during the second game." He also recalled Lajoie's hits, particularly that "in this second game I remember that he choked [the bat] several times." According to Lloyd, when a player does this "you can pretty near figure that he is going to bunt the ball."[43] Judge Williams had tried to bring this point out through other witnesses, but with less success. On cross-examination Lloyd agreed with other witnesses that choking up on the bat does not necessarily mean the batter intends to bunt. He would not concede, however, that it is normal for a third baseman to play back on the outfield grass, saying, "They play behind the base, but very seldom back on the grass."[44]

Red Corriden was the next witness. In his absence, his deposition testimony was read to the jury. He indicated his home as Logansport, Indiana, and occupation, when not playing baseball, as railroad machinist. When the line of questioning reached the events of October 9 in St. Louis, Corriden testified that O'Connor had told him to "play back":

Q. [by Williams] Is that all he said, those two words?

A. [by Corriden] Play back to the edge of the [outfield] grass; he asked me to play back to the edge of the grass. . . .

Q. Then how far back from third base does the grass begin again, after the shaved place, at Sportsman's Park, about how far would you say?

A. I would not say the exact distance, because I do not know. From the third base line?

Q. From the third-base line?

A. I should judge about twenty feet.[45]

Corriden testified that he had no further discussion with O'Connor about positioning until the next day, when his manager told him that "playing in, I would get my leg knocked off."[46] The direction of the examination then turned to Corriden's normal positioning at third base for a right-handed batter such as Lajoie versus a lefty such as Joe Jackson. Corriden testified that he played inside of the bag for left-handers and a little back of the bag for right-handers. That day his normal position was to play "about half way."

> Q. [by Williams] You would stand about the middle part of the shaved place?
> A. Yes, sir.
> Q. And were you playing there when Mr. O'Connor told you to play back for this fellow?
> A. Yes, sir.
> Q. And did you move back of that position after that?
> A. Yes, to the edge of the [outfield] grass.
> Q. How much further back would that be?
> A. About ten feet.
> Q. Further back than you had been playing?
> A. Yes.
> Q. And did you play that position for him [Lajoie] only?
> A. Yes.[47]

With this last line of questioning, Judge Williams placed in the record and before the jury that Jack O'Connor had told his third baseman to play back at least ten feet from where he was told to play other Naps batters during the doubleheader. Those "other" Naps batters included Joe Jackson, which contradicted O'Connor's earlier testimony that he had told Corriden to play back for both Lajoie and Jackson.

Horace Dyer had been in attendance at Red Corriden's deposition. His questioning of the witness now took place in the form of a cross-examination. Early on Dyer established that on the day of the doubleheader, Corriden was aware that Napoleon Lajoie had the reputation of the hardest hitter in the American League. In previous games Corriden told Dyer, O'Conner had told him to play back for "some of the fastest men." Further, he testified that O'Connor had not told him in advance that Lajoie was going to bunt the ball down the third base line, nor had he told him to allow Lajoie to get a hit by fielding slow or the like. Finally, he brought out that Corriden had been called before Ban Johnson to discuss the events of October 9 and cleared of any responsibility by the league's president.[48]

One of the goals of any good defense counsel is to poke holes in the plaintiff's case. Poke enough holes and the plaintiff's case will begin to spring a leak. One such thrust by Judge Williams on behalf of the Browns was to show Jack O'Connor's complicity in Nap Lajoie's hitting achievements during the doubleheader by introducing credible testimony that Rowdy Jack had ordered his pitchers to walk Naps batters to allow Lajoie more appearances at the plate. He planted the seed for this theory by asking O'Connor about it while he was on the stand, knowing full well and caring not that the manager would issue a strong denial. Now he called another rather obscure witness, Sidney Cook, who identified himself as a local insurance man. Cook had been in attendance at the doubleheader with a Mr. Croneheim. Cook told the jury that he was sitting "part of the time in the audience, and part of the time directly over the Browns' bench." He had been seated directly over the bench from the second inning on during game two. When asked about whether while so situated he saw or heard any instructions or statements from Jack O'Connor, he responded as follows:

A. [by Cook] Before the teams went on the field at the beginning of each inning, Mr. O'Connor gave instructions to his pitcher as to what he was supposed to pitch to the different players of the Cleveland team as they came up, which men were to be given bases on balls—certain men were to be hit with the ball, and just what each man was to do. . . .

Q. [by Williams] What was the effect of it?

A. [by Cook] The effect was that certain men—about four or five men were used up each inning—and that it would seem later on that Lajoie was to be brought up to bat every opportunity.[49]

Horace Dyer objected at that point and was able to get witness Cook to say he didn't actually hear O'Connor state that the purpose of his pitching instructions was to get Lajoie more at bats. Further, Cook didn't hear O'Connor give Corriden instructions, but he heard something else that must have quickened the heartbeat of Judge Williams.

Q. [by Williams] Did you hear him make any statement to Mr. Corriden?

A. [by Cook] Yes, sir.

Q. When?

A. After the ball that was hit to Mr. Corriden on which Lajoie was given a sacrifice; when he [Corriden] came in from the field at the end of that inning Mr. O'Connor upbraided him severely for having gotten his hands on the ball—Mr. Corriden.

When Dyer moved to strike the word "upbraided," Judge Williams went him one better:

Q. Tell what was said.

A. He cursed him for getting his hands on the ball; just what he said in words—I don't remember the exact words—the exact words: "Damn it," he says, "why do you make a play"—"why didn't you make a play on that ball," or something like that. . . .

At this point, Judge Williams received an assist from the court when Judge Hitchcock asked for further clarification of what to that point had come out in confusing fashion. Cook then explained that O'Connor was upset because Corriden had fumbled the ball and tried to make a play when the idea was "not to get to the ball in time to throw it to first base to catch Lajoie; and Corriden's answer [to O'Connor] was that he would fall down or break his leg before he would get his hands on another one in time."[50]

To add a bit of icing to the cake, Judge Williams asked Cook whether he heard Harry Howell make any statements. In fact, he had. Right after the play in which Corriden fumbled the ball, "Howell got out from the bench up on his feet and hollered up to the scorer's box and asked what they gave Lajoie on that bunt." This was done with O'Connor on the bench and, although unsaid, within earshot. In final questioning Judge Williams elicited that during the game Cook would pass information to friends in the stands advising them who was about to be walked.[51]

For some time now, the rules of procedure in a civil, or for that matter, criminal, case have required the parties to identify what witness they may wish to call at trial. In 1913 production of a witness list was apparently not a requirement in Missouri. It seems likely that Horace Dyer was surprised by the appearance of Sidney Cook. He was undoubtedly taken aback by the damaging evidence Cook related about Jack O'Connor's actions on the bench during the second game of the doubleheader with the Naps. Cook had gone well beyond anyone else in describing O'Connor as an active participant in an effort to help Lajoie obtain a hit every time he was at the plate, including going out of his way to instruct his pitchers (at least in the second game) to afford the Naps' star a multitude of opportunities to do it. The next day a local newspaper would describe Cook's testimony as "startling."[52] Dyer could hardly let this testimony go unchallenged.

In his opening effort to punch some holes in Sidney Cook's story, Dyer asked the insurance man whether he was a friend of Bob Hedges. To his chagrin, Cook stated he knew him "by sight only." That line of potentially promising questioning closed, Dyer had Cook describe what he could actually see of the Browns' bench.

Q. [by Dyer] Where were you sitting out there at the game?
A. [by Cook] In a box directly over the Brown's [sic] bench.
Q. You mean over the cellar?
A. I mean over the cellar.
Q. How many steps are there down into that?
A. Three or four, possibly. . . .
Q. And you could not see the people on the bench, could you?
A. Yes, sir. . . .
Q. How?
A. By leaning over and looking down. . . .
Q. And you were leaning over and looking down when you heard what you have just testified to?
A. I was.

Cook then told Dyer that O'Connor was not always seated on the bench. He sometimes "was standing around the bench, and sometimes up on the steps; and if I am not mistaken he was on the coaching line at times."[53] Cook could not remember the names of the Naps' players O'Connor instructed his pitchers to pass, nor could he recall how many were walked. He did remember that one player (McGuire) was hit.[54] Later on Cook reiterated that he did not move down from his first game seat to his new perch until the second inning of the second game. He heard O'Connor give instructions to his players from that time until "about the sixth inning."[55]

Dyer's cross-examination had taken some of the edge off Cook's damaging testimony but not all that much. Had Judge Williams stopped this line of inquiry with Sidney Cook, he would have been ahead of the game. Instead, he attempted to bolster Cook's testimony by calling Julius B. Croneheim to the stand. Another local resident, Croneheim told the jury on direct examination that he was a department manager for the Fulton Bag and Cotton Mills. He had accompanied Cook to the games of October 9 and sat with him in the grandstand along the third base line until they moved closer to the field and Browns' bench during the second game. He was quite specific that he heard "instructions given on the Browns' bench" regarding how "the Cleveland players were to go out; one play I remember particularly was that the catcher, McGuire, was to be hit, and it transpired exactly that way." Croneheim confirmed that following the play in which Corriden had fumbled Lajoie's bunt, O'Connor spoke to Corriden when he returned to the bench during the half-inning break. He did not hear O'Connor's exact words, only that he referred to the fumbled ball. Croneheim said, "Corriden replied that he would fall down and break a leg or break an ankle or something of that kind before he would put his hands on another one."[56]

Satisfied, Williams asked another question or two of Julius Croneheim and then sat down. During direct examination Horace Dyer had listened to Croneheim testify that he had heard instructions about pitching a certain way to the Naps from the "Browns' bench." With little to lose, he sought to pin down Croneheim's testimony on that point:

Q. [by Dyer] Will you swear that it was O'Connor that said that?

A. [by Croneheim] I didn't see him say it, no sir; I didn't see him when the remark was made.

Q. And you didn't recognize his voice as, as making the remark?

A. I didn't know his voice at that time.[57]

Dyer had less success getting Croneheim to back off his testimony concerning O'Connor's remarks to Corriden following the fumbled ball. Croneheim stood fast that this particular conversation took place away from the player's bench. Thus, Croneheim could see and hear it.[58] Nonetheless, Croneheim's inability to identify the source of the instructions to the Browns' pitchers raised questions as to how his seatmate Cook was able to be so specific. The defense had gained little by calling this additional witness and probably lost more by doing so.

The next testimony entered by the defense came in the form of the deposition testimony of Ban Johnson. Because Johnson, like Corriden, was out of the jurisdiction of the court, his presence was not required. Nevertheless, the American League's president presented an imposing figure. An in-person appearance might have helped the Browns' cause. During the days leading up to the trial, indications were that he would be in St. Louis for the trial. A news item out of Chicago datelined May 8, the same day as Ban Johnson was deposed and four days prior to trial, discussed the league executive's meeting in Chicago with current Browns manager George Stovall. The latter, Bobby Wallace's managerial replacement midseason 1912, was on suspension following an on-field argument with an umpire during which Stovall grabbed the arbiter's cap and later spat chewing tobacco on him. The article related that Johnson had stated that he planned to meet in St. Louis over the weekend with Browns officials to discuss the Stovall situation.[59] This would have permitted him to be in St. Louis on Monday the twelfth for the start of trial. Instead, he was not present. His testimony would merely be read into evidence.

The deposition had been taken in Chicago by Horace Dyer with Judge Williams in attendance. Dyer presumably had taken it merely to learn what Johnson planned to say in court when he testified on behalf of the defending Browns. Had Dyer known Johnson would not appear in court, he might have asked different questions or been more adversarial in his approach. Some of the early testimony elicited from Johnson explored the makeup of professional baseball and the National Agreement pursuant to which it operated. This agreement included a clause that listed as an objective the perpetuation of the game by installing safeguards to instill public confidence in its "integrity" and "by maintaining a high standard of skill and sportsmanship in its players."[60]

Dyer then turned to the contract in question and established that all "player" contracts were sent to Johnson. However, "it quite frequently occurs that they don't send the contracts to [sic] the managers." Johnson approved the contracts, including those manager contracts forwarded to him, and then returned them to the clubs. He recalled that in 1910 O'Connor was employed as the Browns' manager. He thought a contract for O'Connor was sent but had no record of it.[61] Johnson was shown a letter he had sent to O'Connor in February 1911. It addressed O'Connor's complaint that he had been unjustly dismissed by the Browns. In the letter Johnson advised the former manager that his complaint had been discussed at a recent meeting of American League club owners. As a result of that discussion, O'Connor had been referred back to Hedges to discuss the contract issue. Johnson closed the letter with the following: "I find upon investigation that you were not signed to manage the St. Louis 'Browns.'"[62]

Just what "investigation" did Johnson conduct? asked Dyer. Johnson was evasive, answering, "Well, I presume it was the contracts that showed it; some correspondence that I had with Mr. Hedges on the subject." When asked further about the specific correspondence with Bob Hedges to which he had referred, he began talking instead about the early discussions to bring O'Connor to the Browns from Little Rock, where he had been managing. In that regard, Johnson stated he had recommended O'Connor to Hedges "as to who would make the best manager for the club." Johnson "also had him [O'Connor] in mind at one time for the management of our [American League] Boston club."[63]

At this point Dyer turned to Johnson's investigation of the October 9, 1910, incident in St. Louis. He introduced a copy of a letter Johnson had sent O'Connor on October 11 of that year asking that not only O'Connor but also Corriden and Browns outfielder Hub Northen submit a report explaining their actions.[64] Of course, O'Connor and Corriden eventually delivered their explanations to Johnson in person in Chicago. He now testified that he never was able to get in touch with Northen, but he did have Howell in Chicago as well. Strangely, Dyer never asked the next logical question. He never asked Johnson to state on the record the findings from his investigation, even though the public record showed that Johnson had found "no substantial ground for questioning the accuracy" of the eight hits credited to Lajoie on October 9.[65] Perhaps he had planned to bring that information out at trial, when, as he incorrectly assumed, Johnson would appear to testify in person. Whatever the reason for Dyer's oversight, he ended his questioning with several harmless follow-ups. His opposing counsel, in contrast, waded right into the swamp, asking about the results of Johnson's investigation right out of the box.

> Q. [Cross-examination by Williams] As a result of your investigation of that game and of the conduct of Howell and O'Connor and Corriden, what did you learn?
>
> A. [by Johnson] Well, I notified Mr. Hedges that O'Connor could not continue in the American League. I also wrote him that he would have to dispense with Howell; that I was not satisfied with their conduct that day.
>
> Q. What conduct do you refer to?
>
> A. Why, O'Connor, the manner in which he placed his team, and evidence that was submitted to me in a note that Howell wrote to the scorers and his interest in the scorers' box in the interest of Lajoie. [Johnson then explains the batting race between Cobb and Lajoie and the benefits derived by Lajoie from all the hits he received that day.][66]

After Ban Johnson answered Williams's first two questions, Horace Dyer entered an objection and moved to strike the answers from Johnson's testimony on the ground that they represented conclusions rather than facts developed by him. In a jury trial, criminal or civil, the jury is the trier of the facts, but the judge rules on all points of law. Dyer had raised a point of law at Johnson's deposition. Since at the time it had appeared that Johnson would testify live, the move was primarily a protective one. Williams argued that the testimony was admissible given Johnson's investigative authority as the league's chief officer. The trial judge would rule on the objections if the deposition was used at trial.

Williams continued his questioning. Johnson testified that he "must have" notified Hedges by letter to dismiss O'Connor, but he did not have the letter at hand. When asked to explain why he had found O'Connor at fault, he testified that during their discussion in Johnson's office in Chicago, Corriden "said emphatically that O'Connor had instructed him to play back." O'Connor had denied it, telling Johnson that Corriden was a young ballplayer who didn't know the position. Williams never asked, but the only implication was that Johnson believed Corriden and not O'Connor.[67] The remainder of Williams's questions for Johnson concerned the closeness of the batting race and the fact that a manager could work off a player's contract.

Before Johnson's deposition was concluded, Horace Dyer asked a few more questions, most designed to firm up some points. Johnson admitted that he had never notified O'Connor of the results of the investigation and that he might not have put his orders to Hedges in writing. Further, he agreed that it was well known that Lajoie was one of baseball's hardest hitters. However, Johnson stood fast when asked if third basemen around the league played Lajoie differently than they played other hitters. He did not think that was the case. He exhibited a rather keen knowledge of infield positioning. Dyer attempted to get Johnson to admit he had told O'Connor after the investigation that but for Howell's note, there wouldn't have been anything to the incident. By this he no doubt hoped to show the jury that Johnson had sought O'Connor's dismissal owing to an action by Howell, something outside his client's control. Instead of directly answering the question, Johnson for the first time disclosed that Harry Howell had confessed to him that he had written the note to the scorer.

A. [by Johnson] His name was not signed to it . . . but he confessed to me the writing of the note, and then I had his handwriting and compared it with the card.

Dyer asked the court reporter to read the question again: Had Johnson told O'Connor that Howell's note was the basis for his dismissal?

A. [by Johnson] I don't know that I said that to him. I know that that was the entering wedge.[68]

Dyer concluded the deposition with a few questions about the manager's responsibilities with regard to positioning the players. The attorneys then packed up for their return to St. Louis.

Johnson's deposition testimony was instructive, if not for the jury, then for anyone making a study of Ban Johnson, the person, at that time still the most powerful figure in baseball. His testimony revealed that he had clearly altered his stance regarding his findings in the October 9 matter to suit the circumstances. In October 1910 he wanted to remove the embarrassing St. Louis incident from the sports pages of America with as little stigma and as soon as possible, while still punishing the primary offenders. He sought to accomplish his first goal by whitewashing the incident and clearing the matter from his desk prior to the start of the World Series. The best way to accomplish this was to conduct a couple of interviews for show and then quickly and publicly rule that nothing untoward had occurred. In so doing, he had protected the sanctity of baseball as America's cleanest sport. However, the incident was too damaging to go unpunished, so to accomplish his second goal, he had clandestinely ordered Bob Hedges to fire the main culprits, O'Connor and Howell. Now more than two years had passed, and he found it both necessary and convenient to his league's image to protect the Browns from a monetary judgment. Therefore, he altered his testimony to suit the moment, saying that right from the start, he had determined that there had been wrongful conduct on the part of O'Connor and Howell, which required their dismissal from baseball, and that he had acted accordingly through Bob Hedges. His testimony revealed that at worst Ban Johnson was an outright liar, at best a rank opportunist.

In either case, his actions left the Browns in a bit of a spot as far as O'Connor's lawsuit was concerned. If Johnson appeared in court and testified as he had on deposition, Horace Dyer could still use his pronouncements from October 1910 to skewer his credibility. However, Dyer had not brought up the public record from that period during the deposition. Williams decided to use the deposition in place of an appearance in court by Johnson. Presumably, he liked Johnson's overall deposition testimony, especially his answers to the two questions about finding fault with O'Connor and Howell and ordering their dismissal. Even better he liked it that Dyer had not put a scratch on that testimony. He realized that Dyer had objected to both questions and moved to strike the responses, but he liked his chances with the judge. Certainly, Judge Hitchcock would rule in favor of liberal disclosure. Judge Williams gambled on this by not bringing Johnson to St. Louis. He lost. Judge Hitchcock sustained both objections.[69] As was standard court procedure, the rulings were made before the deposition was read and outside the hearing of the jury. The panel of twelve never heard Ban Johnson on the subject, at least not directly. The evidence had come in through Hedges, but in a manner not nearly as emphatic as Judge Williams had hoped it would be presented through the responses of the well-known and, at the time, highly regarded Johnson. What bearing the sustained objections might have on the ultimate result was yet to be determined.

The reading of Ban Johnson's deposition concluded the Browns' case. The defense rested. Dyer then recalled his client, Rowdy Jack, on rebuttal in hopes of shoring up any cracks in the dam raised by the defense. At the outset O'Connor denied that he had ordered his pitcher, Alex Malloy, to hit Naps manager McGuire or to walk anybody, as alleged by Sidney Cook. He did admit, however, that he had given Corriden "the devil about not getting the ball [bunted by Lajoie] and making a play on it."

Q. [by Dyer] What was said?

A. [by O'Connor] I said, "Damn it to hell, get it up quick"; he [Corriden] said, "God damn it, did you want me to break my leg trying to get a ball?"

Q. He didn't make the statement that he would break his leg?

A. He said he would break his leg getting the ball.

Q. Did he make the remark that he would break his leg before he would get his hands on another ball?

A. No, he didn't make any such remark.

Q. The remark he made was that he would get the next one: is that it?

A. Yes.[70]

Dyer then asked O'Connor to explain how the parties arrived at a two-year contract, rather than the one-year contract alleged by the Browns.

O'Connor testified that, indeed, Hedges wanted him to sign for only one year, but O'Connor insisted that the contract cover two years because, as he claimed he told Hedges, the Browns' club was in such bad shape a one-year deal "would not give me a chance to show what I could do." Hedges at first resisted and then asked for a day to consult with counsel in Cincinnati. The next day the contract was signed. O'Connor testified that he had signed a two-year contract at that time, but the court sustained Judge Williams's objection to that characterization and that portion of the testimony was stricken from the record. The jury, however, heard it. Finally, O'Connor testified that no one had asked him to go to Hedges's office to explain "the game."[71]

Judges Williams then called a defense rebuttal witness of his own. Not wishing to leave the jury with the impression that McGuire had not been hit by a pitch during the game, Williams recalled official scorer Richard Collins to the stand. Earlier Collins had testified that he had been present for the second game of the October 9 doubleheader. (Why he, and not Victor Parrish, who had actually scored both games, was called as a witness was never explained.) Apparently, Collins's memory of events was not the best. Williams attempted to have Collins confirm that McGuire was hit by identifying the box score of the second game from a rival newspaper. Dyer objected, and the best Williams could drag out of Collins was that he had "a very indistinct recollection . . . , but I would not swear to it."[72] After a question or two along this same line on cross by Dyer, the evidentiary portion of the trial ended on a halfhearted note. All that remained was for the attorneys to present their closing arguments—summing up the evidence in the best light for their clients and asking the jury to render a just verdict in their favor—and for Judge Hitchcock to fashion a charge to the jury.

Before sending a jury out to discuss the evidence and render a verdict, the judge instructs (or charges) the jurors as to the law that must be applied to the evidence and to their ultimate findings. If the jurors fail to follow the law, a judge can overturn their decision as not in accord with the law. Some of the law is boilerplate; some is particular to the case. Before the close of evidence, both plaintiff and defendant deliver a proposed set of charges to the jury. Naturally, the proposed instructions are worded to favor the party proposing them. The judge may choose to honor one party's version over another or even to ignore them both. In this case the court took its charges from both parties, although arguably the charge favored the plaintiff. In essence the jury was asked to determine whether the parties entered into a contract for both 1910 and 1911. Further, they were to look into the specific actions of Jack O'Connor on October 9 relative to how he directed his Browns players. Had he favored Napoleon Lajoie and so failed to faithfully perform his duties under that contract? The jurors were permitted to consider whether managerial adjustments allegedly made because of Lajoie's prowess as a hard hitter and Corriden's inexperience at third base were an exercise of a manager's best judgment and not merely a method of favoring Lajoie. The burden was placed on the defendant Browns to establish by a preponderance of evidence that O'Connor sought to increase Lajoie's batting average in order to bring him the American League batting title. The actions put in issue by the court's charge were limited to the positioning of Corriden and did not refer to the allegations of tampering with the Browns' pitchers, allegations Judge Williams had raised throughout the trial. Inasmuch as this was a civil case, nine of the twelve jurors were required to concur on a result in order for the jury to render its verdict.[73]

The jury retired at approximately 6:00 p.m. to deliberate and returned about an hour later with a verdict. The jurors' decision was unanimous in favor of the plaintiff. They had determined that Jack O'Connor's contract with the Browns extended beyond 1910 to 1911 and that O'Connor's management of his team on October 9, 1910, had not violated the terms of that contract. They awarded Jack O'Connor $5,000, the exact amount he had sought when he filed his lawsuit, as damages. The next day the attorneys for the Browns filed a motion seeking a new trial on the basis of a whole slew of legal arguments, none of which caught Judge Hitchcock's fancy. He overruled the motion.

The trial of O'Connor's case had garnered a good deal of newspaper coverage, not only in St. Louis but around the country. Rowdy Jack's victory must have left a bad taste with Ban Johnson and others in baseball's ruling bloc, not excluding Bob Hedges. A wiser and less image-conscious bunch might have licked their wounds and paid the verdict, which by now included interest and costs. Instead, Judge Williams was instructed to file an appeal. Surely a three-judge panel sitting on the St. Louis Court of Appeals would see the error of Judge Hitchcock's way and either rule in favor of the Browns or send the case back for a new trial. On September 8, 1913, the appeal was filed.

Few would submit that Lady Justice rules with a swift hand. It was not until January 4, 1916, that the appellate court handed down its ruling. By then Jack O'Connor's case had sailed the murky waters for more than four years. In the two and a half years since the jury had favored him with a verdict, the former manager had experienced his share of ups and downs. For at least a few days after he received his verdict, O'Connor basked in the glory; a poem trumpeting his victory was just one of the perks:

A Prophet at home is sans honor.
As witness the case of O'Connor,
Said he, with a smile,
As he counted his pile:
"Get the profit—a bas with the honor."[74]

At least one St. Louis newspaper saw O'Connor's win as a direct torpedo hit on Ban Johnson. In a Sunday magazine feature article in the *Star* titled "Beating Out a Bunt on the Baseball Czar," the former manager's win was seen as a possible precursor to a lawsuit in a federal court attacking the system that had prevented O'Connor from obtaining other positions in Organized Baseball once he had been dismissed by the Browns. The fact that the only baseball job Rowdy Jack could obtain after 1910 was with the newly formed and "unsanctioned" Federal League would be the driving force for the suit. The Federal League was coming after the Major Leagues, and its best shot at securing an equal footing was destruction of baseball's reserve clause, a device whereby a player under contract to an American or National League club was essentially that team's property until it no longer needed or wanted his services. According to the *Star*, if a team decided to send a player "to Timbucktoo [*sic*] or the South Sea Islands, and organized baseball happens to have teams in those far climes, the player could be shipped as so much property and his protests drowned in the wavelets that lap against the sides of the ship bound on the long voyage."

In O'Connor, the Federal League saw an opportunity. It was now obvious that the St. Louis native enjoyed great popularity in his hometown. Barred from further employment in the professional game, he had turned to the Federal League. His recent vindication could be the springboard the Feds' St. Louis franchise needed to jump into the pool and land headfirst. Thus the *Star*, mentioning that a move was already under way in Congress to investigate and declare baseball a trust, opined, "It is in the interest of this organization [the Federal League] to have the [proposed O'Connor] case pushed to the limit."[75] O'Connor took a move in that direction. He retained attorneys who announced on June 12, 1913, that in a few days, they planned to file a suit on their client's behalf against each of the eight American League ball clubs. The action would charge the clubs with violation of the Sherman antitrust laws in that baseball's reserve clause restricted the ability of baseball players to earn a living. In this case O'Connor's lawyers said they would seek $25,000 in damages for his banishment from the American League.[76] Ban Johnson reacted to the announcement with an air of indifference, calling the move "ridiculous."[77] It is uncertain whether the lawsuit was ever filed; if it was, little came of it. Such a case was eventually filed and pursued, but not by O'Connor and not in St. Louis. The case was brought by the Federal League against all of Organized Baseball. It was filed on January 5, 1915. The venue chosen was the U.S. District Court for Northern Illinois, seated in Chicago. The case was assigned to a jurist who liked to tangle with the big boys, Judge Kenesaw Mountain Landis. It would play out over a number of years and outlast both the baseball career of Jack O'Connor and the Federal League itself.[78]

Actually, O'Connor found himself once again in serious hot water on a baseball field just more than two weeks after his attorneys announced his intent to sue the American League. On June 28, right before a contest pitting his St. Louis Federal League club against the league's visiting Indianapolis entry, O'Connor—in full Rowdy Jack mode—had a run-in with umpire Jack McNulty, a recent league hire. According to reports, the manager was unfamiliar with McNulty, who was just about to umpire his first Federal League tiff. O'Connor wanted McNulty to prove that he was authorized to umpire the game. The *Kansas City Star* reported, "A dispute followed and all of a sudden O'Connor's fist shot out and landed flush on the umpire's jaw."[79] It took a couple of local officials to break up the scuffle, but the damage was done. McNulty's jaw was busted and so was O'Connor. The manager was fined and suspended indefinitely by Federal League president John T. Powers.[80] McNulty would never return to baseball. Before long O'Connor was back managing his St. Louis club. McNulty, however, had the last say in the matter. On July 24 he filed a lawsuit against both O'Connor and the St. Louis ball club seeking $35,000 in damages for personal injuries and lost wages arising from the blow struck by O'Connor prior to the game.[81] The ball club was eventually dismissed from the case. A judge determined that it was not responsible. Its manager had clearly acted on his own in striking the blow. O'Connor was not so fortunate. In July 1914 he was ordered by a St. Louis jury to pay McNulty $1,500.[82] By then he was no longer managing the St. Louis Feds. The league was now a much more serious challenger for the baseball dollar. Perhaps the owners, wealthy and business savvy, felt they needed to offer the paying public field leaders with a degree of credibility and aura of stability that a rabble-rouser such as Rowdy Jack O'Connor could not provide. When the jury verdict was rendered, he was still with the St. Louis club, but primarily as a scout. That was in 1914. By 1915 O'Connor was permanently out of baseball. The Federal League was not far behind. On December 22 of that year, an agreement was reached between the Feds and the Major Leagues by which the Federal League ceased to exist.[83]

In 1915 not only was Rowdy Jack out of baseball, but the major igniter of his early demise had ceased to exist as well. The Chalmers Award would no longer be given to each league's "most important and useful player." Following the first-place finishes by Cobb and Frank Schulte in 1911, as voted by the panel of sportswriters, the award survived in its latest reincarnation through 1914, but not without further internal strife. In 1912 both Cobb and Schulte voluntarily withdrew from the competition. Perhaps two Chalmers were enough for Cobb. Had he remained in contention, he might have had a third car, as he had another stellar season. He led his league in a number of hitting categories, including batting (.409) and hits (226). The Tigers' outfielder received seventeen votes (tied for seventh place) despite his withdrawal. Lajoie, although batting .368 in 117 games, did not catch the voters' fancy at all and received no votes. The winners in 1912 were outfielder Tris Speaker of the Boston Red Sox for the American League and Larry Doyle, the New York Giants' second bagger, in the National. At the end of the season, a debate ensued between club owners such as the Pittsburgh Pirates' Barney Dreyfuss, who wanted to discontinue the award because it caused jealousy among the players, and the Chicago Cubs' Charles Murphy, who favored the presentation because it tended to keep the players in line, since deportment was a factor in the voting. The debate went so far that Hugh Chalmers offered to withdraw the prizes, but in the end the contest was continued.[84] In 1913 pitcher Walter Johnson of Washington won the American League vote and Jake Daubert, Brooklyn's fine first baseman, won in the National League. In 1914 the Chalmers vehicles were captured by a pair of fiery second basemen, Johnny Evers of the upstart Boston Braves (National League) and Eddie Collins of the dynastic Philadelphia Athletics (American). The pair would face off in a World Series won by the "Miracle" Braves in four games. When the pair drove off in their spanking new vehicles, it was the end of the line. The plan instituted by Chalmers and the National Commission had anticipated a five-year run; that fifth year reached, the Chalmers Award simply faded away.

By early 1916 Jack O'Connor had been sidelined from baseball for more than a year, but he wasn't quite ready to totally fade away. Not just yet. He still had one last iron in the fire. He was used to making a solid buck from the game. It had to be with a degree of anxiety that he waited and then, on January 4, 1916, learned the result in his case against the Browns. By virtue of a unanimous decision, the three-judge panel told the parties in a written opinion authored by Justice P. J. Reynolds, "We see no cause to disturb the verdict of the jury, nor the judgment of the trial court on that verdict."[85] Once again Rowdy Jack had prevailed.

In reaching their decision, the appellate court judges determined that the question of whether Jack O'Connor had breached duties of his employment by failing to manage his ball club in good faith was not a legal question but a question of fact for the jury. Appellate courts are extremely reluctant to overrule the decisions of juries. In this regard the court ruled that there was "no substantial evidence that plaintiff [O'Connor] was desirous of favoring Lajoie in his contest for batting honors over Cobb." To sustain the ball club's charges that O'Connor had acted in bad faith, "the jury would have had to act on the vaguest suspicion." To the contrary, "the jury must have found that there was no substantial evidence that plaintiff [O'Connor] or anyone else could have anticipated, from his manner of holding his bat, that Lajoie intended to 'bunt' all of them." The Browns failed to convince the jurors on this point, and the appellate court saw no reason to disturb their conclusion. Nor did the appeals court feel that the trial judge improperly instructed the jury on the question of whether O'Connor had violated his duties.[86]

In view of its decision with regard to the factual questions surrounding Jack O'Connor's actions on October 9, the remaining issues for the appellate court revolved around the length of the contract. If the contract was limited to 1910, the Browns did not owe O'Connor wages for 1911. In reaching its verdict, the jury had determined that the contract covered both seasons. The Browns, however, had raised a number of issues of construction under contract law based on the differing language of the first and second clauses of the contract. In the opinion of the appellate court, this was a case not of ambiguity but of irreconcilable clauses. The first clause discussed employment for the years 1910 and 1911, whereas the second clause spoke to 1910 only. By law a contract is construed most strongly against the party who drew it up, in this instance, the Browns. In addition, when two clauses in the same contract are in conflict, under the controlling case law of Missouri, the first clause stands. The court concluded that the second clause of the contract by law could be disregarded.

The court went further, however, seeking to determine the construction the parties themselves had given the contract. Here the actions of the parties came to the forefront. In this regard the justices examined Ban Johnson's decision to call Jack O'Connor to Chicago to explain his actions and Johnson's testimony that he subsequently decided O'Connor should no longer manage the Browns. They noted that Hedges had offered O'Connor to the seven other American League clubs before he notified the manager in writing of his dismissal. And, perhaps most significantly, they relied on Bob Hedges's letter of November 29, 1910, informing the manager of the dismissal, in particular, its wording. Hedges had written O'Connor that the ball club had "elected to terminate its contract . . . for the season of 1911." The justices determined that "these proceedings before Johnson and this letter of Hedges are explainable on no other theory than that they understood the employment of O'Connor was for the season of 1911, as well as for that of 1910." Otherwise, "why go to all this trouble and expense? . . . By its course of conduct alone, if for no other reason, defendant put a construction upon the contract by which it is bound."[87]

To borrow an old phrase, the Browns had been "hoisted with their own petard." The O'Connor litigation was finally at an end. Rowdy Jack could pocket his $5,000 and change. Now certainly the controversies surrounding the 1910 batting race were completely resolved—dead and buried with the last remains of many other controversial issues of baseball's storied past.

Chapter Eleven

I wish I had it to do over again.
—Jack O'Connor

The batting race of 1910 did rest quietly, nestled deep in the annals of baseball history, for more than sixty-five years. During that span the main participants, including the automobile company that started it all, had all passed on. In fact, the Chalmers was one of the first to succumb.

In 1910 the Chalmers Motor Company sat in ninth place among American automobile manufacturers, with new car sales in excess of six thousand. By 1915 the annual sales figure exceeded ninety-five hundred. Despite the increase, word among industry insiders was that Hugh Chalmers was a master salesman but directed a company lacking in the engineering and production expertise needed to achieve a lasting place in the industry. One observer, supposedly a close friend, wrote in 1947, "If Hugh had been as fine a manufacturer as he was a salesman, his car would probably be well-known today."[1]

Sales of Hugh Chalmers's iron machines rose in 1915 and peaked in 1916 at more than twenty-one thousand cars. Nonetheless, his company continued to struggle because of poor planning. A rival manufacturer, the Maxwell Motor Company, came to the rescue in the fall of 1917. Hugh Chalmers was given an essentially figurehead position as chairman of the board.

By 1920 the Maxwell Motor Company was in deep financial straits as well. Frustrated bankers turned over the reorganization of struggling

Maxwell, and by necessity Chalmers too, to Walter P. Chrysler, a Kansan who had successfully made the leap from the mechanics department of a railroad to a position of leadership in the Buick Motor Company. Chalmers and Maxwell were combined in 1921 into a new corporation known as the Maxwell Motors Corporation. In 1920 about ten thousand Chalmers vehicles were sold, but that figure dropped to between three thousand and four thousand vehicles over each of the next two years. The Chalmers line was deemed an albatross. The last Chalmers vehicles were manufactured in 1923.[2] It was certainly a sad day for Hugh Chalmers and the company he had championed. Nonetheless, they remain part of the legacy that eventually resulted in the rise of the Chrysler Corporation, by 1929 the nation's third-largest maker of motor vehicles.

When the final automobile bearing his last name rolled out of production in 1923, Hugh Chalmers was fifty years old. In 1910 and for several years thereafter, sales of his company's products had steadily increased. Certainly, the almost daily coverage throughout the 1910 baseball season, followed by the October headlines engendered by the tight batting race, had helped make his vehicle a household name. The concept of the Chalmers prize was born out of Hugh Chalmers's love of baseball. There is little doubt that his love for the game remained long after his participation had ended, when the prize was discontinued after the 1914 season. That same year Chalmers purchased a farm with a large acreage just outside of Detroit. He named his new home "Woodcrest" and held frequent social gatherings there. According to Chalmers's biographer, "Occasional visits were also made by a young baseball player named Ty Cobb, who treated the [Chalmers] children to lessons on batting, catching, and 'rough' language."[3] Chalmers had been out of the automobile business for a number of years when he traveled with his wife by car to see friends in New York in 1932. While there he developed pneumonia and required hospitalization. On June 2, while still in the hospital, he died of a heart attack. He was fifty-nine.[4]

By 1932 most of the participants in the events surrounding the 1910 batting race and that final weekend in St. Louis were no longer in baseball or, like Hall of Fame umpire Billy Evans, who became a general manager in Cleveland and served baseball in various capacities until 1951, were serving the sport in some other capacity. Several were deceased. Two who figured prominently in the primary issues raised by the events were Ban Johnson and his secretary, Robert McRoy. In Johnson's employ as his secretary since 1900, McRoy left Chicago in the fall of 1911 for Boston. The circumstances were far from ordinary. In 1904 John I. Taylor, the son of the publisher of the *Boston Globe*, became the president of the Boston Red Sox. When he purchased the club in April of that year from Henry Killilea, he was nominally the owner, but his family's fortune had funded the purchase. In 1911 Taylor sold a half interest in the team to Jimmy McAleer, a former player and manager, and surprisingly, given his job history, Robert McRoy. Few questioned McRoy's business acumen—he had acted as business manager for several World Series—or his understanding of the game—he had some eleven years as close personal aide and friend to baseball's most powerful man. By now he qualified as a master apprentice. But the job of league secretary did not pay a whole lot. Even if he had been a keen saver and careful money manager, an investor of McRoy's modest means would have had a tough time raising enough funds for a share of the reported buy-in price of anywhere from $125,000 to $150,000. Even McAleer's participation in that economic stratosphere raised eyebrows. Both McRoy and McAleer, however, had one qualification in common: they were close friends with Ban Johnson. Unlike them, Johnson did have the money necessary for such an investment. He also had a penchant for control, in particular, control over a key franchise whose ownership had proved a disappointment. Although Jimmy McAleer would vehemently deny it, his protestations fell on deaf ears. Everyone knew what years later Ban Johnson would admit; he had provided the money for McRoy and McAleer to purchase an interest in the Red Sox.[5]

As McRoy assumed his new position as the treasurer for the Red Sox, his secretarial position in the office of the American League was taken by William Harridge. In 1912 the Red Sox won a World Series under their new ownership scheme, which included the appointment of former Red Sox slugging first baseman Jake Stahl as manager. Stahl, who had managed the Washington Nationals, was lured out of a one-year retirement by a promise of part ownership in the club. Not unsurprisingly, he too was a close friend of the ever-present Ban Johnson.

The 1912 World Series was a controversial one, particularly for Robert McRoy. The Red Sox and their opponents, the New York Giants, would return to Fenway Park, the new home of the Boston club, for Game Seven. Over the years a fixture at any Red Sox home game was the team's rabid fan club, the Royal Rooters, a group that numbered many Boston luminaries, including Mayor John "Honey Fitz" Fitzgerald, the grandfather of future U.S. president John Fitzgerald Kennedy. In 1912 the group's regular roost was the left field bleachers. The Royal Rooters expected to sit in a bloc at this location per usual for the crucial Game Seven. However, when the club members went to claim their tickets, they found that McRoy had sold them to the general public. They were forced to find seats for themselves throughout the stadium. When the Red Sox were routed in Game Seven, forcing yet another contest because of an earlier tie, the Royal Rooters went berserk, parading through the park booing loudly, McRoy the target of their venom. In the end McRoy's feeble attempts at explaining his actions—and even the firm support of his "rabbi" Ban Johnson—failed to erase his sins, which, much like the Japanese attack on Pearl Harbor did for Americans some thirty years later, created a day for the Royal Rooters that would live in infamy.

Fortunately for the Red Sox and McRoy, the Bostonians ultimately prevailed over the Giants and secured baseball's crown. Unfortunately, the success of the 1912 season did not continue into 1913. Injuries and team infighting derailed efforts to repeat as a pennant winner. By midseason the Red Sox had clearly been eliminated from contention. In the front office, team president McAleer seemed uneasy about McRoy's friendship with Jake Stahl. Always present was the imposing shadow of Ban Johnson. McAleer and Stahl clashed, and the manager was released midseason. Johnson was upset about the decision and aired his feelings in a public statement. When Johnson was angry, heads would usually soon roll. In this case the "heads" represented the ownership interests of McAleer, McRoy, and company. In late December 1913 their 50 percent interest in the Red Sox was purchased by Joseph J. Lannin, a Canadian who had built a commercial real estate empire. Those in the know recognized that the deal had been engineered by the actual owner of the one-half interest in the Red Sox, Ban Johnson. According to one newspaper, the fact that McRoy and Stahl knew nothing of the negotiations to sell their Red Sox stock "leads to the belief that they were nothing but figureheads, lending their name to the real owner of the stock [Johnson]."[6]

Robert McRoy's East Coast venture had abruptly ended, but his days as chief bidder for his old boss were not over. In 1916 Ban Johnson turned his attention to Cleveland. By that time the team was known, as today, as the Indians. Longtime owner Charles Somers had fallen on hard times. He needed to sell the team to raise funds to pay back creditors. His friend Johnson came to his rescue by finding a syndicate led by James C. Dunn to purchase the club. Dunn, who had made his fortune in the coal industry and in railroad contracting, was, of course, another Johnson friend. At the outset Johnson even fronted some of the purchase price by way of a loan to the new owners—a group that was said to include none other than Robert McRoy—although Ban held on to some of the stock. Eventually, Dunn became the team president, but his vice president and the man running the Indians was McRoy. Only a few weeks into the season, McRoy, no doubt with Dunn's blessing and Johnson's inside knowledge and influence, engineered a trade that would serve the Indians in good stead for years to come, leading to their first World Championship in 1920.

Under the ownership of Joseph Lannin, the Red Sox franchise returned to greatness, winning the World Series in 1915 and 1916. One of the shiniest stars on that 1915 team was center fielder Tris Speaker, a terrific fielder and hitter who as a young player had made his presence known in the 1910 batting race. Despite his team's winning ways, Lannin was determined to hold down player salaries. This ran counter to Speaker's desire for a raise, and although he was solidly in the Red Sox camp, as the 1916 season started he was not yet under contract. The Indians, no doubt inspired by information provided by Johnson, obtained a flabbergasted Speaker on April 8, 1916, for pitcher Sam Jones, an infielder, and cash. McRoy, who acted as team secretary as well as vice president, had been the primary negotiator for the Indians.[7] The trade would prove to be a crowning achievement for the former league secretary, yet one he sadly would not be around to enjoy. By July 1917 McRoy was a patient at the Sacred Heart Sanitarium in Milwaukee. On December 2 of that year, the keeper of the record for the Chalmers race died of what was described as "a complication of diseases."[8] He was only thirty-five. He left behind a wife and a son named Burton, whose middle name "Bancroft" said a lot about his relationship with his old boss. McRoy's pallbearers included Johnson, as well as White Sox owner Charles Comiskey, Garry Herrmann, and James Dunn.[9]

Whether or not Ban Johnson recognized it as he helped lay his loyal associate Robert McRoy to rest in early December 1917, the balance of power in the American League and thus all of baseball was in the early stages of a seismic shift. A sure sign of change was the sale of the Red Sox in November 1916 by Joseph Lannin to Harry Frazee and Hugh Ward. The pair were theatrical producers with absolutely no ties to Ban Johnson. This time around the American League power broker was on the outside looking in. The sale was just one of a number of transactions and issues that diminished Johnson's stranglehold on the game.

However, while Johnson still held sway, he was confronted with another incident relating to Ty Cobb. This one once again involved Cobb's penchant for confrontation and violence. In May 1912 Cobb left the Tigers' bench during a contest in New York to go after a heckler who had been taunting him mercilessly on this and apparently previous occasions. Initially, Ty tried his best to distance himself from the man. He then traded insults before climbing into the grandstand to administer a savage beating to the man, who turned out to be missing one hand entirely and several fingers on his remaining hand. By mere happenstance, Ban Johnson was a spectator at the game. He did not like what he saw and indefinitely suspended the Tigers' star. This time around, unlike in 1910, Cobb's teammates supported him and even wrote a telegram stating as much. After having played one game without him, they refused to play the next game when he was still not permitted to return to action. Thus was initiated one of baseball's first players' strikes. A woeful team of substitute players had been readied for just such an occurrence. The game was played, and the Athletics won the shameful contest by twenty-two runs. Johnson then intervened. He cancelled the next game and threatened the entire team with banishment from baseball. Cobb encouraged the players' return, and Johnson fixed his punishment as a fine and a suspension to last several more games.[10]

Johnson's power was on the wane when circumstances forced him to make at least two more rulings regarding Cobb. A flowchart of Johnson's power after 1910 would show a gradual downward slope marked by some upward surges rather than a deep descent, although the result, an almost complete bottoming out, was still the same. He was well on the downward descent in 1922, when the issue surfaced as to whether Cobb, now a player-manager for his Tigers, had hit .400 or fallen one hit short. This time around, unlike in 1910, it made no difference in the batting race; George Sisler of the Browns had the batting crown salted away with a .420 average. Nonetheless, the .400 mark was still a signature achievement and much coveted. The dispute arose over a ground ball by Cobb in a May 15 game that was scored a hit by Fred Lieb, the scorer for the Associated Press, whose box scores were carried in newspapers throughout the country. The same play was scored an error by John Kieran of the *New York Tribune*, the official scorer. The discrepancy was never worked out. Whether Cobb finished the year above or below .400 depended on how the hit was scored. In what on the surface might seem an odd stance, Lieb and fellow members of the Baseball Writers' Association of America argued that even though Lieb had scored it a hit, the official scorer's ruling should stand, meaning Cobb would fall short of the magic number. The league's official statistician at the time was a man named Irwin M. Howe. He accepted Lieb's ruling over Kieran's. Johnson backed him up, meaning Cobb had hit .401. The local New York chapter of the Baseball Writers' Association, joined by the national organization, charged that Johnson had acted inappropriately. Johnson fought back. Once again, as in the Frank Baker spiking incident and the 1910 batting race, Johnson had sided with Cobb. Unlike each of those times, however, by now Johnson's power had diminished. According to Cobb biographer Charles Alexander, "Johnson damaged his prestige with the BBWAA [Baseball Writers' Association of America] and especially the New York contingent at a time when he was fighting to preserve his power under the new commissioner system."[11]

In earlier days Ban Johnson would have simply shrugged and said "so what" to the notion that one of his decisions had raised the ire of members of the baseball writing community. By 1922, however, Ban was in no position to alienate another segment of the game without suffering serious damage. Over the years acting impudently had been his modus operandi. The list of those who felt wronged by the league president continued to grow. A number were National League owners such as those in Pittsburgh and Boston who were offended—the Pirates in 1915 over George Sisler, the Braves in 1917 over pitcher Scott Perry—when contract issues governing the playing status of key players were resolved in favor of American League clubs. But the real kickers came when decisions by Johnson negatively affected owners such as Charles Comiskey and Harry Frazee in his own league. In the case of Comiskey, the adverse decision involved Johnson's close friend. In 1918 the contract of Jack Quinn was in dispute between Comiskey's White Sox and the New York Yankees. Although Comiskey followed the advice of the National Commission in handling the matter, the commission's—and as far as Comiskey was concerned Johnson's— decision to award the disputed contract of the pitcher to New York put the finishing touches on what had become a love-hate relationship in the last few years. Thus, in 1919, when Harry Frazee, over Johnson's stern objections, sold unhappy pitcher Carl Mays from the Red Sox to the Yankees, a full-fledged battle broke out with Comiskey, Frazee, and Yankees ownership on the one side and Johnson, still receiving support from the other league owners, on the other. A court of law ruled against Johnson. The ruling seriously weakened the American League president, setting him up for what was to come. In each of these cases, it was not the ruling alone but the arrogant manner in which Johnson acted that wrought such anger and vows of retribution from those who felt wronged.

Now that Johnson was seriously wounded, the end was not far behind. After further threats of lawsuits and a threat by the dissident owners to jump leagues, Johnson was allowed to remain league president but with much of his power stripped. When the Black Sox Scandal erupted in the wake of the 1919 World Series, strong leadership was required to restore the public's confidence in the integrity of the game. A weakened Johnson was unable to muster enough support to fend off the appointment in November 1920 of Judge Kenesaw Mountain Landis, a man who was every bit as strong-minded as Johnson.[12]

The National Commission was dead. Judge Landis now held the reins of power in professional baseball, although at times Ban Johnson failed to recognize it, much to his detriment. One of those times was in 1926, when Johnson took it upon himself to permanently ban from baseball two of his league's and the game's biggest stars. Again Ty Cobb was involved, this time in a much more serious conflict than an argument over a few points one way or the other in his batting average. In November 1926 Cobb resigned as manager of the Tigers and called it quits as a player too. His stint as a manager had not been nearly as productive as his years as the game's star hitter. As a result, his decision to leave the game was accepted, even though many observers felt there were still some hits left in his bat. When, just a few weeks later, Tris Speaker resigned as player-manager of the Cleveland Indians, people began to scratch their heads. Cobb's abrupt departure was brought back into the mix. As would later come out through Commissioner Landis, former Detroit pitcher Dutch Leonard had implicated the pair in a conspiracy with him and pitcher-outfielder "Smoky" Joe Wood to fix a ballgame way back in 1919. Leonard believed Cobb and Speaker were reasons he no longer was in the league, and now he sought his revenge.

Eventually, Leonard's evidence, a "Dear Dutch" letter written in 1919 by Cobb discussing the incident, found its way to Ban Johnson, who sought to bury the matter under the rug by paying Leonard to remain silent and give up the letter. Ban held the evidence for the remainder of the 1926 season, then confronted Cobb and Speaker, and obtained their agreements to retire. When Landis became aware of what was going on, he took off in a different direction. First, he interviewed Leonard, and then, after Cobb and Speaker started having second thoughts about keeping quiet, he acceded to their demands for a formal hearing of the alleged "conspirators" and an additional witness. Leonard persisted in refusing to appear so that the accused could confront their accuser. When the hearing was over, Cobb and Speaker urged that the matter be made public. Landis complied, realizing how difficult it would be to maintain secrecy, given the high profile of the individuals involved. The sporting press went wild. Support from fellow players and the public tilted strongly in favor of the two stars. The release of information that Johnson had tried his best to bury proved an embarrassment for Johnson, whose credibility took a major hit. That his nemesis, Landis, appeared to ride to the rescue of the now much-sympathized victims only added to Landis's power and undermined Johnson's already tenuous position. In early 1927 Johnson's attempts to keep Cobb and Speaker from playing again in his American League were overridden by Landis with the support of the owners when Johnson made the mistake of going to the press with his feelings. Johnson was stripped of his powers by an almost unanimous vote of American League owners. To save face, he was given a leave of absence for medical reasons. By July, now actually sick and quite depressed, Ban Johnson tendered his resignation, effective at the end of the 1927 season. Instead of being banned from further American League play, Cobb played in Philadelphia for the Athletics; Speaker landed with the Washington Senators.[13] Less than four years later, on March 28, 1931, Ban Johnson succumbed to diabetes. The record keepers of the 1910 batting race, Johnson and McRoy, were gone. Their tale of the tape died with them.

By the time Ban Johnson's presidency ended, one of his loyal owners, Bob Hedges, had been out of baseball for more than a decade. When the deal to sell the Browns to a St. Louis syndicate fell through in 1911, Hedges continued to pursue a magic elixir for his struggling ball club by finding the right manager. Bobby Wallace was finally chosen to replace Rowdy Jack. In midseason 1912 Wallace was replaced by George Stovall, a man known to ruffle his share of feathers. Stovall lasted through 1912 and almost all of 1913 before he was replaced by Jimmy Austin for a few games and then a young-but-wise-before-his-years Branch Rickey, who remained through 1915. During Rickey's tenure, the already crowded baseball scene in St. Louis was squeezed even tighter by the presence of a Federal League franchise owned by Phil Ball, a man who had amassed considerable wealth manufacturing ice machines for large companies such as meatpackers and brewers. After the 1915 season, the Federal League and the two major circuits entered an agreement whereby the Feds essentially ceased to exist. Hedges saw an opportunity to turn a profit in the transition, which he did handsomely by selling his team and ballpark to a syndicate largely controlled by Ball. The longtime owner of the Browns did not return to the game but remained in St. Louis, where he later took an executive position with a bank. On April 23, 1932, just over a year after Ban Johnson's death, the patrician Hedges, age sixty-three, died of lung cancer.[14]

Jack O'Connor remained out of the game too. Bob Hedges's manager in 1910 spent his remaining years as a tavern owner and a boxing promoter. He had talked little about his banishment from the American League until he reluctantly granted a lengthy interview in 1933 to Dick Farrington for the *Sporting News*. About the former manager's state of mind, Farrington wrote that some twenty-three years later, O'Connor, by now pushing sixty-four, lived quietly with his regrets over the incident that resulted in his downfall, leaving no doubt he would have acted differently if he had had an opportunity for a do-over: "I might have been well fixed today, perhaps still in the game, had I smashed that thing before it had a good start. . . . I wish I had it to do over again."[15]

Indeed, the abrupt end to a lengthy baseball career that had paid O'Connor well for his services eventually took its toll. When O'Connor died of cancer and heart disease at seventy on November 14, 1937, it was reported that his last illness had left him with so little money that "former associates and relatives" had to pay for his funeral.[16] The man of many nicknames, certainly one of baseball's more colorful and most raucous performers, was fittingly buried in his beloved St. Louis.

Back in 1910, when Bob Hedges terminated the contract of Jack O'Connor, he did so with little regret. Not so when at the same time he dismissed the long faithful and consistently popular Harry Howell. After he had attempted to convince Ban Johnson to allow him to umpire American League games, Howell played a bit of Minor League ball and then called balls and strikes in the Minors through 1914. In 1915 he was hired to umpire by the Federal League. In July a call by Harry so enraged manager Fielder Jones of the league's St. Louis entry that following his ejection from the game, Jones resigned. The resignation was temporary, but later in the month, Howell was released, only to return after a short time.[17] By the end of the year, the Federal League's run was over. In 1916 Howell umpired in the Northwestern League, his last baseball stop.

Howell must have seen something he liked in the Pacific Northwest when he worked the Northwestern League circuit. He eventually settled in Seattle. Now married to a woman named Marie, he worked as a steamfitter in that city's shipyards. Later he moved across the state of Washington to Spokane. For a time he was a mining engineer, but over the years he held a number of jobs as varied as bowling alley manager and truck driver. Nonetheless, he stayed connected to baseball, advising the owner of Spokane's Minor League club, developing a baseball card game with the man, and coauthoring a guide for young players. Despite the work, money was a problem in Harry's last years. For a time Harry and his wife lived rent-free in a hotel owned by the owner of the Spokane club.[18] Marie died in 1942. Harry developed gangrene of his left foot and died of heart failure at age seventy-nine in Spokane on May 22, 1956.

John "Red" Corriden was just a baseball pup when the roof caved in and he was called before Ban Johnson in October 1910. He had survived the investigation and was a member of the Chicago Cubs infield when he played his last Major League game on May 15, 1915. In 1914 he enjoyed his best season in the Majors, playing in 107 games, the majority as a shortstop, and hitting .230. His lifetime average in 223 Major League games was .205. Corriden finished out the 1915 season with Louisville of the American Association, a double-A team at the top of the Minor League rung. He played regularly for the Colonels through 1917. He then remained in the American Association as an outfielder for St. Paul in 1918 and 1919. He finished out his playing career in the outfield for a pair of teams in the single-A Western League, St. Joseph (1921–22) and Des Moines (1923–24). He was a player-manager in Des Moines, where his teams finished fifth and then seventh.

After what must have been considered a less than impressive start to his managerial career, it appeared Corriden was finished with the game, but he was far from it. In 1928 he resurfaced as a coach with Indianapolis of the American Association. By 1930 he was the team's manager. An eighth-place finish did not dissuade ownership from bringing him back the next season; however, he was removed midseason when the team failed to improve. In 1932 Red climbed back to the Majors, this time as a coach with the Chicago Cubs. He remained with the Cubs until 1941, when he landed in Brooklyn as a coach for the Dodgers. In 1947 he traveled across the bridge to the Bronx, where he coached for the Yankees.[19] At each of these stops, Red seemed popular with the players, especially the Yanks, who gave him a new nickname. One scribe wrote about him as "Lollypop John, whose face resembles a boxing glove after a four-round prelim. . . . Corriden is the ONLY [sic] member of the field staff who is admired by each and every Yankee."[20] Perhaps Red's popularity chafed Yankees manager Bucky Harris, who in 1947 and 1948 bridged the Yankees' managerial gap between legendary managers Joe McCarthy and Casey Stengel, because Corriden was not with the Yanks in 1948.

During the 1949 season, the intrepid Corriden coached for the San Diego Padres of the Pacific Coast League. In 1950 he landed a job as a coach on Jack Onslow's staff with the Chicago White Sox. In early May, when matters turned starchy and a verbal battle broke out between Onslow, who had led the team to but a sixth-place finish in his first year at the helm, and the team's general manager, Frank Lane, Onslow was fired. Red Corriden was named the new manager. He fared little better than Onslow. The 1950 White Sox once again placed sixth, their record under Corriden a rather dismal 52-72. Understandably, the White Sox looked elsewhere for 1951. Corriden's Major League managing career was over. Still, in less than one season, he had won five more games managing in the American League than did his first big league manager, Jack O'Connor. Unknown is whether Corriden instructed any rookie third basemen to play back on the outfield grass for "dangerous" right-handed hitters.

In his last baseball years, Red Corriden scouted for the Brooklyn Dodgers. He had not been retired all that long when he sat down in front of his television in his Indianapolis home on September 28, 1959, to watch one of his pet projects, Dodgers rookie Larry Sherry, work in relief against the Milwaukee Braves in a three-game playoff for the pennant. Red's wife Ethel found him slumped in his easy chair. He was pronounced dead of a stroke that same day. He was seventy-two.[21]

Ty Cobb's illustrious baseball career was nearing an end when Judge Landis reinstated him in 1927, enabling him to sign a contract to play for the Philadelphia Athletics of Connie Mack. By the time he played his last game on September 11, 1928, his legacy was unmatched. Including the batting crown he was awarded in 1910, Cobb won an astounding nine straight American League batting titles (1907–15), an achievement that will almost certainly never be duplicated. All told he won twelve batting titles, earning his other crowns in 1917, 1918, and 1919. During a career that spanned twenty-four seasons, Ty batted a remarkable .366. When Ban Johnson announced that Ty Cobb had won the 1910 batting race, Napoleon Lajoie had just been nosed out by the man who would finish his career with baseball's all-time highest batting average. One Cobb biographer, Richard Bak, offers this assessment: "There are several ways to measure Ty Cobb's greatness as a hitter. Perhaps the most telling is his domination of the batting title."[22]

Of course, consistently hitting for a high average was only a part of the Georgia Peach's game. Every time he ran the base paths, he provided a thrill for some, an increase in blood pressure for others, raising almost as much controversy as dust. As a player-manager for the Tigers from 1921 to 1926, he was less successful. His charges finished their highest for him in 1923, when they placed second to the New York Yankees. His teams never finished below sixth, but they finished at sixth twice, in his first year at the helm (1921) and his last (1926). Like many stars of the game, it was much easier to use his great talent to play the game than to produce similar results from others.

Cobb's frustrating stab at managing, as well as the unsettling Dutch Leonard affair in late 1926, meant that when Ty retired as a player in 1928 at age forty-one, he was probably retired from baseball for good. During his career Ty had been a tough negotiator at contract time. Often he was one of the last to sign on the dotted line, if not an outright holdout. As the game's main attraction for more than a decade, he commanded a top salary, which he invested wisely. After the Tigers had played at home, Cobb would head for the bar at the swanky Hotel Pontchartrain in downtown Detroit, an after-work watering hole for young industrialists with names like Ford, Buick, Dodge, and Chevrolet. The young baseball player knew that the world of commerce was the playing field on which these new tycoons honed their game. He listened and learned. In later years, as Ty recounted his tale, he told readers, "Fortunes were made overnight in early Detroit. You could toss your money in almost any direction and not miss."[23] That is exactly what the young investor did, striking gold by putting his chips on companies like the emerging General Motors and an infant company called Coca-Cola. The value of Ty's stock in these and other Cobb holdings, including real estate, increased over the years, and his assets would prove depression proof.[24] By the time Cobb retired, he was a "millionaire" in an era when the appellation clearly separated the men from the boys.

A player of Cobb's caliber, especially one who evoked an opinion either positive or negative from almost everyone who was at all aware of him, was not soon forgotten. Decades after his retirement, he is among a handful of baseball players such as Babe Ruth and Lou Gehrig that needs no introduction to the average American citizen, baseball fan or not. Even before his retirement, Ty was welcomed back to Detroit by a grateful Tigers franchise and adoring fans who had quickly forgotten that many had booed this same man only one season before. On May 10, 1927, a large crowd arrived at Navin Field for Ty Cobb Day. Earlier there had been a parade and special luncheon. Before the game, the fans smiled and clapped loudly as the guest of honor, now wearing the uniform of the Philadelphia Athletics, accepted a number of gifts, including—what else?—a new automobile. As soon as the festivities were over, Ty, fresh off a suspension for allegedly bumping an umpire while arguing a call, turned to the task of beating the pulp out of his old team by playing the game in the only manner he knew, full bore with no quarter given.

In 1935 a poll was taken of more than 225 members of the Baseball Writers' Association to select the first group of baseball greats to be inducted into a proposed Hall of Fame. When the poll results were announced, five players had received the minimum votes required. They were Babe Ruth, Honus Wagner, pitchers Walter Johnson and Christy Mathewson, and Ty Cobb. Ty was the top vote-getter, only four votes shy of a unanimous choice.

His youngest son, Jimmy, felt nothing in his father's gloried baseball career topped that vote as Cobb's proudest moment. Thus, it was strange that Cobb was late for the start of the festivities at the dedication of the new National Baseball Museum and Hall of Fame in the small, quaint village of Cooperstown, New York, on June 12, 1939. Upon arrival he complained of travel delays. Some years later he admitted he had arrived late to avoid having his photograph taken with Commissioner Landis, who he felt had dragged his feet in 1926 in bringing the conspiracy issues to a conclusion.[25] Had he arrived on time, he would have been photographed with fellow inductees, including an old adversary, Nap Lajoie, who had been elected to the Hall of Fame along with Tris Speaker in 1937.

Cobb's wealth and star status allowed him to lead a life of luxury, free to do pretty much whatever he wanted to do with his time. In that regard he enjoyed the outdoor life, hunting, fishing, and playing golf. He traveled the world as well. Eventually, he moved his family, which included his wife, Charlie, and five children, from Augusta to Atherton, a California town near San Francisco. In retirement Cobb found new outlets for his tempestuous disposition, frequently kicking up a fuss on the golf course and, apparently, at home. Beginning in the 1930s, Charlie Cobb filed for divorce on several occasions, but each time the petition was withdrawn. In March 1947 she sued Ty for divorce once again. This time she stayed the course. The marriage was dissolved later that year. In 1949 Ty entered a new union, this time with a younger woman. The marriage ended in divorce almost seven years later. Over the years the relationship between Cobb and his children, particularly Ty Jr., who had shown, much to his father's chagrin, no interest in baseball, was strained. The two had little in common but had reconciled by 1952, when the younger Cobb died of a brain tumor at age forty-two. A younger son, Herschel, had died less than two years before. These and other losses served to fill the aging baseball star with regret.

Certainly Cobb's temperament played a part in his difficulties with family and friends. Over the years an ever-increasing affinity for drink played its part as well. Cobb was now a heavy drinker who had created a lonely existence for himself. Not too long after his second divorce, Cobb moved back to Georgia, but by now his health was in serious decline. In 1959 he was diagnosed with prostate cancer.

Over the years a number of writers had written biographies of Cobb. None had apparently completely caught their subject's fancy. Now faced with his own mortality, Ty wished to author an autobiography. To facilitate the project, he chose a sportswriter named Al Stump to assist him. The writing project, which took place over the course of almost a year, resulted in a collaboration titled *Ty Cobb: My Life in Baseball*. It was published in 1961, the same year that Cobb lost his battle with cancer. The great ballplayer died on July 17 at age seventy-four. He was buried in his hometown of Royston.

Al Stump produced a magazine article and a biography out of his association with Ty Cobb. The article, which appeared in *True—The Man's Magazine* in December 1961, was sensationalistic in keeping with the tenor of a "men's" magazine. Titled "Ty Cobb's Wild 10-Month Fight to Live," it describes an old, mean-spirited, mentally ill man fighting constant pain with significant alcohol and medication. The magazine article plus Stump's 1994 biography, *Cobb: The Life and Times of the Meanest Man Who Ever Played Baseball*, and the movie based on that book form a large part of the current perception of Tyrus Raymond Cobb.[26] Many feel that Stump's writings about Cobb are loaded with inaccuracies and that the perception they leave about the man is overstated, if not entirely wrong.[27]

A pair of historians who tackled the prevailing perception of Cobb concluded that "it too often separates Cobb from the context of his time and has served to inflate this deeply troubled figure into a monster despite the justification for a more objective examination of Cobb's actions on and off the field."[28] Nonetheless, the feeling persists that Cobb's popularity, at least among his fellow players, is pretty much as stated by noted baseball historians Harold Seymour and wife Dorothy Seymour Mills, who wrote that Cobb "was about as popular among them as a mosquito in a bedroom."[29]

Whether the public perception of Ty Cobb was accurate or not, someone who certainly benefitted from it, fairly or unfairly, at least in Cobb's time was Napoleon Lajoie in 1910. The 1910 season might be seen as the infielder's last hurrah as a ballplayer at the forefront of the game. His statistics held up reasonably well in the two or three seasons that followed but began to noticeably decline in 1914, when, at age thirty-nine, he batted .258 and saw a precipitous drop in almost every offensive category. In 1912 he was still in stride, however, hitting .368. On June 4 of that year, his tenth anniversary in a Cleveland uniform, he was honored with a "Lajoie Day." Before the game, he was presented with an unusual gift: a nine-foot tall floral horseshoe. The piece was held in place with 1,009 silver dollars, coins donated by the fans. The day was a highlight for Nap, who was playing for a manager he liked—Harry Davis, the former first sacker for the Philadelphia Athletics.

Harry Davis, much to Lajoie's chagrin, did not last the season of 1912; he was replaced by outfielder Joe Birmingham. Birmingham had been with Cleveland since 1906. At one time Lajoie, who was a decade older, had been his manager. Birmingham was immediately successful, as the team finished 21-7 under his leadership. However, Lajoie and Birmingham did not get along. At one point during the 1913 season, Lajoie was benched. Nap had quite uncharacteristically exploded, publicly airing his grievances with Birmingham. According to Lajoie biographer J. M. Murphy, Nap believed "Birmingham had not put out fully when Davis had had the club, and that he'd been in an 'anti-Davis' clique that had hurt the team." He also was particularly upset that Birmingham, an average hitter, was attempting to instruct him and others in the art of batting. Lajoie was quoted as saying, "It's ridiculous when a bush league player like him [Birmingham] tries to tell a club of old veterans how to play ball. I was hitting .300 when he was in primary school. He did the same with Joe Jackson as he did with me, and Joe was hitting .400."[30]

These and other words uttered by Lajoie with particular venom at the man in charge of his team did not bode well for the old-timer. Nonetheless, Nap played in 137 games in 1913 and batted a respectable .335 for a manager he did not respect. The team, at least by Naps standards, played well too, finishing in third place. By 1914 that was all forgotten. The team, finishing dead last after winning but fifty-one games, collapsed, and so did Lajoie, with a .258 average, the lowest of his career to date. There was one highlight for Nap: near the end of the season, on September 27, he became the third player in baseball history to accumulate three thousand hits. The first two were Cap Anson and Honus Wagner. There was little fanfare at the time for the feat, but the game was stopped so that he could be given the ball. (Later reviews of statistics would reveal that he had reached the three-thousand-hit plateau ten days earlier.)[31] Cobb joined the elite club in 1921.

As a direct result of the 1914 disaster, Joe Birmingham lasted through only a portion of the next season, Lajoie not even that long. In January 1915 his contract was purchased by Connie Mack under an arrangement whereby Mack would pay half of Lajoie's substantial $9,000 salary and his former employer Charles Somers the rest.[32] A few months later, F. C. Lane of *Baseball Magazine* wrote, "Never before had a player so represented a club, so utterly dominated its career. Never before was a player's name so identified with that of the club he represented."[33] Lane predicted that the Cleveland club would be known for years as the Naps, but that was not the case. In short order owner Somers asked sportswriters for a new name. They chose to call the club the "Indians."[34] The new name stuck.

Now age forty, Lajoie was returning to his first American League team and manager. He was not unhappy about the prospect. He said just that to F. C. Lane, telling the writer that under normal circumstances he would have remained silent: "To leave [Cleveland] as if you were a second-story man is different." He then unloaded on Joe Birmingham: "My hitting last year was poor, but that wasn't odd. Any man who has played under Birmingham for a year or so is lucky to hit for a hundred."[35]

Lajoie's new team was a far different club from the minidynasty that had represented the American League in the World Series in four of the past five seasons, winning three of them. The 1914 Athletics had been swept by the Boston Braves, leaving Mr. Mack with a host of problems, including declining attendance and rising salary demands from a bevy of star players coveted by the emerging rival Federal League. To deal with the problem, Mack had dealt many of his star players to other clubs, including his star second baseman Eddie Collins, the 1914 winner of the Chalmers for top American League player. The Athletics now had a gaping hole at second base and a roster suddenly lacking star power. Napoleon Lajoie was purchased to fill both voids. Alas, the Lajoie of 1914 was nowhere near the Lajoie of 1901. Mack was getting a player who had slowed quite a bit with the bat and perhaps even more in the field. Despite his best efforts, Nap would be incapable of helping his new team avoid a slide from the top of the ladder to the bottom. In 1914 the Athletics won the pennant with a record of 99-53. The club, minus many of its top performers, fell to last place in 1915 with only 43 wins against 109 losses. Any illusions that the A's were getting the diamond-studded version of the Big Frenchman when he arrived in 1915 were dashed early on when Lajoie bobbled five ground balls on April 22 versus the Red Sox in Boston. The five-error game was a career worst. At the plate he fared better, hitting .280 in 129 games and driving in sixty-one runs. A highlight was a return to Cleveland, where he was favored with another "day" and greeted by a large and adoring crowd.

Lajoie returned to the Mackmen in 1916, but by then even more components of the championship teams were gone. The club repeated its last-place finish, recording a woeful 36-117 record. When Nap took the field on August 22 for game number 2,480 in a twenty-one season career, he was unknowingly playing his last Major League game. Fittingly, the opponent was Cleveland. The next day, in pregame drills, he was injured. He did not play again. In his last Major League season, he played in 113 games and batted .246, exactly 180 points below his American League record average in 1901. Over his long and illustrious career, Lajoie had averaged .338, a figure that produced three—and some say four—batting titles, not counting the contested 1910 contest. He would gladly have traded some or all of those titles for one team accomplishment that never came his way: an American League pennant. He branded it "the greatest disappointment of my baseball life."[36] Cobb, in contrast, had played on three pennant winners, all early in his career and none resulting in a world title.

In 1917 Lajoie did not return to the A's. About his brief time with the club he said, "I was more of a coach than a player."[37] Thus it was a fairly easy transition in 1917 to a managing job in the upper-level Minors with Toronto of the International League. Here Nap captured his first league title, winning the league crown with a victory on the last day of the season. The team's batting leader was its first baseman, Napoleon Lajoie, who had apparently recovered from his injury enough to bat at a league-best .380 clip. Naturally, the combination of his hitting and managerial results piqued the interest of several big league clubs, but nothing came of it. A return to Toronto for the 1918 season seemed likely. However, concerns for the International League's viability and a portending salary cut fueled by the ongoing and heightening war in Europe resulted in Nap's resignation. The snafu with Toronto included an abortive attempt by the club to sell his rights to the Brooklyn Dodgers. Instead, and with his own full approval, Lajoie started the season as the playing skipper for the Indianapolis Indians of the American Association, the team his Toronto club had just lost to in an improvised playoff between pennant winners of the top-level Minor League circuits. Nap's stay in the Indiana capital was short. It proved to be his swan song as both a player and a manager. He recalled, "I started out managing [and playing] again in 1918 with Indianapolis, but on July 21 the league had to fold because of the World War, and I packed up my uniform for the last time and said goodbye to the game."[38]

In the years that immediately followed, Nap and his wife, Myrtle, returned to Cleveland, where the couple maintained a small farm with horses in South Euclid. There was a brief flirtation with New York Giants manager John McGraw about a return to the playing fields for his National League club and a feeler or two from a nearby semipro league, but that was it.[39] Lajoie and baseball had entered into an agreed separation. Over the next several years, he was employed in the tire business. In addition, he served on the Cleveland Boxing Commission and resisted attempts to encourage him to run for the post of county sheriff. Eventually, the Lajoies sold their farm and moved to another Cleveland-area community, Mentor-on-the-Lake. Nap was out of the tire business by the mid-twenties. Since he and Myrtle were free to move around, they began spending winters in Florida, at first in the Lake Worth area. By the 1940s the Sunshine State was their permanent home. They eventually purchased a home in Daytona Beach and later downsized to another residence in Holly Hill, a suburb of Daytona.

Although the now bespectacled Lajoie was open to interviews, frequently greeting visiting scribes wearing a white T-shirt, favorite pipe in hand, he seldom attended Major League ballgames. One game he did see must have been viewed with mixed emotions by the retired veteran. On October 9, 1920, ten years to the day from his eight—or was it nine?—hit day in St. Louis, Nap was in the stands as his former club, behind pitcher Stan Coveleski, bested the Brooklyn Robins 5–1 in Cleveland in Game Four of the 1920 World Series. The Indians would win the World Championship that year, an experience its longtime headliner could now enjoy only vicariously as he no doubt reflected on the one that got away in 1908.

Lajoie had accumulated nowhere near the wealth of Ty Cobb. Nevertheless, he and his wife lived quite comfortably. He had not bet his money on Coca-Cola, but his star status and a conservative lifestyle left him with more than most retired players of that era. He played a lot of golf in his leisure time and enjoyed a game of bridge. Unlike Cobb, Nap had a stable marriage and did not take solace in a bottle. In 1937 he was elected to the Hall of Fame. At the induction ceremony in Cooperstown in 1939, Lajoie arrived in plenty of time for the photo shoot and kept his remarks short. He seemed to be enjoying life and had a great time mixing with the other greats of the game.

But all good things must eventually end. In 1954 Myrtle Lajoie died of cancer. Not one to live alone, Nap had one of his nieces and her husband move in with him. In his last years, the greatest Nap of them all was seen in attendance at Little League games in parks around Daytona. He preferred to watch the youngsters perform in those venues than the professionals playing in nearby spring training sites. In late January 1959 Lajoie came down with pneumonia and was hospitalized. He seemed to be recovering but relapsed and died at age eighty-four on February 7. He was buried in Daytona Beach. In view of his baseball interests during his last years, it was fitting that his casket was carried to its last resting place by Little Leaguers.[40]

The scandal created in 1910 in the main by this cast of characters, all deceased by the early 1960s, may have been unique in the annals of baseball. In the eyes of one baseball expert, Daniel E. Ginsburg, who researched and wrote an in-depth book about baseball gambling and game fixing, it was one of the worst. According to Ginsburg, the 1910 batting controversy "was one of the most sordid ones in the history of baseball, because [unlike the 1919 Black Sox Scandal] the motive was not personal gain for the corrupt individuals, but spite against a fellow player."[41]

Over the years there would be other attempts by opposing teams in baseball and other sports to aid an individual player in establishing some record or finishing first in the standings in one category or another. For example, in 1968 Detroit's raffish Denny McLain, his impressive thirty-first victory well in hand, admittedly grooved a pitch to Yankees slugger Mickey Mantle, enabling the aging outfielder to slam home run number 535 and move into sole possession of third place on the all-time home run list.[42] In a National Basketball Association (NBA) game in 1997, the Washington Bullets stood by and watched as Philadelphia 76ers guard Allen Iverson swished a three-point shot to reach forty points. This permitted Iverson to set a rookie record with five straight forty-point games. Earlier his team called three timeouts in the last minute and constantly fed him the ball to get him close enough for the Bullets to offer their assist.[43]

Somewhat similar but even more unsavory were the events that occurred at the close of the 1929 baseball season, when outfielders Chuck Klein of the Philadelphia Phillies and Mel Ott of the New York Giants entered the last day of the season tied for the National League home run lead. The two teams were conveniently facing each other. In inning five of game one, the twenty-four-year-old Klein homered to take the lead. In game two, Phillies hurlers walked Ott on five occasions. He had one official at bat and singled, but the actions of Klein's pitching teammates went a long way in preventing Ott from opportunities to tie Klein or win the home run crown outright.[44] In this case the Phillies were doing what they could to help a teammate. Certainly their actions, as well as those of Denny McLain and the two NBA teams, did serious disservice to the idea of fair play and healthy competition. None, however, came as close to the events of October 9, 1910, as the charges levied at the end of the 1976 season by outfielder–designated hitter Hal McRae of the Kansas City Royals.

As it had in 1910, the batting race in the American League in 1976 came down to the last game of the season. This time it was a three-man race involving teammates Hal McRae and the Royals' great third baseman George Brett, as well as perennial batting champion Rod Carew of the Minnesota Twins. Just over a point separated the three with McRae, an African American, in the lead and Carew, a black man of Panamanian descent, bringing up the rear in an attempt to win his fifth straight batting title. Of course, with typical baseball karma, the Royals and Twins were facing off against each other. In the ninth inning, in what would likely be the last at bat for each Royals player, Brett, already 2 for 4 on the day and batting ahead of McRae, sent what appeared to be a routine fly ball toward Twins left fielder Steve Brye. According to reports, Brye was playing Brett deep. Brett lifted the ball high and of medium depth. Brye started in, appeared ready to make a routine catch, and then suddenly stopped. The ball fell several feet in front of him, took a high bounce on the artificial turf and went over Brye's head to the outfield wall.[45] Brett rounded the bases for an inside-the-park home run. McRae batted next. He was also 2 for 4 for the day. He grounded out, finishing second to Brett in the batting race and just ahead of Carew, who also went 2 for 4 in this final contest.

When Brett crossed the plate, McRae congratulated him. However, when McRae headed for the Kansas City dugout following his ground out, he targeted Twins manager Gene Mauch with a "clench-fist" gesture. When he repeated it, Mauch came up out of the dugout. Both he and McRae had to be restrained. After the game, McRae claimed the Twins' actions in letting Brett's ball drop in were racially motivated: "I know what happened. It's been too good a season for me to say too much, but I know they let that ball fall on purpose. . . . It's changing gradually, but I know how things are, so I can accept them. It's too bad things like this have to happen in 1976."[46]

Mauch denied McRae's accusations. He defended his player Brye and the Twins defended their manager Mauch. Outfielder Brye said Mauch told him to play shallow: "I was just too deep and it was my fault, my mistake all the way."[47] Rod Carew, who was as interested in the outcome of the day as McRae and Brett, told reporters, "That's a bunch of crap when they talk about racial stuff. . . . Gene [Mauch] said he wanted me to win the [batting] championship."[48] What Carew didn't say, however, was that by the bottom of the ninth inning, given the score, the only players who could have won the title were McRae and Brett. Newly crowned champion Brett seemed to agree with his teammate, thinking just "maybe the Twins made me a present of the batting championship. . . . I mean, I wanted to win, but I didn't want it to be this way."[49]

Given the allegations, Major League Baseball thought an investigation was in order. Then-commissioner Bowie Kuhn referred the matter to the office of Lee MacPhail, American League president. MacPhail's findings echoed those of predecessor Ban Johnson, rendered some sixty-five seasons earlier: "This office has questioned many people with respect to the [incident]. Although it is not always possible to know with certainty what governs men's action, there is no evidence or reason to believe that any plays in the game of October 3 at Kansas City were unfairly motivated. Lacking such, it is unjust to imply otherwise, simply by citing one missed play."[50]

That was it then, save for one interesting comment that later came to light. At some point Rod Carew told a reporter that just before the next to last game of the 1976 season, he had had a conversation about the tight batting race with none other than Hal McRae. The Royals had clinched the American League pennant the night before. Thus, regulars such as McRae and George Brett were getting the night off. Carew said McRae told him, "No way you're going to win another title. We're going to walk you the next two games and George and I aren't going to play."[51] It was said that when Twins manager Mauch heard this, he approached Royals manager Whitey Herzog and the pair agreed that the contenders would not be intentionally walked. As a matter of record, over the final two games, Carew was walked just one time in the first inning of that last game, and as it turned out, when Carew went 3 for 4 in the next to last game to pull closer to the top, Brett and McRae did play the final game. Nevertheless, sportswriter Bob Fowler, writing for the *Sporting News*, raised the specter of a scenario by which the allegedly aggrieved McRae had planted the seed for those actions of the Twins he now complained about.[52]

Shades of 1910 appeared in 1976 in at least one additional setting, this time under a category that might be labeled "lessons learned." As with any close batting race, there were allegations of bias and questionable calls with favoritism toward the hometown heroes. In this case, knowing that the race would be up for grabs on the last day, the American League took precautions to avert a controversy. Normally there was one official scorer. This time there were three, the number in use by that time for playoff and World Series games. One of the scorers was from Minnesota. Although there were no controversial scoring decisions, McRae still found something to complain about. Fortunately, no automobile was involved.

Of course, by 1976 a number of tweaks had been made to the way games were officially scored, but in truth not all that much had changed substantively. There was that immediate uproar during the winter of 1910–11, but as often happens with brush fires like the Chalmers affair, once the embers cooled the calls for change died with the flames. Over the years there would be calls for change that sounded eerily similar to those raised during the heat of the 1910 batting race. In 1912 one baseball writer ventured that "the main difficulty in the present system is that the official scorer is a club official and not a league official."[53] A decade later cries of favoritism by local official scorers, this time of the St. Louis variety, accompanied the batting crowns achieved in 1920 by George Sisler of that city's American League Browns and Rogers Hornsby of the National League Cardinals. The league presidents, Ban Johnson and John Heydler, were implored to consider a system whereby the league and not the clubs would appoint each official scorer.[54] A partial solution was offered in 1930. Although the two big leagues were not ready to install a system like that in place for umpires, whereby the league would hire and pay scorers to travel the circuit, they did agree to a new plan. Henceforth, each league president would name the reporter from each big league city who would do the scoring. In addition, two "competent and experienced men" would be named as alternates, thus avoiding the sometimes controversial situations whereby a busy scorer delegated the job to a much less experienced colleague.[55] This approach was formally adopted in 1957, when it became a requirement pursuant to the official rules of the game that "the league president shall appoint an official scorer for each . . . game."[56] Seven years earlier, in 1950, official scorers had finally been formally accorded the status of "an official representative of the league."[57] For a time the almost exclusive bailiwick of active sportswriters who were members of the Baseball Writers' Association, today official scorers include but are not limited to retired sportswriters and active sportswriters who agree not to report on the game.[58] The official rules also require the scorer to decide all judgment calls within twenty-four hours and to file a formal report on a prescribed form to the respective league office within thirty-six hours of the completion of the game.[59]

As one season turned to another, the number of official box scores and the statistics contained therein accumulated at a rapid rate. So too the interest in what those numbers reflected about the game and the performance of its players. There was still interest—mixed in with mounting criticism of their importance—in individual batting averages, but also an increasing interest in many other hitting and fielding categories. In early 1912 it was reported that Ban Johnson, perhaps in part to avoid the confusion stemming from the 1910 batting race, which produced a profusion of sometimes radically different batting figures as the season progressed, wanted to have a statistician compile American League statistics during the season.[60] These "official" figures could be released to the public as fans followed their respective teams and favorite players. The man hired for the job turned out to be Irwin M. Howe, a former printing salesman.[61] His outfit became known as the Howe Baseball Bureau. The National League, less scarred perhaps than its brethren by the 1910 statistical morass, did not follow suit until 1918, when it also hired a couple of former salesmen with a penchant for keeping score of baseball games, Al Munro Elias and his brother Walter. Known as the Elias Sports Bureau, the brothers' company eventually corralled the work of the American League as well and entered the twenty-first century as the official number cruncher for Major League Baseball.[62]

Chapter Twelve

The passage of 70 years, in our judgment, also
constitutes a certain statute of limitations.
—Bowie Kuhn

In April 1981, after a slumber that exceeded that of Rip Van Winkle, a story broke that put the whole 1910 batting controversy back into play, where it remains today. Once again the controversy was initiated from outside, rather than inside, the game. This time the originators were individuals tracking the statistical record of baseball.

Interest in keeping and studying baseball statistics was not confined to the men hired by the various leagues to keep track on an official basis. Over time a number of baseball fans directed their interest to the compilation of statistics, and several of them published their results. More than one would revisit the statistics compiled in past seasons. One way to do so was to obtain the "official" records of Major League Baseball kept on microfilm at the league offices and at the library at the National Baseball Hall of Fame in Cooperstown. The record sheets for the National League date back to 1903, and the American League records begin in 1905. The statistic sheets for each year are commonly known as day-by-days (DBDs).[1] Men such as American League secretary Robert McRoy, working on behalf of league president Ban Johnson, kept two kinds of statistical counts culled from the score sheets sent to the league office by the official scorers. There was a team sheet for each of the eight teams in the secretary's league. A separate line was used to record the numbers for each game a team played in that season. For example, the total at bats and total hits were entered for each game. There were also individual player sheets. There was a separate sheet for each player on each team. The individual data for that player for each game were set forth on separate lines with the first column listing the date of the game. In the case of a doubleheader, the same date was entered, but the player's individual results for each of the two games was entered on its own line. Data for a player's batting average could be extracted by adding the columns for at bats and for hits and dividing the latter by the former.

The team and individual DBD sheets were a feast for sore eyes to anyone who loved baseball statistics, particularly those of the historical variety. One such person was Pete Palmer, by day a computer programmer and radar-systems engineer. During the 1970s, when he wasn't programming under one military contract or another, Palmer edited Hy Turkin and S. C. Thompson's *Official Encyclopedia of Baseball*. First published in 1951, the book was, as the title implied, baseball's first true encyclopedia. Included among the tome's more than six hundred pages were the individual statistics for thousands of the men who played the professional game.[2]

One of Pete Palmer's particular interests was compilation of home-and-away statistics for individual players. One night in the late 1970s, he was combing through a number of reels of microfilm from the Baseball Hall of Fame that included the DBDs from the 1910 season. In particular, Palmer was interested in the home-and-away figures for Sam Crawford, the outfield mate of Ty Cobb.[3] When he examined Crawford's DBD sheet for results from the Tigers' long September home stand that began on September 12, something did not add up. One more game was listed than was actually played. When he looked closer at Crawford's sheet, he found that only a single entry appeared for a doubleheader the Tigers had played in Detroit against the Boston Red Sox on September 24. However, there was a double entry for the twenty-fifth, when only a single game was played against the Red Sox. His interest piqued, Palmer's eyes slid down the page to the end of the month. The last entry for September should have been for a home game against New York on the twenty-eighth. However, the last entry was for the twenty-fourth. This then was the extra game that had raised Palmer's eyebrows in the first place. It could mean a major error had occurred in the statistical count, but to Palmer's relief, each number in that row had been crossed out.

For most interested observers, noting the correction on Crawford's sheet would have been enough. The dates were a bit askew, but so what? The totals would otherwise be correct. But Palmer was not just any interested observer, he was an investigative analyst. Each statistic held a story for him. These were not just numbers; they represented baseball history. He looked further, checking out the individual DBD sheets for the other 1910 Tigers. He found that with one exception, the entries for the games of September 24 and 25 were listed and handled in the same manner as on Sam Crawford's sheet. On each, the statistics from the extra game were crossed out. The lone exception, however, was a stunner. The sheet for Ty Cobb, the announced winner of the closely contested and controversial 1910 American League batting crown, was noticeably different. On Cobb's DBD sheet, as on all the other Tiger sheets, there were four entries for the games of the twenty-fourth and twenty-fifth when in fact only three games had been played, but unlike all the other sheets, Cobb's sheet showed the extra entry for the twenty-fourth left standing and included in the statistical count. Cobb had been credited with two hits in three times up in that additional game. This meant that Cobb had been incorrectly awarded with two hits. Back on October 15, 1910, when Ban Johnson announced that Ty Cobb was the winner of the 1910 batting title and accompanying Chalmers prize, he told the public that Cobb's average was .384944, whereas Lajoie's final tally was .384084.[4] As the news media would quickly point out, the league office had divided Cobb's totals incorrectly.[5] Cobb's correct average based on at-bat and hit totals of 509 and 196, respectively, should have been stated as .385068. The error in division was obviated when the official statistics for 1910 were announced in late November 1910 and the averages of Cobb and Lajoie rounded off. In round numbers, Cobb had hit .385 and Lajoie .384. Lajoie's average was based on 227 hits in 591 at bats. If Palmer's discovery regarding Cobb was accurate—and there was absolutely no reason to think otherwise—Ty's recalculated average should have been based on 194 hits in 506 at bats. In the corrected version, with matching DBDs for Sam Crawford and other Tigers players, Cobb had hit .383339, almost a full point less than Lajoie. Rounded off, Lajoie's 1910 batting average stood at .384; Cobb's corrected average .383. The record books were wrong.

As Pete Palmer leaned back in his chair, he realized his discovery of inaccuracies in Cobb's 1910 hit total raised another question—one of more current importance. The discovery not only cast a shadow on a controversial batting race that had occurred some seventy years before, but it sullied one of baseball's storied numbers. For years Ty Cobb's career hit total of 4,191 stood as one of baseball's most unassailable records. The thought that the game's numbers mavens had been wrong about the figure all along cast doubt on the accuracy of many of the statistics generated in the early decades of what had become commonly known as "the modern era" (1901 and after). The discovery of the error was magnified by its timing. Cobb retired in 1928. Now decades later Pete Rose, a National Leaguer who rivaled Cobb's competitive spirit like few others, was piling up hit totals at such a pace that before long he would seriously challenge Cobb's cherished record. Palmer had unwittingly stumbled upon evidence that compelled him to conclude that Cobb's recognized hit total was incorrect. It seemed Pete Rose was shooting for the wrong figure.

Palmer did not sit on his find. He shared it with others, including Cliff Kachline, a writer and editor who at the time was the official historian at baseball's Hall of Fame. Kachline conducted an independent study of the batting numbers for Cobb and Lajoie for 1910. He carefully compared box scores carried in the *New York Times* or the *Sporting News* with the individual DBDs. He also looked at the game accounts as they appeared in the newspapers. In addition to the extra two hits in three at bats of September 24-25 credited to Cobb, he found two extra hitless at bats. Kachline concluded that Cobb's corrected totals should have been 194 hits in 508 times up, instead of 196 for 509. His average then should have been .38189 instead of .384944. For Lajoie he found an extra hitless at bat, making Lajoie's actual batting figures 227 for 592. Since his hit total remained the same, the extra at bat dropped Lajoie's average from .384084 to .383450.

Despite the drop in Lajoie's numbers, Kachline's calculations revealed that Lajoie's lead over Cobb had actually increased.[6]

Palmer also corresponded with Leonard Gettelson of New Jersey. Gettelson was a grocer who kept baseball statistical records as a hobby. He assisted the *Sporting News* in compiling *Daguerreotypes* and other record books that the baseball weekly published and sold to the public. Before his death in December 1977, he too labored to determine the correct batting numbers for Cobb and Lajoie in 1910. Like Palmer and Kachline, Leonard Gettelson was a member of the Society for American Baseball Research (SABR). Some three years later, the behind-the-scenes work of these three men would become public and raise a minor uproar in the baseball world.

On April 18, 1981, the weekly edition of the *Sporting News* carried a story by Paul Mac Farlane, an associate editor. It was titled (in bold type) "LAJOIE BEATS OUT COBB." The subhead read, "After 70 Years, Researchers Prove Lajoie Really Did Win."[7] The article set forth in detail the errors discovered in the tracking of Cobb's 1910 batting statistics. Mac Farlane's description of the discovery process takes great pains to place his newspaper and Gettelson in the forefront of the discovery, but does give due to Palmer and Kachline as well.[8] The article included reproductions of the portions of the Cobb DBD in question. It also mentioned Cliff Kachline's review and findings of additional errors, although Mac Farlane gave no specific credit for those findings. The article also fully discussed the October 9 doubleheader in St. Louis between the Browns and Cleveland, including allegations of favoritism toward Lajoie and Ban Johnson's investigation concluding that all Lajoie's hits were fairly obtained.

The errors on the 1910 individual DBDs for the Tigers and the difference in treatment of entries on Ty Cobb's sheet when compared to those of each of his teammates who, like Cobb, played in both ends of the doubleheader of September 24 and the single game of September 25, 1910, raised a question for serious fans of baseball history. Was the failure to correct the obvious error on Ty Cobb's 1910 DBD a mere oversight, or was it instead an intentional act on the part of an American League official, presumably Ban Johnson, to maintain a status quo he had created by signifying the accuracy of the figures for Cobb and Lajoie hurriedly released in October, when he declared Ty Cobb the 1910 batting champion?

Mac Farlane stated the issue regarding Ban Johnson's actions way back in 1910 this way: "It is not known exactly when the duplicate entries were discovered. Was it immediately after the season ended, when Johnson ordered the check of Cobb's record? If so, did Johnson order retention of the two 'phantom' hits? Or was the discovery made weeks or months later, when the statistics were being audited for publication as the final, official averages? If that was the case, were Cobb's two extra hits retained to avoid embarrassment of another reversal, this time in Lajoie's favor?"[9]

It should be noted that neither Paul Mac Farlane nor anyone else has ever raised a question about the double entry itself. It seems certain that it was an unintentional mistake. An examination of the individual DBDs of the Boston Red Sox, the Tigers' opponents in the doubleheader of September 24 and the single game on the twenty-fifth, supports this assertion. The Red Sox's sheets reveal that for those players playing in all three games in question only one game was entered for the twenty-fourth and two for the twenty-fifth, just as on the Tigers' sheets.[10] However, record keeper McRoy did not compound his error on the Red Sox's sheets by later adding another column for the twenty-fourth at the end of the month, as he had on the Tigers' sheets. Thus, on the Red Sox's sheets, the number of games entered for the twenty-fourth and twenty-fifth are wrong, but the total games (three) is correct, meaning the statistics are accurate. In all likelihood, given the importance of Cobb's batting statistics to the batting race, McRoy at the end of September took another look at the Tigers' records and saw only one game entered for the twenty-fourth. He thus added the second game after the figures for the last game the Tigers played in September. He did not notice that he had already entered the batting results for the second game from the twenty-fourth incorrectly as the second game listed as played on the twenty-fifth.

Nonetheless, a pure conspiracy theorist would still find nirvana in the first posit of Paul Mac Farlane, that is, that Johnson had known early on that an unintentional error had been made and took full advantage of it to obtain the result he wanted. If indeed he acted with intent at that early stage, he probably felt justified in view of the actions of O'Connor and the Browns on October 9. A more likely fact pattern, although much less titillating, is Mac Farlane's second hypothesis. In this fact pattern, Johnson announced the final figures as he knew them to be true. Only later, through an audit by either McRoy or an independent auditor preparatory to release of the final 1910 statistics for the entire American League, was McRoy's mistake found.[11] It seems unlikely that McRoy would have taken it upon himself to correct all of the Tigers' DBDs save Cobb's. He more likely went to his boss Ban Johnson, who directed him to do so. After all, Johnson's guiding principle when he investigated the October 9 doubleheader had been to keep damage to baseball's image to a minimum by certifying the results of those games quickly and authoritatively. Shortly thereafter, he had crowed about the accuracy of his league's record keeping in announcing Ty Cobb as the winner. In his mind justice had been served and the integrity of the game preserved—and all in time for the 1910 World Series. Why stir it all up again just a few weeks later? No one would ever see the records, would they? He felt so confident that he left only Cobb's sheet uncorrected.

Of course, it was now some seven decades later, and any idea of what had happened in the days and weeks following October 9, 1910, behind the closed doors of the American League offices was pure conjecture and would remain so forever. What was not pure conjecture was that Ty Cobb's hit totals for 1910 and for his career were now incorrect. Moreover, procedures were in place and had been used previously to correct the errors that were popping up more and more frequently as the ability to comb through old official baseball record sheets and to compare them to box scores and newspaper accounts became more sophisticated. The Official Baseball Records Committee, aka the Special Baseball Records Committee, created and supported by Major League Baseball, had been authorized by Commissioner William Eckert and in place since 1968.[12] In January 1980 the thirteen-member committee, which included Paul Mac Farlane of the *Sporting News* and Cliff Kachline (the committee chairman) of the Baseball Hall of Fame, had approved twenty-one revisions to the career record of Tris Speaker, a contemporary of Cobb and Lajoie and one of the serious contenders for the Chalmers prize in 1910.[13] In December 1980, some eleven months later, the discrepancies in the Cobb hit totals for 1910 were brought before the committee. According to Mac Farlane, the issue was discussed but never voted on. Instead, Bowie Kuhn, the former Wall Street lawyer who had been baseball's commissioner since early 1969, issued a statement. During his reign, Kuhn had continued to support the work of the records committee. Since it was his committee, he obviously felt he could decide the parameters of its authority. Kuhn said,

> While we appreciate the devotion of various statisticians in researching this case (and others), the league presidents (N. L. President Charles Feeney as well as [Lee] MacPhail) and I have determined that the recognized statistics on Cobb and Lajoie in 1910 should be accepted. We cite the following reasons:
>
> 1. President Ban Johnson of the American League reviewed this batting championship at the close of the season and ruled that Cobb was the rightful winner. President Johnson said, in part: "I will certify to the National Commission that Cobb has a clear title to the leadership of the American league batsmen for 1910. . . ."
>
> 2. The passage of 70 years, in our judgment, also constitutes a certain statute of limitations as to recognizing any changes in the records with confidence of the accuracy of such changes.
>
> 3. Since a variety of questions have been raised through the years about the accuracy of the statistics of that period, the only way to make changes with confidence would be for a complete and thorough review of all team and individual statistics. That is not practical.
>
> For these reasons, we all feel the official records as reflected in the record books should remain the same.[14]

Commissioner Kuhn was a seasoned lawyer. Words were his calling in trade. As these words rolled off his pen and entered the public sector, his tongue must have stuck like glue to the inside of his cheek. He had formed a select group to deal with errors in records. They had done just that, making changes in Tris Speaker's records as well as others. Then suddenly there was a statute of limitations on statistical errors. All at once only a complete review of all individual and team records could make any change practical and acceptable. Kuhn could have been forthright, acknowledging what clearly was an error in Cobb's 1910 hit total and ordering the committee to vote for that change. He could have announced that Cobb's title would remain, in spite of statistical evidence to the contrary, because Lajoie's claim was seriously tainted. Instead, he apparently felt his hands had been tied by Johnson some seventy years before when he certified that Lajoie's hits had been fairly obtained and then had Bob Hedges do the dirty work to clean house back in St. Louis. And then there was that large elephant in the room, that "4,191" thing. That magic number put fans in seats in ever increasing numbers as Pete Rose continued to mount a serious attack on Cobb's record—a record signified by a number that by mandate of the baseball commissioner was not about to change. So Commissioner Kuhn issued a contrived statement that much like Johnson's statement on October 15, 1910, was nothing if not a charade.

American League president Lee MacPhail was more to the point, issuing his own brief statement: "If we had a project to examine all records, and the Cobb-Lajoie error was one of the results, then I'd approve the change. But just to zero in on one isolated record after all these years seems unfair. Ban Johnson certified Cobb as the champion and I'm sure he had good reasons for it. Unless we examine all the records completely, we shouldn't change only this one."[15]

However, as Mac Farlane quickly pointed out, MacPhail had raised no objections when the records committee "zeroed" in and made changes to star pitcher Walter Johnson's earned run average and the legendary Babe Ruth's runs-batted-in total.

By publishing the findings of the statisticians and Kuhn's response, the *Sporting News* was taking the issue to the public. It announced through Mac Farlane's article that in all future record books it published, the newspaper planned to reduce Cobb's hit total by two and make the adjustment of one extra at bat for Lajoie. It would also list Lajoie as having the higher average, as well as note that Cobb was "declared leader by Johnson."[16]

Out of frustration at the failure of baseball's establishment to follow his newspaper's lead, Mac Farlane wrote, "So the issue remains. After 70 years, the odor may linger over Lajoie's seven safe bunts, but the questions over Cobb's phantom 2-for-3 are larger."[17]

The *Sporting News* continued its campaign in follow-up issues. In its next weekly issue, the paper reported that Bowie Kuhn had reacted to its position regarding a record revision stating he was "disappointed that *The Sporting News* had elected, contrary to our recommendations and request, to take the actions it has in regard to the Cobb-Lajoie matter."[18]

Baseball's "bible" struck back one week later in a lengthy editorial, charging that "Kuhn's new all-or-nothing approach [requiring a complete review of all records before making a revision] collides head on" with the committee's mandate. The editors argued that a news release in early April by the records committee needed clarification. The committee had charged that the newspaper was in "open defiance of a decision made by the commissioner and league presidents and supported by an 11–1 vote (one abstention) of the members of the Official Baseball Records Committee." The editors pointed out that the committee had not followed its own protocol in this case. Normally, the committee voted and the commissioner and league presidents reviewed the committee's decision. Here Kuhn had rejected any change prior to committee vote. Thus, the committee members knew that they were "serving on what amounted to a kangaroo court." The editors concluded that the verdict supporting the commissioner should not have come as a shock "since six of them [the committee members] have baseball jobs."[19]

Judging from letters to the *Sporting News* from its readers, there was little unanimity on the issue of revising Ty Cobb's hits total. Opinions ranged from that of one reader who thought the article "a waste of newsprint" to that of baseball scandal expert Daniel E. Ginsburg, who thought the article "well researched and well written." There was even one reader who saw the paper's campaign as motivated by "bias, jealousy and hate" for Cobb.[20]

Whatever the true agenda of the *Sporting News*, the weekly filed an appeal with the Official Baseball Records Committee. It was rejected by a 13–1 vote. The single vote in favor of revising Cobb's hits total was from—no surprise here—Paul Mac Farlane of the appealing entity. He and his paper decided that in the future its record books would carry the original Cobb number (4,191) and reflect Cobb as the 1910 batting leader, but with notations that both entries are in dispute. The publication ended the editorial in its January 2, 1982, issue with the declaration, "The score isn't final yet." But, indeed, nothing had changed by September 11, 1985, as Pete Rose, by that time back with his original team, the Reds, singled to left center against the San Diego Padres. The hit—career number 4,192—broke the still existing, official record of 4,191 held by Ty Cobb.

As Rose began that 1985 season and excitement mounted over his run at the record, some in the baseball community thought his task at least a hit or two easier. The usual suspects weighed in. Paul Mac Farlane, by now director of historical research at the *Sporting News*, cast venom at the records committee and commissioner's office one more time: "They can't live with fact." Cliff Kachline, no longer at the Hall of Fame, was now the executive director of SABR. By 1985 SABR was a group of five thousand serious baseball researchers that included a high percentage of college professors and a number of professionals from various fields. Kachline, who continued to examine Cobb's career numbers over the years, had discovered that the Tigers' star had been innocently cheated out of one hit in 1906. He now believed that Cobb's correct career hits total was 4,190. He was adamant that changes in the official record should be made. "There's no question Cobb's record is not right," he told a Cincinnati reporter. "When you do research, you have no control over what you find. But a good researcher must be bound by a sense of justice."[21]

Obviously, not everyone agreed with Mac Farlane and Kachline. There was no doubt where Major League Baseball stood. Serious students of the game supported the league's stance as well. One of these supporters is David Q. Voigt, a sociology professor from Albright College in Reading, Pennsylvania, who has written extensively about baseball history. Shortly before his death in September 1989, baseball commissioner Bart Giamatti appointed a new three-member committee. Its charge was to oversee any changes in the game's statistical records. In addition to Voigt, the members were George Kirsch, a history professor at Manhattan College in New York City, and Joseph Durso, a baseball writer for the *New York Times*. Several years prior to his appointment, Voigt had given strong evidence on his position with regard to errors like those presented by Ty Cobb's 1910 batting statistics. In 1983 he penned an article in which he stated, "Historians must reconstruct the past by keeping faith with the logic system under which their subjects lived."[22] In the article, Voigt lists the errors found in Cobb's record. He finds their correction wanting in light of the anti-Cobb sentiment, as well as the actions of Jack O'Connor and his merry band of Browns during the October 9 doubleheader with the Naps. Voigt, in fact, mentioned that article in commenting on his selection for the records committee, telling the *Sporting News*, "I wrote a piece for SABR... which I titled 'Fie on the [*sic*] Figure Filberts.' My theme was that going back and changing statistics was a crime against Clio, the muse of history. To me, historical error has its own integrity."[23]

In so arguing, Voigt and those who support him tend to give the cloak of "integrity" to acts by Ban Johnson, a man with the authority to rule otherwise, who first certified that all Lajoie's hits were fairly obtained and later, when almost certainly presented with clear errors in Cobb's 1910 hit total, intentionally chose not to rectify the record before the release of that season's official statistics.

Not everyone agrees with Voigt's reasoning. Noted baseball historian John Thorn, who succeeded Jerome Holtzman as the official historian for Major League Baseball, is quoted as saying, "there can be no statute of limitations on historical error."[24] Apparently, baseball commissioner Bud Selig, the man who appointed Thorn, agrees with him. In 1999, under Selig's watch, an error in Hack Wilson's runs-batted-in numbers from his record-breaking 1930 season with the Chicago Cubs was corrected. The error surfaced because of the diligence of the resolute Cliff Kachline. As a result, Wilson's total as recognized by Major League Baseball went from 190 to 191. At the time Selig acknowledged that he was "sensitive to the historical significance that accompanies the correction of such a prestigious record, especially after so many years have passed." Nevertheless, he thought that "it is important to get it right."[25]

Selig confirmed his adherence to the principle of getting it right in July 2010, when members of a volunteer baseball statistics organization known as Retrosheet, staffed by a number of members of SABR's Records

Committee, discovered two significant errors in official scoring from the 1961 season. Roger Maris, while in the process of a season during which his sixty-one round-trippers broke Babe Ruth's long-standing home run record, was erroneously awarded a run batted in when a run was scored on an error. The revised figure lowered his season total to 141. As a result, he fell into a tie for the American League lead with Jim Gentile, the slugging first baseman for the Baltimore Orioles. Although Maris lost sole possession of one position atop the 1961 season leader board, he gained another when the same group of researchers found that star center fielder Mickey Mantle of the Yankees was mistakenly credited with a run actually scored by a teammate. When this error was corrected, Maris, who had been tied with Mantle at 132, now led that category. In each instance, the changes in the individual player and season statistics were recognized by Major League Baseball and new leaders were crowned. In fact, Gentile, now seventy-six, even received the $5,000 bonus check he had been promised by the Orioles back in 1961, to be awarded if he won the league RBI crown.[26]

It thus seems clear that per his public record, Selig would support a change in Cobb's 1910 and career hit totals. Nonetheless, more than a hundred years after the 1910 season, Cobb's hit total for the year as recognized by Major League Baseball remains at 196, as does his career hit total of 4,191. His 1910 batting average remains at .385 for first place.[27] This is not the case in many baseball encyclopedias and online websites staffed by serious baseball statistical researchers.[28] Several of these authoritative sources carry Cobb's career hit total as 4,189 and his 1910 hit total as 194. His average for that season is .383, behind Lajoie's average of .384, although Cobb is still carried as the 1910 batting leader. However, given the significantly different treatment of the results of the 1910 American League batting race, it might be said that with regard to Ty Cobb's batting title, "uneasy lies the crown."

Epilogue

I don't want to say any more about it.

—Napoleon Lajoie

It does not take too much reflection to recognize that the reason Major League Baseball persists in ignoring the obvious in its treatment of the statistics generated during the 1910 batting race is the stench that surrounds it, an odor spread in part by baseball's establishment in the name of Ban Johnson. However, Commissioner Bud Selig or a successor would not have to be a Houdini to escape the straitjacket Johnson created way back in 1910. The fly in the ointment is that Bowie Kuhn lumped the issue of the batting title and Cobb's hit count together, rather than handling them separately. The editors of *Total Baseball* (8th edition), which include Pete Palmer and John Thorn, explain the way they and presumably many others have decided to handle the dilemma created by the discovery of the errors in Ty Cobb's 1910 hitting record and the method chosen by Johnson to handle it:

> Asked at the time [1981] how we would have resolved the dispute over the 1910 batting race, we responded in this way: remove Cobb's two redundant hits and alter his batting average accordingly, effectively dropping it beneath Lajoie's, and correct his lifetime hit total as well; however, retain Cobb's batting championship, for two reasons—one, because Lajoie's flurry of bunts were highly suspect, and two, because

Cobb was awarded the title *in his day*, and awards should be permanent, not contingent. Furthermore, a reasonable case can be made that Ban Johnson, if he had believed that Lajoie's tainted hits would have been sufficient to produce a batting championship, would have nullified them; after all, he did banish from baseball the Browns' manager who had instructed his rookie third baseman to play exceptionally deep.[1]

What this all means is that after years of silence, pundits from the 1980s on have spoken volumes about the handling, or in many cases mishandling, of the 1910 batting race. Once thought dead, the issues raised in the last weekend of that season are alive again. During their lifetimes, neither Cobb nor Lajoie had any idea of the discrepancies in their 1910 statistics. How would these two razor-edged competitors, who in late season 1910 claimed to think so little of the competition for the prize that they refused to be photographed behind the wheel of it in the presence of one another, react to this enduring controversy? Of one thing we can be certain: their "aw shucks" facade was a total sham. Cobb took the last two games off just to preserve his win. Lajoie, at the very least, lobbied the official scorekeeper for the additional bunt single that in the end might have changed everything. He never once took a full swing at a pitch after realizing the bunt was an open option for a base hit.

Napoleon Lajoie did not cause the animosity toward Cobb that plagued Ty's early baseball days, but in 1910 Nap definitely benefitted from it. Over the years, in the various articles and entries in baseball history books describing the Chalmers batting race, little has been made of Ty Cobb's unusual restraint. Few have acknowledged the dignified manner in which he handled an obvious attempt on the part of his baseball contemporaries to take away a prize he thought he had honestly secured. Likewise, little—perhaps way too little—has been made of Lajoie's willingness to take advantage of the opportunities to win the batting title presented by the Browns, including those overt attempts to wring one more hit out of the official scorer.

The pair met at least once more during their lifetimes, in 1957, in a private session at Nap's Florida home. It was a meeting of old friends recounting old times like only they were equipped to do. The session was described by Lajoie's biographer, J. M. Murphy: "They sat for half a day on the Lajoie breezeway. How tragic that their words were not preserved forever on a tape recorder. Two of the game's giants—both would be dead within four years—who thrilled literally millions by their storied diamond deeds, seated there quietly, the passing traffic on Daytona Avenue blissfully unaware of their presence, swapping tales of games long ago that were seared into their memories forever."[2]

Lajoie later summarized the topics of his conversation with Cobb that afternoon in Florida.[3] He did not mention the batting race of 1910, but it is hard to believe it did not lurk somewhere just underneath the surface. Over the years Cobb spoke little about the finish of the 1910 season, although it was covered in some detail in his autobiography.[4] He didn't have to discuss the affair much because in the end he had been declared the winner of the batting crown. Lajoie, during an interview in 1953 with Lee Allen, which appeared in two parts in the *Sporting News*, told the baseball historian, "The [Chalmers] story's been told a number of times, and I don't want to say any more about it." He then proceeded to cast doubt on the one at bat that day not scored a hit. Finally, in a classic line, hopefully delivered tongue in cheek, he told Allen, "I've always understood that the automobile I got ran a lot better than the one they gave to Ty."[5]

It is a good bet then that at least one participant in the 1910 debacle, Napoleon "Larry" Lajoie, would be delighted with the continuing scrap over the final batting average figures. Lajoie's nephew Lionel once caught Lajoie in a less measured moment: "When [Uncle] Napoleon had that close race with Ty Cobb, he was given a Chalmers car, but he didn't want to accept it. It was [his wife] Myrtle who made him accept. He just thought that he, not Cobb, had won that championship and was angry that Cobb had been ruled the winner."[6]

It would be nice to end an analysis of Cobb, Lajoie, and the controversial 1910 batting race with a large stamp that reads, "Resolved!" Alas, it is not possible. More than a hundred years later, the "official" final paragraph of the affair remains unwritten. Major League Baseball likes to call itself "The Show." When the final act was reached in Cobb versus Lajoie in 1910, the show turned into a case of pure unadulterated hippodrome. Is this what Hugh Chalmers really wanted when he offered to trade an automobile for base hits in an effort to gain some fame for his fledgling company? It really matters little, for by now it is fair to assume that the controversy over the 1910 batting race cannot be resolved to everyone's satisfaction. Instead, it takes its place among the game's more inglorious moments, dwarfed in importance in later days by the issues of gambling and cover-ups raised by the Black Sox Scandal of 1919, the pall cast upon the game by its failure to even begin to integrate until the 1940s, and more recently the assault on baseball's sacred batting and pitching records by players who used performance-enhancing drugs. In each case the controversies rage on, never to be fully resolved. In each case the issues raised are as much a part of the fabric of the game as is the horsehide that covers the ball.

Acknowledgments

The phrase "it takes a village" is probably overused these days, but there are instances when it is particularly apropos. I believe it applies to the collaborative efforts that result in a finished work of nonfiction. In my case, it took a village to bring this book to print. I need to take a moment to thank the "villagers" for their time and support.

I was fortunate that Steve Gietschier and Steve Steinberg, esteemed baseball historians with substantial writing experience, agreed to read my initial manuscript. They each offered valuable insight and made helpful suggestions that influenced the final product. Steve Steinberg also lent his considerable expertise on photographs of the period. Offering assistance on the overall scope of the project was Gary Gillette. A special thanks to Pete Palmer for taking the time to talk with me about his important statistical discovery, which serves as a major part of the story.

One of my objectives when I started research on this book was to uncover the records of the lawsuit St. Louis Browns manager Jack O'Connor filed against his employer arising from his dismissal following the controversial doubleheader on the last day of the 1910 season. That I was successful in that regard can be attributed to the dogged pursuit of the court records by Kathy Grillo, manager, Circuit Court Clerk's Office, St. Louis. She was assisted by the able staff of the appellate court system for that circuit.

I had a lot of help mining for gold in the various newspapers of the day. Thanks are not enough for the yeoman service provided in that regard by longtime SABR member Fred Schuld of Cleveland. Fred's knowledge of

Cleveland baseball and willingness to help locate relevant material in the Cleveland newspapers of the day were invaluable. He also was helpful as I sought information about the passenger ships that plied the waters of Lake Erie in the early 1900s. Likewise, the research assistance provided by Stephanie Nord and Malissa Glush was invaluable in helping me review the old newspapers of St. Louis and Detroit, respectively, in order to add different perspectives of the exciting end to the 1910 season.

Anyone who completes a work of nonfiction owes a debt of gratitude to the dedicated people who staff our various libraries, public and private. The mecca for any baseball researcher is the National Baseball Library in Cooperstown. My thanks go to the staff of that library. Those who provided assistance this time around included present or former staffers Claudette Burke, Gabriel Schechter, Russell Wolinsky, Freddy Berowski, Kim McRay, and John Horne. My hometown Westerville Public Library stepped to the plate time and time again to obtain microfilm and books through the inter-library loan system. Library staffers also provided a pleasant atmosphere in which I could spend the many hours necessary to review the microfilm they had obtained for me. Those who were particularly helpful were Erik Johansen, Mindy VanHouten, Beth Weinhardt, and Nina Thomas. Equally helpful were the following with their respective libraries in parenthesis: Ann Sindelar (Western Reserve Historical Society), Dawn Eurich (Detroit Public Library), Mary Wallace (Walter Reuther Library), Aspasia Luster (Augusta Public Library), and Margaret Baughman (Cleveland Public Library). Steve Moore deserves a nod of thanks for assisting me with downloading photographs. Thanks also to Ken Voyles of the Detroit Athletic Club.

A number of SABR members and other baseball aficionados lent a hand in some significant way. They are the late Gene Carney, Len Levin, Lyle Spatz, Lee Lowenfish, Mark Stang, Jerry Wood, Dan Levitt, Tom Swift, Rex Hamann, Herb Moss, R. J. Lesch, Norm Coleman, Wesley Fricks, Pete Cava, Ron Selter, Steve Klein, Bill Burgess, David Vincent, Stew Thornley, and Andy Wirkmaa. These last three were quite helpful in answering questions I had about baseball scorers and scoring.

As I have in each of my three baseball books, I want to extend a special thanks to Dr. Charles C. Alexander for encouraging me to write about baseball, readily answering my questions about the history of the game, and most recently writing a foreword for this book.

I previously thanked Gabriel Schechter for help he provided when he was with the National Baseball Library. Gabriel also provided his expertise in double-checking the facts that appear in the text. If something still slipped by, as invariably happens, it is totally my fault and certainly unintentional.

No book is presented in its best light without valuable input from a highly competent and dedicated editorial staff. The staff of the University of Nebraska Press definitely fits that bill. I wish to particularly thank Rob Taylor for his editorial work and for giving the project wings. Courtney Ochsner also provided significant guidance as the book took shape. As the project neared completion, Sabrina Stellrecht as project editor and Julie Kimmel as copyeditor brought their considerable skills to the fore.

Last and absolutely not least, no village is complete without family. In my case, wonderful family members who never cease to amaze me in the support they give to my baseball-writing adventures. My son-in-law, Rob, serves as an early reader. His baseball knowledge and common sense always seem to steer the work in the right direction. My daughter, Kim, is a Grade A editor and comes to the rescue when my meager computer skills force me out on the ledge. My wife, Marcia, not only gives me valuable editing help as the first person exposed to the manuscript but always encourages me and allows me to go the extra mile until I am satisfied that I have done my best.

It is plain to see that in writing about Cobb, Lajoie, and their race for the Chalmers, I have had a lot of help from the inhabitants of the village. For that I am eternally grateful.

Notes

PREFACE

1. John E. Wray, Wray's Column, *St. Louis Post-Dispatch*, October 10, 1910.

PROLOGUE

1. *New York Times*, October 16, 1910.
2. *Detroit Free Press*, October 9, 1910, and October 12, 1910. According to sportswriter E. A. Batchelor, Cobb was motoring with friends. *Detroit Free Press*, October 13, 1910.
3. Murphy, "Napoleon Lajoie," 30.
4. "More Praise for Lajoie," May 1915, source unknown, Napoleon Lajoie Clippings File, National Baseball Hall of Fame Library, Cooperstown NY.
5. *Detroit Journal*, October 11, 1910. As previously noted in the text, the Naps actually needed to sweep the three-game series to clinch the pennant.

CHAPTER ONE

1. Ty Cobb and Napoleon Lajoie quotes and photograph, *St. Louis Republic*, October 10, 1910.
2. Hammond, *Hugh Chalmers*, 4.
3. Hammond, *Hugh Chalmers*, 8-9. Reports differ, however, as to how much of Thomas's interest in the company Chalmers initially purchased. Here it is said the opportunity offered was purchase of "a majority interest." "Chalmers; Chalmers-Detroit (us) 1908-1924 Chalmers Motor Car Co., Detroit, Michigan," *The New Encyclopedia of Automobiles, 1885 to the Present*, 131, states that Chalmers purchased one-half of the stock owned by Thomas. Likewise, Hyde, *Riding the Roller Coaster*, 19. An entry titled "Lot 31: 1909 Chalmers-Detroit Thirty Touring" on Motorbase.com describes an arrangement whereby Chalmers bought out Thomas. A fourth scenario has Chalmers, Thomas, and the Bezner-Chapin group with an equal split, one-third each. See Foster, "Birth of Hudson."

4. Hammond, *Hugh Chalmers*, 17.

5. A fifth child died at age three. Hammond, *Hugh Chalmers*, 11.

6. *Sporting Life*, September 18, 1909, 2.

7. *Sporting News*, March 3, 1910, 1.

8. *Sporting Life*, March 12, 1910, 1. Over the years numerous otherwise accurate reports of the events surrounding the race for the Chalmers state that a vehicle was presented to the leading batsman in each league, but such was not the case. See for example, Bak, *Ty Cobb*, 67.

9. Although it is possible that Chalmers initially offered an automobile to the batting champion of each league, there is no question that by late March 1910 only one vehicle was in play. A letter dated March 29 from H. W. Ford, the secretary and advertising manager of Chalmers, to Garry Herrmann specifically refers to a Chalmers car "to be given to the champion batsman of the major leagues." Box 83, File 15, August Herrmann Papers, National Baseball Hall of Fame Library, Cooperstown NY.

10. *Sporting News*, March 31, 1910, 6. See also *Sporting Life*, April 2, 1910, 1.

11. *Sporting Life*, April 2, 1910, 4.

12. See Strohl, "Ultimate Loving Cups," 28–31. The cup was awarded annually through 1912. The winner from 1910 to 1912 was Ty Cobb.

CHAPTER TWO

1. *Baseball Magazine*, July 1910, 87.

2. DeValeria and DeValeria, *Honus Wagner*, 166.

3. *Baseball Magazine*, July 1910, 87.

4. A ballplayer's slugging percentage represents the average number of bases achieved per official at bat. It is determined by dividing the player's total number of at bats into his total bases. The player's on-base percentage is calculated by dividing the number of times the batter reaches base via a hit, walk, or hit-by-pitch by his total number of at bats, walks, hit-by-pitches, and sacrifice flies. Dickson, *Dickson Baseball Dictionary*, 597–98, 794.

5. Schwarz, *Numbers Game*, 11.

6. Schwarz, *Numbers Game*, 4. It was called an "abstract." See also Morris, *Game of Inches*, 2:154.

7. Schwarz, *Numbers Game*, 8–9.

8. Schwarz, *Numbers Game*, 11, quoting Henry Chadwick's entry in the 1872 edition of his *Beadle*. See also Schiff, *Father of Baseball*, 79. However, in his *Game of Inches*, Peter Morris attributes this last quote to H. A. Dobson, identifying Dobson with the *New York Clipper*. Author Morris writes that Dobson voiced his opinions regarding batting average, including the quote, in an 1871 letter to Nick Young, the league secretary of the National Association. At 2:157–58. Apparently, Young ignored Dobson's plea. It was not until 1874 that a Boston paper—Morris states the *Globe*—made use of batting averages in their current form. At 2:158, citing Thorn and Palmer, *Hidden Game of Baseball*, 17. The National League adopted the computation in 1876.

9. *St. Louis Globe*, October 3, 1910.

10. Schwarz, *Numbers Game*, 28.

11. Schwarz, *Numbers Game*, 16.

12. Schwarz, *Numbers Game*, 17.

13. Unnamed Boston newspaper quoted in Schwarz, *Numbers Game*, 17.

14. Lane, "Why the System of Batting Averages Should Be Changed," 41-42.

15. Sanborn, "Some Needed Changes in the Baseball Records," 402.

16. Moreland, "Need of a Better Scoring System," 16. See also Lyons, "Problem of Official Scoring," 55-60.

CHAPTER THREE

1. *Detroit Free Press*, March 4, 1910.

2. Alexander, *Ty Cobb*, 85.

3. *Detroit Free Press*, March 24, 1910. Also the issue of March 30, 1910, in which said newspaper published in full a letter dated March 27 from Cobb to the paper.

4. *Atlanta Constitution*, October 3, 1909, in which Cobb sings the praises of the vehicle, bragging that "it is the greatest car I ever saw—bar none." However, Cobb's interest in automobile brands was not limited to sale of Hupmobiles. Shortly after the 1909 World Series, he drove an automobile from New York to Atlanta in an endurance race. *Augusta Chronicle*, February 13, 1910. See also Alexander, *Ty Cobb*, 85, identifying the vehicle in the contest as a Chalmers 30. An article in the November 6, 1909, *Augusta Chronicle* describes Cobb's trip in a "Chalmers-Detroit car." This was followed one day later by an advertisement containing the contents of a telegram dated November 6 from Cobb to Chalmers-Detroit: "Arrived first. Two blowouts, one puncture all trouble we had. Cars creating lots of excitement." *Augusta Chronicle*, November 7, 1909. During the same off-season, he reportedly purchased stock in General Motors. Bak, *Ty Cobb*, 67.

5. *Detroit Free Press*, March 29, 1910.

6. *Detroit Free Press*, March 1 and March 2, 1910.

7. Alexander, *Ty Cobb*, 11.

8. Cobb, *My Life in Baseball*, 280.

9. Cobb, *My Life in Baseball*, 47.

10. *Sporting News*, February 24, 1927, 8.

11. Alexander, *Ty Cobb*, 19-20.

12. Cobb, *My Life in Baseball*, 52.

13. Although numerous Cobb biographies mention that Amanda Cobb shot her husband, William, with a shotgun, the evidence clearly indicates that the weapon fired was a pistol. For a detailed analysis, see Cobb, "Georgia Peach," 84-101.

14. Alexander, *Ty Cobb*, 45.

15. Bak, *Ty Cobb*, 28.

16. Alexander, *Ty Cobb*, 65.

17. Alexander, *Ty Cobb*, 68. Biographer Al Stump, whose research on Cobb's life has often come under scrutiny owing to questions of its veracity, adds that a bit of the asphalt spilled onto Cobb's pant leg. He also reports an additional incident that occurred at the Pontchartrain. This time Cobb allegedly kicked a black hotel maid in the abdomen when she flared up on hearing Cobb use a racial invective. Cobb apparently was ordered to leave the premises, but the matter was kept out of the press when the aggrieved woman was paid off. Stump, *Cobb*, 160–61.

18. Stump, *Cobb*, 161.

19. Alexander, *Ty Cobb*, 74.

20. Alexander, *Ty Cobb*, 79, citing Ty Cobb, taped interview with William Emerson Jr., Cornelia GA [early 1958], Ty Cobb Collection, National Baseball Hall of Fame Library, Cooperstown NY.

21. Alexander, *Ty Cobb*, 80.

22. Bak, *Ty Cobb*, 59.

23. Bak, *Ty Cobb*, 85–86.

24. *Detroit Free Press*, April 9, 1910.

25. *Detroit Free Press*, April 12, 1910.

CHAPTER FOUR

1. Thorn et al., *Total Baseball*, 957.

2. Lane, "Behind the Scenes in Organized Baseball," 50–51. Much to the chagrin of baseball historians and statisticians, the official score sheets were not kept. They were thrown away after the statistics were transferred to the daily sheets. "Official" box scores of each American League and National League game appeared in the weekly editions of *Sporting News*. They probably were a reflection of the score sheets turned in by the official scorers, but there is no way to check their accuracy. Pete Palmer, telephone interview by the author, July 7, 2009.

3. Lyons, "Problem of Official Scoring," 59–60. It should be noted that at least in 1910 official individual statistics were released by the American League office in midseason.

4. In 1911 the American League retained Irwin Howe of Chicago to record its official statistics. Schwarz, *Numbers Game*, 41.

5. *Sporting Life*, January 25, 1908, 5.

6. See April 14, 1910, entry in day-by-day records of Ty Cobb, American League Records, National Baseball Hall of Fame Library, Cooperstown NY. The discrepancy was noted in the late 1970s by baseball researcher Cliff Kachline, historian of the Baseball Hall of Fame, Cooperstown NY, who compared box scores from *Sporting News*, box scores and game accounts from the *New York Times*, and the official American League (day-by-day) sheets for Ty Cobb and Napoleon Lajoie for the 1910 season. See Paul Mac Farlane, "Lajoie Beats Out Cobb," *Sporting News*, April 18, 1981, 11.

7. *Detroit Free Press*, April 15, 1910.

8. *Sporting Life*, May 28, 1910, 11.

9. *Detroit Free Press* and *Chicago Tribune*, July 12, 1910.
10. Unofficial National League averages through games of July 7, compiled by George L. Moreland, *Sporting Life*, July 16, 1910, 9.
11. Murphy, "Napoleon Lajoie," 5. Murphy points out that Lajoie's birth date is often misstated as September 5, 1875. As to the three unknown Lajoie offspring, Murphy mentions that family members speculate they were born sometime between 1854 and 1863, while the family lived in Canada.
12. Murphy, "Napoleon Lajoie," 8.
13. Lee Allen, "From Hack Seat to Pedestal in Game's Hall of Fame (Part One)," *Sporting News*, November 4, 1953, 13.
14. Murphy, "Napoleon Lajoie," 12. See also J. M. Murphy, "Nap Lajoie's Major Leap," *Providence Journal-Bulletin*, date unknown, Napoleon Lajoie Clippings File, National Baseball Hall of Fame Library, Cooperstown NY.
15. Murphy, "Napoleon Lajoie," 13–16. See also Lajoie's Minor League records at www.baseball-reference.com.
16. Lajoie claimed that Selee sent outfielder Tommy McCarthy to check him out and that the player told his manager Lajoie "isn't going to hit." Allen, "From Hack Seat to Pedestal (Part One)," 13. The assertion seems dubious since McCarthy, who did at one time play for Boston, was a member of the Brooklyn Nationals at the time. Biographer J. M. Murphy's account differs somewhat and seems more logical. He has Selee himself in attendance at the July 31 game and doesn't mention McCarthy. He says Pittsburgh offered to purchase Lajoie but at a price too low for Marston's tastes; New York also balked at the price. Murphy, "Napoleon Lajoie," 14.
17. Allen, "From Hack Seat to Pedestal (Part One)," 13.
18. Murphy's statement and quoted material from the *Philadelphia Evening Reporter* appear in Murphy, "Napoleon Lajoie," 17.
19. *Sporting Life*, September 4, 1897, 13.
20. Allen, "From Hack Seat to Pedestal (Part One)," 13. In relating this story to Lee Allen, Lajoie identified his pitching teammate as "Bollicky" Bill Taylor. Since this particular Taylor had not pitched for the Phillies in some ten years, it is more likely that the pitcher in question was Jack Taylor, who won more than ninety games for the Phillies from 1892 through 1897.
21. Jones and Constantelos, "Napoleon Lajoie," 659.
22. Louisa, "Elmer Flick," 649–50.
23. Murphy, "Napoleon Lajoie," 13–14.
24. Allen, "From Hack Seat to Pedestal (Part One)," 14.
25. Archie Bell, "Bashful Larry Trains on Hard Shell Crabs," source and date unidentified, Napoleon Lajoie Clippings File, National Baseball Hall of Fame Library, Cooperstown NY.
26. The four cities losing a franchise were Cleveland, Baltimore, Louisville, and Washington.
27. Allen, "From Hack Seat to Pedestal (Part One)," 14.

28. Allen, "From Hack Seat to Pedestal (Part One)," 14.

29. Allen, "From Hack Seat to Pedestal (Part One)," 14.

30. Allen, "From Hack Seat to Pedestal (Part One)," 14. But Mack later is said to have claimed the offer was for $4,000 a year. Murphy, "Napoleon Lajoie," 20.

31. Allen, "From Hack Seat to Pedestal (Part One)," 14.

32. For a brief discussion of the findings of John Tattersall, a steamship executive who moonlighted as a baseball statistician, relative to Lajoie's 1901 season batting average, see Schwarz, *Numbers Game*, 99, 104-5.

33. The American League adopted the foul strike rule in 1903. Lajoie once told a writer that he felt the adoption of the rule sliced twenty-five points off his average. Lane, "Inside Facts of the Great Lajoie Deal," 56.

34. *Philadelphia Ball Club v. Lajoie et al.*, 51 Atlantic Reporter 973, at 974 (Pa. Sup. Ct., 1902).

35. This was an era of "syndicate" baseball during which one individual or group might possess ownership interest in more than one team. Somers was a Cleveland industrialist who early on had monetary interests through direct investments or financial assistance in the American League clubs in Cleveland, Boston, Philadelphia, and Chicago. According to Ban Johnson's biographer, "Ban Johnson built the American League, but Charles Somers paid the bills." Murdock, *Ban Johnson*, 49-50.

36. Because Lajoie played in only 87 games (385 at bats) whereas Delahanty played in 123 (539 at bats), the latter is generally considered the American League's batting average leader for 1902. See Thorn et al., *Total Baseball*, 62-63. But see www.baseball-reference.com, which lists Lajoie first.

37. Allen, "From Hack Seat to Pedestal (Part One)," 14.

38. "Naps" or "Napoleons" received 365 votes, while runner-up "Buckeyes" garnered 281 and "Emperors" picked up 276. Lewis, *Cleveland Indians*, 44.

39. Murphy, "Napoleon Lajoie," 26. According to Murphy, although Armour complained of Lajoie's lack of aggression, he stressed that the second baseman was a great player.

40. Murphy, "Napoleon Lajoie," 26. Lajoie was once quoted as saying, "In 1905, I got a job [managing] that I didn't like for a minute." Lin McLean, "A King among Swatters," *Cleveland Leader* (Illustrated Sunday Magazine), May 14, 1911, 13.

41. Murphy, "Napoleon Lajoie," 27. Murphy connects the current practice of white-only "sanitary hose" beneath colored stirrups to Lajoie's 1905 travails.

42. Murphy, "Napoleon Lajoie," 27.

43. Some authorities write that the Cobb-for-Flick offer was made in 1908. See Lewis, *Cleveland Indians*, 51-52, and Schneider, *Cleveland Indians Encyclopedia*, 15. The scenario in 1907, however, with Jennings new on the scene as manager, Cobb in constant turmoil with teammates, and Flick holding out, makes more sense as an environment for such a trade. See Alexander, *Ty Cobb*, 51, and Murphy, "Napoleon Lajoie," 27-28.

44. Murphy, "Napoleon Lajoie," 28.

45. Lee Allen, "From Hack Seat to Pedestal in Game's Hall of Fame (Part Two)," *Sporting News*, November 11, 1953, 11; Murphy, "Napoleon Lajoie," 28.

46. *Cleveland Plain Dealer*, April 28, 2003.

47. See Prologue, 3–6.

48. Schneider, *Cleveland Indians Encyclopedia*, 17; Murphy, "Napoleon Lajoie," 31.

49. Murphy, "Napoleon Lajoie," 31.

50. Murphy, "Napoleon Lajoie," 31. The full text of Lajoie's letter is reprinted in *Sporting Life*, August 28, 1909, 7.

51. Quote from unnamed "contemporary" source appears in Jones and Constantelos, "Napoleon Lajoie," 660.

52. Murphy, "Napoleon Lajoie," 30.

53. *Cleveland Plain Dealer*, April 20, 1910.

CHAPTER FIVE

1. Attendance figures from *Cleveland Plain Dealer*, April 22, 1910; ballpark capacity listed in Selter, *Ballparks of the Deadball Era*, 87.

2. Selter, *Ballparks of the Deadball Era*, 81–82. See also Lowry, *Green Cathedrals*, 69–72; and Dewey and Acocella, *Total Ballclubs*, 217–24.

3. Lewis, *Cleveland Indians*, 67.

4. Selter, *Ballparks of the Deadball Era*, 87–88.

5. Seymour, *Baseball*, 123. See also Swift, *Chief Bender's Burden*, 79–81.

6. The term was first used in 1906 and is a synonym for the term "inside baseball." Dickson, *New Baseball Dictionary*, 272. See also Schaefer, "Legend of the Lively Ball," 92–93.

7. These attributes were included in a patent application filed on June 18, 1909, by Ben Shibe, a partner in baseball manufacturer A. J. Reach & Co. Schaefer, "Legend of the Lively Ball," 94. See also Hample, *Baseball*, 110–11, which adds that the patent was granted six weeks later. Author Hample maintains that Ban Johnson did not learn of the use of the cork-centered ball in his league until December 8, 1910, the date Reach ran an ad proclaiming its use in the World Series. At 111.

8. "Cork-Center Base Ball," 141.

9. *Cleveland Plain Dealer*, May 7, 1910.

10. George Reach's quote in the *Philadelphia Bulletin*, made when he was eighty-one (otherwise undated), appears in Macht, *Connie Mack and the Early Years of Baseball*, 488. Baseball historian Robert Schaefer writes that the cork-centered ball was "surreptitiously" used during the latter half of 1910 and "totally without authorization, slipped into several World Series games" that year. Schaefer, "Legend of the Lively Ball," 94. See also "Cork-Center Base Ball."

11. League batting averages were taken from statistics available at www.baseball-reference.com. The use of the new ball (manufactured by Spalding) in the National League in September 1911 is discussed in Schaefer, "Legend of the Lively Ball," 94–95.

12. Rose, *Cleveland*, 680.

13. Rose, *Cleveland*, 679.

14. Beasley and Stark, *Made in Detroit*, 178.

15. Hatcher, *Lake Erie*, 130–31.

16. Hatcher, *Lake Erie*, 132.

17. Kavanagh, *Walter Johnson*, 151.

18. Stanton, *Ty and the Babe*, 218–19.

19. *Cleveland Plain Dealer*, July 2, 1910.

20. *Cleveland Plain Dealer*, July 3, 1910. See also *Detroit Free Press*, July 3, 1910.

21. Bevis, *Sunday Baseball*, 116–51 and 169–73. Bevis contends that one reason Ban Johnson pushed Napoleon Lajoie to Cleveland in 1902 following the court decisions in Pennsylvania was his desire to increase attendance in Sunday-baseball-deprived Cleveland. At 143.

22. Bevis, *Sunday Baseball*, 172–73.

23. Bevis, *Sunday Baseball*, 168–69. However, Bevis notes that the Tigers played only two Sunday games at home in 1907 and received no Sunday days in their World Series appearances in 1907, 1908, or 1909.

24. *Detroit Free Press*, July 4, 1910.

CHAPTER SIX

1. *Cleveland Plain Dealer*, July 3, 1910.

2. *Detroit Free Press*, July 17, 1910; *Sporting Life*, July 30, 1910, 7.

3. *Detroit Free Press*, July 13, 1910.

4. Alexander, *Ty Cobb*, 93.

5. *Sporting Life*, August 20, 1910, 9. See also *Detroit Free Press*, August 6, 1910.

6. Reports vary as to exactly what played out on the field between Jones and Cobb. One newspaper reported that when Jones either ignored the sign (Cobb's claim) or missed it (Jones's version), Cobb struck out. *Detroit News*, August 6, 1910. See also Ritter, *Glory of Their Times*.

7. Alexander, *Ty Cobb*, 94. See also *Detroit Times*, August 6, 1910.

8. *Detroit Free Press*, August 6, 1910.

9. Ritter, *Glory of Their Times*, 40–41. In this same interview, conducted several decades after 1910, Jones describes, but does not date, an incident that was probably his 1910 run-in with Cobb over the missed signal. In Jones's version Cobb was upset because he was in the midst of a batting slump. Cobb was at bat against Red Sox pitcher Ray Collins, and Jones was on first watching Cobb for a hit-and-run sign, which he alleges Cobb did not flash. After the pitch, Cobb stepped from the batter's box to loudly chastise Jones for missing the signal and not taking off for second on the pitch. When the next pitch was a called strike, Cobb left the plate, returned to the bench, and refused to play further with Jones. This required a substitute batter. Cobb sat out the next game. Club president Frank Navin had to intercede before Cobb would play again. Although Jones's later description of the spat is similar to

the 1910 version, it seems that the intervening years may have clouded his memory. A review of the box score for the August 2, 1910, game with the Red Sox (Collins as pitcher) does not support that Cobb, who was 0 for 4, left the game. In addition, Cobb had gone 2 for 3 and 1 for 4 in the previous games, countering Jones's charge that he was in a slump and actually removed himself because he was facing a tough pitcher. At 42–43.

10. *Sporting Life*, August 6, 1910, 11.

11. *Detroit Free Press*, August 6, 1910.

12. Cobb's letter in part is reprinted in *Sporting Life*, August 13, 1910, 5. Although most fans and newspaper writers supported Jennings's position on this matter, the *Detroit Free Press* reported that one unidentified afternoon Detroit paper felt the criticism of Cobb was unjust. *Detroit Free Press*, August 9, 1910. That paper was the *Detroit News*. In its August 8, 1910, edition, sports columnist H. G. Salsinger defended Cobb, claiming that the young outfielder had received "a heap of unjust criticism."

13. *Detroit Free Press*, August 7, 1910.

14. *Detroit Free Press*, August 8, 1910. Club president Frank Navin was quoted in the article, saying, "Cobb acted hastily and was quick to acknowledge his error."

15. *Cleveland Plain Dealer*, August 1, 1910.

16. J. Ed Grillo's comments are reprinted in *Cleveland Plain Dealer*, July 25, 1910.

17. *Sporting Life*, August 6, 1910, 11.

18. *Cleveland Plain Dealer*, August 19, 1910.

19. *Sporting News*, August 4, 1910, 1.

20. See *St. Louis Star*, October 16, 1910.

21. Stump, *Cobb*, 345. At the same time, Stump, whose veracity has been frequently attacked, reported that retired "eastern sportswriters" had confessed to him that a scoring bias did exist for Cobb at home and against Cobb on the road.

22. Moreland, "Need of a Better Scoring System," 16.

23. At that point Snodgrass needed 2.3 at bats per game in the remaining forty Giants games to qualify for the Chalmers automobile. He would accomplish that goal, batting 396 times in 1910. He ended the season with a .321 batting average. See www.baseball-reference.com.

24. *Cleveland Plain Dealer*, September 8, 1910.

25. *Sporting Life*, September 17, 1910, 1. This report spells the eye specialist's name "Gilliam." Separate reports in Detroit newspapers spell the name "Gillman." The (undated) articles written by sportswriters H. G. Salsinger and E. A. Batchelor are part of a scrapbook labeled "Detroit Baseball Co., 1910," Ernie Harwell Collection, Burton Historical Collection, Detroit Public Library, Detroit MI.

26. *Sporting Life*, September 17, 1910, 5, and *Detroit Free Press*, September 8, 1910. Cobb biographer Al Stump, whose veracity has frequently been questioned, has said that his subject once told him the source of these rumors was Cobb himself. Cobb apparently wrote in confidence to a friend that he could see well out of his left eye only and planned to see a specialist for a stomach ailment he suspected was the

cause of the "smoky" vision in his right eye. The friend breached the confidence, and the contents of the letter became public. A portion of Cobb's letter is quoted in Stump, *Cobb*, 194. See also Cobb, *My Life in Baseball*, 95–96. In the letter, Cobb writes in closing that if he doesn't win the batting race "no better, cleaner contestant could win than Lajoie." At 96.

27. *Cleveland Leader*, September 8, 1910.

28. *Cleveland Plain Dealer*, September 13, 1910. A photo of Cobb in street clothes appears in an otherwise unidentified newspaper clipping, dated September 13, 1910. In keeping with reports that Cobb's eye problem was confined to his right eye, Cobb is wearing sunglasses in which the left lens is missing. The article is part of a scrapbook labeled "Detroit Baseball Co, 1910," Ernie Harwell Collection, Burton Historical Collection, Detroit Public Library, Detroit MI.

29. *Sporting Life*, September 24, 1910, 11.

30. *Cleveland Plain Dealer*, September 13, 1910.

31. E. A. Batchelor, *Detroit Free Press*, September 13, 1910.

32. *Detroit Free Press*, September 14, 1910.

33. *Sporting Life*, September 24, 1910, 2.

34. *Sporting Life*, 9, 11.

35. *Detroit Free Press*, September 22, 1910.

36. The column appeared in part in *Sporting Life*, October 8, 1910, 2.

CHAPTER SEVEN

1. *Detroit News*, October 6, 1910.

2. *Detroit Free Press*, September 25, 1910. Also see *Sporting News*, September 29, 1910, 4, reporting games of September 24, 1910. The box score for the second game differs only in not listing Cobb for a "sacrifice hit."

3. *Cleveland Plain Dealer*, September 25, 1910.

4. *Cleveland Plain Dealer*, September 27, 1910; *Detroit Free Press*, September 28, 1910.

5. *Cleveland Press*, September 27, 1910. The article incorrectly identifies this as the fifth Vanderbilt Cup Race. The 1910 race was the sixth and last of these international road races run on a raceway in Long Island NY. The first such race was in 1904, and a race was held in each subsequent year except for 1907, when the competition was canceled. The races drew large crowds ranging in size from 25,000 to 250,000 spectators. After 1910, the races were held annually at various locations throughout the country. See www.vanderbiltcupraces.com.

6. *Boston Globe*, September 29, 1910. A report of the game in the *Cleveland Plain Dealer*, September 28, 1910, states that a pitched ball (not a foul tip) struck Lajoie on the right shoulder.

7. *Cleveland Leader*, September 29, 1910.

8. *Cleveland Plain Dealer*, September 29, 1910.

9. *Cleveland News* and *Cleveland Press*, September 29, 1910.

10. *Sporting Life*, October 8, 1910, 11.

11. *Detroit Free Press*, September 29, 1910.

12. Joe Jackson, Sporting Facts and Fancies, *Washington Post*, September 30, 1910.

13. *Detroit Free Press* and *Cleveland Plain Dealer*, October 2, 1910.

14. *St. Louis Globe-Democrat*, October 3, 1910.

15. *St. Louis Times*, October 3, 1910.

16. *Detroit News*, October 5, 1910.

17. *Detroit News*, October 3, 1910.

18. *Detroit News*, October 5, 1910.

19. *Detroit News*, October 3, 1910.

20. *Detroit Free Press*, October 4, 1910.

21. *Cleveland Plain Dealer*, October 4, 1910.

22. *Cleveland News*, October 5, 1910.

23. *Cleveland News*, October 5, 1910. It appears that the *Cleveland News* report was accurate, at least in this regard, as the entries in the official American League day-by-day individual statistical sheet for Ty Cobb for 1910 recorded that on both August 29 and 30, he was 2 for 4. The box scores in the *Detroit Free Press* for August 29 and 30 are in accord, whereas the box scores purported by papers such as *Sporting Life* to be "official" 1910 American League box scores show Cobb batting 1 for 4 in each of these games. Ty Cobb's 1910 day-by-days and the American League box scores were provided by the National Baseball Hall of Fame Library, Cooperstown NY. These differences in the box scores were later verified by Cliff Kachline of the National Baseball Hall of Fame, who compared box scores and accounts from newspapers with the entries on the league's official sheets and found that on the twenty-ninth the *New York Times* box shows Cobb reaching first base in the first inning via an error by "Hauser," while the official scorer ruled it a hit. A similar variance occurred in scoring the game of the thirtieth. This time, the newspaper listed Cobb as reaching base in the ninth inning on an error by "Barry" of the Athletics, while the official scorer determined it was a base hit. The extensive research notes of Cliff Kachline were provided by baseball statistician Pete Palmer.

24. *Cleveland Press*, October 6, 1910.

25. Again, it appears that the *Cleveland News* report by Ed Bang is accurate. A box score in the *Cleveland Plain Dealer* for August 21, 1910, records five at bats for Lajoie. This is the figure recorded by the American League in its 1910 day-by-days. However, the so-called official American League boxes show Lajoie with six at bats on August 20. Napoleon Lajoie's 1910 day-by-days and the American League "official" box scores were provided by the National Baseball Hall of Fame Library, Cooperstown NY. Cliff Kachline of the National Baseball Hall of Fame determined that the difference exists because a number of newspaper box scores (*Cleveland Leader*, *Sporting News*, and *Sporting Life*) showed Lajoie with six times at bat with no sacrifice hits, whereas others (*Cleveland Plain Dealer* and *Washington Post*) showed five at bats, plus a sacrifice hit. Mr. Kachline's research notes were provided by Pete Palmer. See note 23.

26. *Cleveland News*, October 5, 1910.

27. *St. Louis Times*, October 6, 1910.

28. John "Rowdy" O' Connor biography, Daguerreotypes, *Sporting News*, January 31, 1935, 2.

29. Dick Farrington, "O'Connor Looks Back at Lajoie's 'Eight Hits,'" *Sporting News*, February 23, 1933, 3.

30. Alexander, *Turbulent Seasons*, 146.

31. See *1892 Spalding Guide* entry cited in Ginsburg, *Fix Is In*, 78. According to the entry, the Columbus ball club had suspended O'Connor the day before without pay for "disgraceful conduct."

32. According to Ban Johnson's biographer, the American League president at first hoped to convince Barney Dreyfuss to transfer his team to the new league. Thus, he initially did not try to convince individual Pirates players to jump their team. When this strategy was rebuked by Dreyfuss in the summer of 1902, Johnson went to his alternative plan involving O'Connor. Murdock, *Ban Johnson*, 58–60.

33. Ban Johnson, as told to Irving Vaughn, "Thirty-Four Years in Baseball—The Story of Ban Johnson's Life (Article 1)," *Chicago Tribune*, February 24, 1929.

34. Vaughn, "Thirty-Four Years in Baseball (Article 1)." See also Murdock (*Ban Johnson*), who writes that Dreyfuss and his associate, Harry Pulliam, went to the Lincoln Hotel and camped out in the lobby, hoping to catch O'Connor and the players in their act of betrayal. Sensing that possibility, O'Connor took his teammates up a freight elevator. The meeting and signings were concluded, and everyone left the hotel by this same freight elevator with the Pirates' executives no wiser. At 60. Years later, in an interview, O'Connor claimed that before Dreyfuss suspended him, he asked how much he had signed for with the Highlanders and then offered "a new [Pirates] contract, telling me to write in my own figures." O'Connor refused and only then was suspended. Farrington, *Sporting News*, February 23, 1933, 3.

35. Farrington, *Sporting News*, February 23, 1933, 3.

36. Unidentified news article, date unknown, Jack O'Connor's Clippings File, National Baseball Hall of Fame Library, Cooperstown NY.

37. *St. Louis Times*, October 6, 1910.

CHAPTER EIGHT

1. *Cleveland News*, October 6, 1910.

2. Cobb once said, "Doc White gave me trouble for a long time. He had a drop ball that fooled me continually." Cobb, *Memoirs of Twenty Years in Baseball*, 112.

3. *Cleveland Plain Dealer*, October 7, 1910. The designation "special" likely came from the *St. Louis Post-Dispatch*, which carried it in its October 7 edition.

4. *Detroit Journal*, October 7, 1910.

5. *Cleveland Plain Dealer*, October 9, 1910.

6. Stump, *Cobb*, 195.

7. *Cleveland Plain Dealer*, October 9, 1910.

8. *Detroit Free Press*, October 9, 1910.

9. *Detroit News*, October 7, 1910.

10. *Cleveland Plain Dealer*, October 7, 1910.

11. The spelling of the scorer's last name appears variously in newspapers of the time and other accounts as Parrish or Parish. The former will be used in this text for conformity.

12. *Cleveland Plain Dealer*, October 9, 1910.

13. *Detroit News*, October 9, 1910. St. Louis sportswriter H. W. Lanigan termed the St. Louis players' efforts to field the pop fouls "slovenly hiking." *St. Louis Times*, October 10, 1910.

14. *St. Louis Star*, October 9, 1910.

15. *St. Louis Times*, October 10, 1910. There has been some confusion about whether Evans's comments refer to his observations during the single game on October 8 or the next day's doubleheader. The confusion appears derived from the dateline (October 10) on some of the articles that mix Evans's statement into coverage criticizing the Browns' play in the doubleheader. However, sportswriter H. W. Lanigan, in reporting on both the single game and the doubleheader in the piece referenced herein, is specific in describing the timing of the Evans quote, saying, "Umpire Evans stated after Saturday's game. . . ." See also *Detroit News*, October 10, 1910, to same effect.

16. *St. Louis Republic*, October 9, 1910.

17. Attendance figures in 1910 are estimates at best. The Browns' home attendance for 1910 is listed by www.baseball-reference.com as 249,889 for seventy-seven home dates. Subtracting the estimated 10,000 fans in attendance for the two games played in Sportsman's Park on October 9 results in an average of 3,198 fans per game.

18. *St. Louis Post-Dispatch*, October 9, 1910. Still, one baseball historian posits that many Browns "fans" rooted for Lajoie over Cobb because they resented that in 1908 Cobb was granted the American League batting crown over Browns rookie Dode Criss. Criss, however, had batted only eighty-two times in attaining his .341 average, as opposed to Cobb's 581 at bats and .324 average. Fleitz, *Silver Bats and Automobiles*, 183.

19. News clipping, source unknown, April 14, 1906, Jack O'Connor Clippings File, National Baseball Hall of Fame Library, Cooperstown NY.

20. Alexander, *Ty Cobb*, 48.

21. While submitting that there is no evidence to support the supposition, baseball historian David Fleitz offers that another incentive for the Browns might have been a betting interest on Lajoie over Cobb for the batting crown. Fleitz, *Silver Bats and Automobiles*, 183–84. Jack O'Connor specifically denied any wagering on the October 9 games. See chapter 10, p. 169.

22. Farrington, "O'Connor Looks Back at Lajoie's 'Eight Hits,'" 3.

23. *St. Louis Times*, October 10, 1910.

24. Schul, "Bobby Wallace," 776.

25. *Detroit News*, October 10, 1910; *Detroit Journal*, October 10, 1910.

26. *St. Louis Post-Dispatch*, October 10, 1910.

27. *St. Louis Times*, October 10, 1910.

28. Wallace had started the year at third base. He played some third base for the Browns in 1909. He and Hartzell switched positions in mid-June 1910, when Wallace returned to his primary position of shortstop.

29. *Cleveland Plain Dealer*, October 7, 1910.

30. Napoleon Lajoie's biographical sketch in Daguerreotypes, *Sporting News*, date and page not identified, Napoleon Lajoie's Clippings File, National Baseball Hall of Fame Library, Cooperstown NY. See also Lajoie's sketch in the newspaper's 1934 compilation of Daguerreotypes, 5–6.

31. Ring Lardner's comments appeared in an article dated September 7, 1910, otherwise unidentified, which apparently later appeared in *Sports Collectors Digest*, Napoleon Lajoie's Clippings File, National Baseball Hall of Fame Library, Cooperstown NY.

32. Cobb, *Busting 'Em and Other Big League Stories*, 132. The book was ghostwritten by John N. Wheeler.

33. *Cleveland Plain Dealer*, May 18, 1910.

34. *Cleveland Plain Dealer*, October 10, 1910. The comments appear after the game write-up in a column titled Notes of the Game.

35. *Cleveland Leader*, October 10, 1910.

36. *St. Louis Times*, October 10, 1910. Had Lajoie been awarded a ninth hit for the doubleheader, he would be one of nine men in baseball history with nine hits in a twin bill. Three were pre-1901. The first of the six post-1901 performances was by Ray Morehart of the Chicago White Sox on August 31, 1926. See www.baseballalmanac.com for the complete list.

37. *St. Louis Times*, October 10, 1910.

38. *St. Louis Post-Dispatch*, October 10, 1910.

39. *St. Louis Star*, October 10, 1910. For a detailed review of the Louisville incident, see Ginsburg, *Fix Is In*, 37–51.

40. *Detroit Times*, October 10, 1910.

41. *Cleveland Plain Dealer*, October 10, 1910.

42. *Cleveland Leader*, October 10, 1910.

43. *Detroit Journal*, October 10, 1910.

44. *Cleveland Plain Dealer*, October 10, 1910.

45. *St. Louis Times*, October 10, 1910. See also *St. Louis Post-Dispatch*, October 10, 1910, which reported that after the games, Hedges "had little to say" but was "evidently displeased with the affair."

46. *Detroit Free Press*, October 12, 1910.

47. *Cleveland Press*, October 10, 1910, and *Detroit Journal*, October 11, 1910. Portions also appear in *Detroit Times*, October 10, 1910.

48. *St. Louis Star*, October 10, 1910.

49. *Cleveland Press*, October 10, 1910. The snippet claims that Somers summoned Lajoie to his office ten days prior to deliver this instruction.

50. *St. Louis Republic*, October 13, 1910. Although this report does not mention it, a column titled Sports Salad, written by Joe S. Smith for the October 13 edition of the *Detroit Journal*, states that Parrish claimed the note was delivered by "a Negro boy."

51. *St. Louis Republic*, October 13, 1910. In his article on Jack O'Connor, written more than two decades later, Dick Farrington relates a somewhat similar tale involving Naps manager Jim McGuire and the Browns' regular official scorer Richard Collins of the *St. Louis Republic* in which the night after the game McGuire was in the newspaper's offices. McGuire supposedly tried to no avail to persuade Collins to change his colleague's scoring of the sacrifice. No further support for this encounter is forthcoming. Farrington, "O'Connor Looks Back at Lajoie's 'Eight Hits,'" 3.

52. *Detroit Free Press*, October 11, 1910.

53. *Detroit News*, October 12, 1910.

54. *Detroit News*, October 12, 1910.

55. *Detroit Times*, October 10, 1910.

56. *St. Louis Star*, October 10, 1910.

57. *St. Louis Post-Dispatch*, October 11. 1910.

58. *St. Louis Post Dispatch*, October 11, 1910. Somewhat similar statements by Herrmann appeared on the same date in his hometown *Cincinnati Enquirer*. In that article Herrmann expressed regret that he ever accepted Hugh Chalmers's offer, saying that initially the National Commission was under the mistaken impression that two automobiles would be offered, one for each league. Herrmann did not explain how that would have alleviated the current predicament.

59. *St. Louis Republic*, October 10, 1910.

60. *Chicago Tribune*, October 12, 1910.

61. *Detroit Free Press*, October 12, 1910.

CHAPTER NINE

1. Santry and Thomson, "Byron Bancroft Johnson," 390–91. See also Murdock, *Ban Johnson.*

2. Santry and Thomson, "Byron Bancroft Johnson," 390.

3. *St. Louis Star*, October 10, 1910.

4. *Detroit Free Press*, October 11, 1910.

5. *Detroit News*, October 11, 1910.

6. Editorial from *Philadelphia Inquirer*, October 10, 1910, quoted in *Hartford Courant*, October 11, 1910.

7. *Washington Post*, October 11, 1910.

8. *Cleveland Plain Dealer*, October 11, 1910.

9. *St. Louis Globe-Democrat*, October 11, 1910.

10. *Boston Globe*, October 11, 1910.

11. *St. Louis Times*, October 11, 1910.

12. *St. Louis Times*, October 13, 1910.

13. *Chicago Tribune*, October 12, 1910.

14. See Sallee and Jones, "Harry Howell," 780–81, in which it is noted that while the slipperiness of Howell's ball enabled him to achieve the Browns franchise record for lowest career ERA, it also made the ball extremely hard to handle for Browns infielders. As a result, he often gave up more unearned runs than the average Browns hurler.

15. *Detroit Free Press*, October 14, 1910.

16. *Detroit Free Press*, October 14, 1910.

17. *St. Louis Post-Dispatch*, October 13, 1910. Dudley Criss is undoubtedly seldom-used Browns right-hander Dode Criss. He appeared in but six games in 1910, all in relief.

18. *St. Louis Post-Dispatch*, October 13, 1910.

19. Murdock, "Youngest 'Boy Manager.'" Also see chapter 8 of this text for a description of the game scenario that does not support Peckinpaugh's "flock" of walks but does reveal a late inning walk and hit batsman, which enabled Lajoie an additional at bat and resulted in a bunt for hit number eight.

20. Anderson, "Billy Evans," 397.

21. *St. Louis Times*, October 10, 1910.

22. *Detroit Free Press*, October 13, 1910.

23. *Chicago Tribune*, October 13, 1910.

24. *Detroit News*, October 13, 1910. As to Evans, Salsinger is apparently under the impression, shared by some but not all, that Evans's remark about favoritism toward Lajoie referred to the Sunday doubleheader rather than to Northen's late-inning drop of a Lajoie fly ball on Saturday. See earlier discussion.

25. Reprinted in *Washington Post*, October 13, 1910.

26. HEK [Hugh Keough], "In the Wake of the News," *Chicago Tribune*, October 12, 1910.

27. Reprinted in *Detroit Times*, October 14, 1910.

28. Reprinted in *Detroit Times*, October 14, 1910.

29. Stump, *Cobb*, 198.

30. *Chicago Tribune*, October 14, 1910.

31. *Chicago Tribune*, October 14, 1910.

32. *Chicago Tribune*, October 11, 1910.

33. *Cleveland Leader*, October 12, 1910.

34. *Washington Post*, October 12, 1910.

35. At least two Cobb biographers write that noted Chicago sportswriter Hugh Fullerton expressed his anger and frustration by doing more than just writing about the Browns-Naps doubleheader. Lacking confirmation, the story remains apocryphal but bears notation. According to one version, Fullerton, a crusader for honest baseball, had been the "co-scorekeeper" of a midseason 1910 game involving Detroit. During the game, Fullerton gave Cobb credit for a "questionable hit." The other

scorekeeper changed it to a "fielder's choice," thus taking away a hit for Cobb. On learning of the St. Louis affair, Fullerton found the old score sheet and changed it back to indicate that Cobb had a hit. He mailed it to the league office, lobbying Johnson to make the change. Stump, *Cobb*, 197. Author Stump, whose credibility has often come under attack, does not state whether Johnson accepted the amended score sheet. However, another Cobb biographer whose book antedated Stump's by almost two decades claims that Johnson accepted the revised sheet submitted by Fullerton and "that slight paperwork made the difference." This version has Fullerton in attendance at the St. Louis doubleheader. This is unlikely. If Fullerton indeed was an official scorer or co-scorer in 1910 for an American League team, it would most likely have been the White Sox. Thus, he would presumably have been in attendance and scoring the White Sox–Tigers contest in Chicago on October 9. At any rate, this version has Fullerton approaching Cobb a few days after October 9 to tell him of his plan. Supposedly, Cobb told him to let it go, but Fullerton went ahead and made the change anyway. McCallum, *Ty Cobb*, 74.

36. Statement of E. V. Parrish, *St. Louis Republic*, October 13, 1910.
37. *Chicago Tribune*, October 15, 1910.
38. Statement of E. V. Parrish, *St. Louis Republic*, October 13, 1910.
39. *Chicago Tribune*, October 15, 1910.
40. *St. Louis Post-Dispatch*, October 14, 1915.
41. *St. Louis Post-Dispatch*, October 14, 1915.
42. *St. Louis Star*, October 14, 1910.
43. *St. Louis Times*, October 14, 1910.
44. J. E. Wray, Wray's Column, *St. Louis Post-Dispatch*, October 15, 1910.
45. *Chicago Tribune*, October 16, 1910.
46. *St. Louis Post-Dispatch*, October 16, 1910.
47. *Detroit Times*, October 17, 1910.
48. Editorial in *Detroit Free Press*, October 17, 1910.
49. Editorial in *Detroit Times*, October 18, 1910.
50. J. E. Wray, Wray's Column, *St. Louis Post-Dispatch*, October 17, 1910.
51. *Cleveland Press*, October 17, 1910.
52. *St. Louis Republic*, October 16, 1910.
53. *New York Times*, October 16, 1910.
54. *Cleveland Leader*, October 14, 1910.
55. *Detroit News*, October 16, 1910.
56. *Cleveland Leader*, October 16, 1910.
57. *Washington Post*, October 17, 1910.
58. *St. Louis Post-Dispatch*, October 16, 1910.
59. *St. Louis Post-Dispatch*, October 16, 1910. Quotes are from Bob Hedges's written statement carried in its entirety.
60. Ban Johnson's statement appears in the *Chicago Tribune*, October 16, 1910. The story carrying the statement is not entirely clear as to the date of the statement's

release. The story, datelined "St. Louis, Mo., Oct. 15," indicates that Johnson made the statement "last night." This would indicate that Johnson issued the statement on the evening of October 14. It is, however, unlikely that Johnson would make public Hedges's letter until he issued his own statement regarding the results of his investigation. Because the story was carried in the October 16 issue of the *Tribune*, it is more likely the statement timing the release as "last night" was added by the staff of the *Tribune* and that Johnson's reaction to Hedges's letter about his plan to dismiss O'Connor followed Johnson's earlier statement clearing O'Connor.

61. Farrington, "O'Connor Looks Back at Lajoie's 'Eight Hits,'" 3.

62. *St. Louis Republic*, October 16, 1910.

63. *Chicago Tribune*, October 17, 1910.

64. See, for example, an article carried in the *St. Louis Star*, October 16, 1910. It referred to a rumor that Ty Cobb curried favor with official scorers during the 1910 season by entertaining them.

65. *St. Louis Star*, October 19, 1910.

66. *St. Louis Globe*, October 22, 1910.

67. J. E. Wray, Wray's Column, *St. Louis Post-Dispatch*, October 22, 1910.

68. *St. Louis Times*, October 23, 1910.

69. *Sporting Life*, December 3, 1910.

70. *Sporting Life*, November 11, 1910. See also *Baltimore Evening Sun*, October 22, 1912, which says that Lajoie was still driving the Chalmers with said license number two years later.

71. *Sporting Life*, November 11, 1910.

72. *Atlanta Constitution*, October 23, 1910.

73. *Atlanta Constitution*, October 26, 1910.

74. Alexander, *Ty Cobb*, 96–97.

75. *Cleveland News*, October 17, 1910.

76. The most tie games in a season was the ten ties played by Detroit's 1904 American League entry. The 1910 Naps with their nine ties are tied with the St. Louis Cardinals for second all-time. Games more frequently ended in ties in the early days of baseball for a number of reasons, including darkness, rain on poorly conditioned fields left unprotected and without proper drainage, and teams' need to meet train schedules on the day of the last game of a series.

77. Over the years a number of the batting statistics for 1910 have been adjusted. An example is "runs scored," for which Lajoie's total has been increased to 94, second behind Cobb in that category. See, for example, the American League batting leaders by year at www.baseball-reference.com.

78. *New York Times*, October 21, 1910.

79. *St. Louis Post-Dispatch*, October 22, 1910.

80. *Sporting Life*, December 12, 1910, 8.

81. *Sporting News*, December 21, 1910, 1.

82. *Sporting Life*, December 31, 1910, 1.

1. The petition, contract, and letter, as well as all other court documents not otherwise identified are contained in the court records for *John O'Connor, Plaintiff vs. St. Louis American League Base Ball Company, Defendant*, Case No. 74234, Circuit Court, City of St. Louis, Missouri, Division No. 3, hereinafter referred to as "Circuit Court Records," or in the appellate court records for *John J. O'Connor, Respondent vs. St. Louis American League Base Ball Company, Appellant*, Case No. 14244, St. Louis Court of Appeals (decided January 4, 1916), hereinafter referred to as "Appellate Court Records."

2. *Sporting Life*, February 11, 1911, 1. According to an item in *Sporting Life*, March 18, 1911, 4, Heydler specifically opposed the "traveling scorer project."

3. *Baseball Magazine*, July 1911, 26.

4. See excerpt from editorial in *Chicago Tribune* reprinted in *Sporting Life*, April 1, 1911, 4.

5. H. W. Ford, letter to August Herrmann, October 4, 1910, August Herrmann Papers, Box 83, File 15, National Baseball Hall of Fame Library, Cooperstown NY.

6. Hugh Chalmers, letter to Ren Mulford Jr., May 12, 1911, August Herrmann Papers, Box 83, File 15, National Baseball Hall of Fame Library, Cooperstown NY. See also Deane, *Award Voting*, 6-7.

7. Hugh Chalmers, letter to August Herrmann, May 12, 1911, enclosing letter of same date from Chalmers to Ren Mulford Jr., August Herrmann Papers, Box 83, File 15, National Baseball Hall of Fame Library, Cooperstown NY. See also Mulford, "Chalmers Baseball Trophy," 79-82. According to Mulford, the idea of using sportswriters originated with Ban Johnson and Chicago White Sox president Charles Comiskey. At 80.

8. Okkonen, *Ty Cobb Scrapbook*, 57.

9. Okkonen, *Ty Cobb Scrapbook*, 56. See also Alexander, *Ty Cobb*, 99.

10. The remark, allegedly repeated by Cobb to a Detroit sportswriter, is set forth in Stump, *Cobb*, 199.

11. *Sporting Life*, October 28, 1911, 5.

12. *Washington Post*, February 5, 1911.

13. Sallee and Jones, "Harry Howell," 781. See also *Sporting Life*, July 15, 1911, 15, regarding Howell playing second base for St. Paul.

14. *Sporting Life*, August 19, 1911, 5.

15. See Ben Adkins quotes in *Sporting Life*, December 31, 1910, 1.

16. See Steinberg, "Robert Hedges," SABR Baseball Biography Project. See also *Sporting News*, January 12, 1911, 2, and July 4, 1940, 4. In the latter article, Montague Lyon, a former vice president of the Browns and an attorney who was consulted concerning the deal, is quoted as saying the agreed purchase price between Hedges and the prospective purchasers was $300,000.

17. See Corriden's entry at www.baseball-reference.com.

18. Circuit Court Records.

19. *St. Louis Times*, May 12, 1913.

20. Appellate Court Records, Appellant's Abstract of the Record, 16–22.

21. Appellate Court Records, Appellant's Abstract of the Record, 22.

22. Appellate Court Records, Appellant's Abstract of the Record, 26.

23. Appellate Court Records, Appellant's Abstract of the Record, 26.

24. Appellate Court Records, Appellant's Abstract of the Record, 27.

25. Appellate Court Records, Appellant's Abstract of the Record, 31.

26. Appellate Court Records, Appellant's Abstract of the Record, 31–32.

27. Appellate Court Records, Appellant's Abstract of the Record, 35.

28. Appellate Court Records, Appellant's Abstract of the Record, 36.

29. Appellate Court Records, Appellant's Abstract of the Record, 37.

30. Appellate Court Records, Appellant's Abstract of the Record, 37–39.

31. Farrington, "O'Connor Looks Back at Lajoie's 'Eight Hits,'" 3.

32. Appellate Court Records, Appellant's Abstract of the Record, 41.

33. Appellate Court Records, Appellant's Abstract of the Record, 41–43.

34. Appellate Court Records, Appellant's Abstract of the Record, 46–53.

35. Appellate Court Records, Appellant's Abstract of the Record, 60.

36. Appellate Court Records, Appellant's Abstract of the Record, 61.

37. Appellate Court Records, Appellant's Abstract of the Record, 62–67.

38. Appellate Court Records, Appellant's Abstract of the Record, 71–75.

39. Comments appear in undated news article datelined May 12, 1913, Jack O'Connor's Clippings File, National Baseball Hall of Fame Library, Cooperstown NY. The article goes on to say that the judge reprimanded Hedges four times for evasive answers during the testimony. The judge did overrule a number of objections interposed by Judge Williams on behalf of the defense. Such frequent attempts to block testimony, in and of themselves, might leave an impression of evasiveness. The record does reveal one time that Judge Hitchcock actually reprimanded Hedges for an evasive answer. Appellate Court Record, Appellant's Abstract of the Record, 68.

40. Appellate Court Records, Appellant's Abstract of the Record, 84–85.

41. Appellate Court Records, Appellant's Abstract of the Record, 87.

42. Appellate Court Records, Appellant's Abstract of the Record, 90.

43. Appellate Court Records, Appellant's Abstract of the Record, 91.

44. Appellate Court Records, Appellant's Abstract of the Record, 93.

45. Appellate Court Records, Appellant's Abstract of the Record, 99–100.

46. Appellate Court Records, Appellant's Abstract of the Record, 101.

47. Appellate Court Records, Appellant's Abstract of the Record, 103.

48. Appellate Court Records, Appellant's Abstract of the Record, 103–7.

49. Appellate Court Records, Appellant's Abstract of the Record, 108–9.

50. Appellate Court Records, Appellant's Abstract of the Record, 109–10.

51. Appellate Court Records, Appellant's Abstract of the Record, 110–11.

52. *St. Louis Times*, May 13, 1913.

53. Appellate Court Record, Appellant's Abstract of the Record, 112.

54. Appellate Court Record, Appellant's Abstract of the Record, 113.

55. Appellate Court Record, Appellant's Abstract of the Record, 115.

56. Appellate Court Record, Appellant's Abstract of the Record, 117.

57. Appellate Court Record, Appellant's Abstract of the Record, 118.

58. Appellate Court Record, Appellant's Abstract of the Record, 119-20.

59. *St. Louis Globe*, May 9, 1913. Stovall was suspended by Johnson from May 5 to May 22, 1913. He was reinstated with a rather mild hundred-dollar fine and the condition that he author a letter of apology to the umpire, Charlie Ferguson. Constantelos, "George T. Stovall," 663-64.

60. Appellate Court Record, Appellant's Abstract of the Record, 121-22, quoting paragraph 2, clause 1.

61. Appellate Court Record, Appellant's Abstract of the Record, 123-24.

62. Appellate Court Record, Appellant's Abstract of the Record, 125, quoting letter dated February 16, 1911, from B. B. Johnson to John J. O'Connor.

63. Appellate Court Record, Appellant's Abstract of the Record, 125-26.

64. Appellate Court Record, Appellant's Abstract of the Record, 127-28.

65. Ban Johnson's statement in *Chicago Tribune*, October 16, 1910.

66. Appellate Court Record, Appellant's Abstract of the Record, 129-30.

67. Appellate Court Record, Appellant's Abstract of the Record, 131-32.

68. Appellate Court Record, Appellant's Abstract of the Record, 138-39.

69. Appellate Court Record, Appellant's Abstract of the Record, 129-31.

70. Appellate Court Record, Appellant's Abstract of the Record, 140-41.

71. Appellate Court Record, Appellant's Abstract of the Record, 142-43.

72. Appellate Court Record, Appellant's Abstract of the Record, 143-44.

73. Appellate Court Record, Appellant's Abstract of the Record, 146-50.

74. L. C. Davis, Sports Salad, *St. Louis Post-Dispatch*, May 16, 1913.

75. *St. Louis Star*, May 18, 1913.

76. *Chicago Tribune*, June 13, 1913. See also *Washington Post*, June 13, 1913.

77. *Chicago Tribune*, June 13, 1913.

78. See *Federal Baseball Club of Baltimore v. National League*, 259 U.S. 200 (1922). Following the 1915 baseball season, the bulk of the Federal League franchises entered into an agreement with the two major leagues to dissolve. The lawsuit was pursued to its conclusion by Baltimore's entry in the Federal League when that franchise remained unhappy with the terms of the settlement. In its decision, the U.S. Supreme Court ruled against the Baltimore club, deciding that Organized Baseball was not subject to the Sherman Act because it was not involved in interstate commerce. As such, it was not violating the nation's antitrust laws.

79. *Kansas City Star*, June 29, 1913.

80. *Chicago Tribune*, June 30, 1913.

81. *Chicago Tribune*, July 25, 1913.

82. *Sporting News*, April 23, 1914, 2.

83. See *Federal Baseball Club of Baltimore v. National League*.

84. A series of letters discussing the issue of discontinuing the Chalmers Award is contained in Box 83, File 16, August Herrmann Papers, National Baseball Hall of Fame Library, Cooperstown NY.

85. *O'Connor v. St. Louis American League Baseball Co.*, 181 Southwestern Reporter 1167 (1916), at 1175.

86. *O'Connor v. St. Louis American League Baseball Co.*, 1173.

87. *O'Connor v. St. Louis American League Baseball Co.*, 1175.

CHAPTER ELEVEN

1. Lewis, *Motor Memories*, 70–71. This quote and other information regarding the demise of Hugh Chalmers's company are taken from Hyde, *Riding the Roller Coaster*, 16–23.

2. Hyde, *Riding the Roller Coaster*, 22–23.

3. Hammond, *Hugh Chalmers*, 14.

4. Hammond, *Hugh Chalmers*, 46.

5. The admission was made by Ban Johnson on September 11, 1919, when he testified under oath in a case involving former Boston Red Sox pitcher Carl Mays. For information about this and Johnson's involvement in the sale and ownership of the Red Sox over the years, see Lynch, "A Question of Ownership." See also Lynch, *Harry Frazee, Ban Johnson and the Feud*, 31–40.

6. Lynch, "Question of Ownership," quoting from an article that appeared in the *New York Tribune* shortly after the transaction.

7. Lynch, "Question of Ownership." In his column The Round-Up, *Washington Post*, December 7, 1917, J. V. Fitzgerald claims McRoy got the idea Speaker was available from a paragraph he saw in a "Western newspaper" quoting Lannin as saying he might sell Speaker for the right price.

8. *Boston Globe*, December 3, 1917.

9. *Chicago Tribune*, December 6, 1917.

10. Alexander, *Ty Cobb*, 105–7.

11. Alexander, *Ty Cobb*, 164–65.

12. Descriptions of the reduction of Ban Johnson's power can be found in a number of books listed in the bibliography. For a brief description, see Santry and Thomson, "Byron Bancroft Johnson," 391–92. For a more detailed version, see Murdock, *Ban Johnson*, 159–225.

13. The Cobb-Speaker conspiracy affair is covered in detail in Alexander, *Ty Cobb*, 183–94. See also Murdock, *Ban Johnson*, 214–25, for a more sympathetic treatment of Johnson's fall from power.

14. Steinberg, "Robert Hedges," in Jones, *Deadball Stars of the American League*, 769. See also Huhn, *The Sizzler*, 56–57.

15. Farrington, "O'Connor Looks Back at Lajoie's 'Eight Hits,'" 3.

16. Unsourced news article, dated November 25, 1937, Jack O'Connor's Clippings File, National Baseball Hall of Fame Library, Cooperstown NY.

17. Wiggins, *Federal League of Base Ball Clubs*, 242–43.

18. Sallee, "Harry Howell."

19. Contract Cards, John Corriden's Clippings File, National Baseball Hall of Fame Library, Cooperstown NY.

20. Unsourced, 1947 (otherwise undated) article by Ben Epstein titled "Corriden Is Good Will and Good Humor Man," John Corriden's Clippings File, National Baseball Hall of Fame Library, Cooperstown NY.

21. John Corriden's Medical Certificate of Death, Division of Vital Records, Indiana State Board of Health, John Corriden's Clippings File, National Baseball Hall of Fame Library, Cooperstown NY. See also McMahon, "Old Scout Expired as Protégé Won in '59 Playoff," 17.

22. Bak, *Ty Cobb*, 135.

23. Cobb, *My Life in Baseball*, 179.

24. Alexander, *Ty Cobb*, 155, 213.

25. Alexander, *Ty Cobb*, 218–19.

26. Stump, *Cobb*. The movie *Cobb* was directed by Ron Shelton and released in 1994. Cobb was portrayed by actor Tommy Lee Jones.

27. For example see Cobb, "Georgia Peach," 84–101. See also Alexander, *Ty Cobb*, 238–39, as well as pages x–xii of Dr. Alexander's introduction to the 1993 reprint of Cobb, *My Life in Baseball*.

28. Klinetobe and Bullock, "Complicated Shadows," 21.

29. Seymour, *Baseball*, 285.

30. Murphy, "Napoleon Lajoie," 39. The quotes appear to be taken from an interview Lajoie gave to F. C. Lane of *Baseball Magazine* in early 1915. See Lane, "Inside Facts of the Great Lajoie Deal."

31. The game was stopped on September 27 because it was then thought that his hit that day was number three thousand. Subsequent revisions would determine that the number of hits originally credited to Lajoie in 1901, but subsequently lowered, were indeed accurate. By this measure, Lajoie collected his three thousandth hit on September 17, 1914. Murphy, "Napoleon Lajoie," 40.

32. Murphy, "Napoleon Lajoie," 57.

33. Lane, "Inside Facts of the Great Lajoie Deal," 51–52.

34. There is some question whether the name was chosen to honor Cleveland Spiders player Louis Sockalexis, believed to be the first Native American to play in the Major Leagues, or merely to honor Native Americans in general.

35. Lane, "Inside Facts of the Great Lajoie Deal," 58, 62.

36. Allen, "From Hack Seat to Pedestal (Part Two)," 11.

37. Allen, "From Hack Seat to Pedestal (Part Two)," 12.

38. Allen, "From Hack Seat to Pedestal (Part Two)," 12.

39. Murphy, "Napoleon Lajoie," 65.

40. Murphy, "Napoleon Lajoie," 70.

41. Ginsburg, *Fix Is In*, 76.

42. Numbers Games, *Sporting News*, April 28, 1997, 5.

43. Numbers Games, *Sporting News*, April 28, 1997, 5.

44. Brandon, "Walter 'Peck' Lerian," 54.

45. Joe McGuff, "Misplayed Ball Clouds Brett's Batting Title," *Sporting News*, October 16, 1976, 31. See also Ginsburg, *Fix Is In*, 80–81.

46. McGuff, "Misplayed Ball Clouds Brett's Batting Title," 31.

47. McGuff, "Misplayed Ball Clouds Brett's Batting Title," 31. But see Nemec, *Rules of Baseball*, 198–99, in which the author states that Brye waffled and "eventually acknowledged that most" American Leaguers preferred Brett for the batting championship because he played full-time, whereas McRae was primarily a designated hitter.

48. McGuff, "Misplayed Ball Clouds Brett's Batting Title," 31.

49. McGuff, "Misplayed Ball Clouds Brett's Batting Title," 31.

50. Bob Fowler, "One Misplay . . . Could It Wreck Brye's Career?" *Sporting News*, October 23, 1976, 34.

51. Bob Fowler, "Did McRae Plant Seeds for Own Beef?" *Sporting News*, October 30, 1976, 26.

52. Fowler, "Did McRae Plant Seeds for Own Beef?," 26.

53. Lyons, "Problem of Official Scoring," 58.

54. See Nat Fleischer, "Charge Sisler and Hornsby Were Helped by Favoritism," *New York Evening Telegram*, January 11, 1921.

55. Gould, "Why Not Make Official Scoring Really 'Official'?" 438.

56. Rule 10.01 (a), Professional Baseball Official Playing Rules.

57. Rule 10.01 (c), Professional Baseball Official Playing Rules.

58. According to the late Jerome Holtzman, the Baseball Writers' Association voted in 1979 to discontinue supplying scorers from its ranks. He adds that by the 1980s all newspapers barred their writers from scoring owing to conflict of interest. Holtzman, *Jerome Holtzman on Baseball*, 129.

59. Rule 10.01 (a), Professional Baseball Official Playing Rules.

60. *Sporting Life*, February 17, 1912, 4, reporting on an item in the *Philadelphia Times*.

61. Schwarz, *Numbers Game*, 41, writes that Howe actually "serviced" the American League in 1911. If true, it seems the move by Johnson was directly connected to the problems raised by the 1910 batting race.

62. Schwarz, *Numbers Game*, 41.

CHAPTER TWELVE

1. See Selter, *Ballparks of the Deadball Era*, 9, for a more detailed explanation.

2. The *Official Encyclopedia*'s individual statistics were limited to games played, as well as batting averages for hitters and won-lost figures for pitchers. Schwarz, *Numbers Game*, 54. The encyclopedia was not the first compilation of baseball statistics. That honor goes to *Balldom* by George L. Moreland, published in 1914. (For more on Moreland, see chapter 2.) The first comprehensive treatment of individual statistics was

the controversial 1969 *MacMillan Baseball Encyclopedia*. For a detailed discussion of the history of baseball statistical encyclopedias, see Schwarz, *Numbers Game*, 91–109. See also Smith, "Number of Changes," 36–37.

3. Pete Palmer, telephone interview by the author, July 7, 2009. See also Schwarz, *Numbers Game*, 156–57, and John Thorn, Pete Palmer, and Joseph M. Wayman, "The History of Major League Baseball Statistics," in Thorn et al., *Total Baseball*, 958.

4. Ban Johnson's statement in *Chicago Tribune*, October 16, 1910.

5. *Detroit Times*, October 17, 1910.

6. Undated typewritten statistics sheets of Cliff Kachline, 1–3. The sheets were provided to the author by Pete Palmer.

7. Paul Mac Farlane, "Lajoie Beats Out Cobb," *Sporting News*, April 18, 1981, 3.

8. Mac Farlane, "Lajoie Beats Out Cobb," 11. Mac Farlane credits Gettelson with "detecting . . . the error before his death." The newspaper alleged it discovered the find when it acquired Gettelson's library after his 1977 death and saw written correspondence about it between Palmer and Gettelson. The article appears to claim that Palmer's discovery was independent from Gettelson's and "dovetailed with facts already discovered at TSN." Kachline's work was mentioned in connection with Palmer, as was the contribution of Alex Haas, another SABR member who provided the box scores from the *New York Times*.

9. Mac Farlane, "Lajoie Beats Out Cobb," 11.

10. Individual day-by-days for the 1910 Boston Red Sox (on microfilm), National Baseball Hall of Fame Library, Cooperstown NY.

11. There are numerous mentions of an "audit" in 1910 for the American League batting records. See, for instance, Schwarz, *Numbers Game*, 156. This author was unable to identify whether the audit was conducted by Robert McRoy, the league secretary, or an independent auditor, such as Irwin Howe, who later became the league's statistician.

12. Voigt, "Fie on Figure Filberts," *Baseball Research Journal*, 32.

13. Additional members of the committee in 1980 were Seymour Siwoff, the National League's statistician; Bob Wirz, director of information for the baseball commissioner's office; Joe Reichler, special assistant to Commissioner Bowie Kuhn; Bob Fishel and Blake Cullen, American and National League public relations directors, respectively; Harry Simmons, Kuhn's administrative assistant; former ballplayer and Hall of Famer Ralph Kiner, a broadcaster for the New York Mets; Jack Lang, of the *New York Daily News* and an officer in the Baseball Writers' Association; Red Foley, a *New York Daily News* writer; baseball statistician Allan Roth; and Leonard Koppett, a sportswriter and columnist for the *Sporting News* specializing in "quantitative analysis of [baseball] statistics." Mac Farlane, "Lajoie Beats Out Cobb," 11.

14. Mac Farlane, "Lajoie Beats Out Cobb," 11.

15. Mac Farlane, "Lajoie Beats Out Cobb," 11.

16. Mac Farlane, "Lajoie Beats Out Cobb," 3.

17. Mac Farlane, "Lajoie Beats Out Cobb," 11.

18. *Sporting News*, April 25, 1981, 37.

19. Editorial, *Sporting News*, May 2, 1981, 14. The "abstention" mentioned in the quoted material was presumably exercised by Paul Mac Farlane.

20. Readers Michael J. Strehl, Daniel E. Ginsburg, and Steve Hatcher, Voice of the Fan, *Sporting News*, May 9, 1981, 4.

21. Paul Mac Farlane and Cliff Kachline quoted in Michael Graham, "Record Books Still Wrong on Cobb's Career Hit Total," *Baseball Digest*, June 1985, 43.

22. Voigt, "Fie on Figure Filberts," 33.

23. *Sporting News*, March 5, 1990, 8. A similar position was taken by a fellow member of the official records committee, Leonard Koppett. The sportswriter and baseball author has opined that "official" means "from the office." It does not mean "accurate." Koppett is quoted in Smith, "Number of Changes," 37.

24. Schwarz, *Numbers Game*, 167.

25. Schwarz, *Numbers Game*, 171.

26. Greg Couch, "Jim Gentile Walks Off a Champ, as Do Baltimore Orioles," AOL News. com, August 6, 2010, http://www.aolnews.com/2010/08/06/jim-gentile-walks -off-a-champ-as-do-baltimore-orioles/. See also Mike Dodd, "News Flash: Roger Maris, Mickey Mantle Lose RBI, Runs Scored Titles," USA Today.com, July 27, 2010, http://content.usatoday.com/communities/dailypitch/post/2010/07/news-flash -roger-maris-mickey-mantle-lose-rbi-runs-scored-crowns-/1#.UdxtgW3rCoo.

27. See Ty Cobb's career and 1910 season statistics at MLB.com.

28. See for example, Thorn et al., *Total Baseball*; baseball-reference.com; or Retrosheet. com. For a different approach, see *ESPN Baseball Encyclopedia*, ix. It recognizes four mistakes in Cobb's career total and records "the net result" as 4,189.

EPILOGUE

1. Thorn, Palmer, and Wayman, "History of Major League Baseball Statistics," 958.

2. Murphy, "Napoleon Lajoie," 69.

3. Murphy, "Napoleon Lajoie," 69.

4. Cobb, *Ty Cobb*, 95–98.

5. Allen, "From Hack Seat to Pedestal (Part Two)," 11.

6. Murphy, "Napoleon Lajoie," 35.

Bibliography

Alexander, Charles C. *Turbulent Seasons*. Dallas: SMU Press, 2011.

———. *Ty Cobb*. New York: Oxford University Press, 1984.

Allen, Frederick Lewis. *The Big Change: America Transforms Itself 1900-1950*. New York: Harper & Brothers, 1952.

Allen, Lee. *The American League Story*. New York: Hill and Wang, 1965.

Anderson, David. "Billy Evans." In Jones, *Deadball Stars of the American League*, 397-98.

———. "William 'Kitty' Bransfield." In Simon, *Deadball Stars of the National League*, 199-200.

Bak, Richard. *Cobb Would Have Caught It*. Detroit: Wayne State University Press, 1991.

———. *Ty Cobb: His Tumultuous Life and Times*. Dallas: Taylor, 1994.

"Barney Dreyfus [*sic*] on Official Scoring." *Baseball Magazine*, July 1911, 26.

Beasley, Norman, and George W. Stark. *Made in Detroit*. New York: G. P. Putnam's Sons, 1957.

Bevis, Charlie. *Sunday Baseball: The Major League's Struggle to Play Baseball on the Lord's Day, 1876-1934*. Jefferson NC: McFarland, 2003.

Brandon, T. Scott. "Walter 'Peck' Lerian, 1928-29 Philadelphia Phillies." *National Pastime: Monumental Baseball*, 2009, 46-56.

Burgess, Bill, III. "Did All of Ty Cobb's Team Mates Hate Him?" BaseballGuru.com. http://baseballguru.com/bburgess/analysisbburgess04.html.

Cobb, Tyrus Raymond. *Busting 'Em and Other Big League Stories*. Jefferson NC: McFarland, 2003.

———. "Is There Any Luck in Baseball?" *Baseball Magazine*, July 1911, 11-12.

———. *Memoirs of Twenty Years in Baseball*. Edited by William R. Cobb. Marietta GA: William R. Cobb, 2002.

———. *My Life in Baseball: The True Record*. With Al Stump. Lincoln: University of Nebraska Press, 1993.

Cobb, William R. "The Georgia Peach: Stumped by the Storyteller." *National Pastime: Baseball in the Peach State*, 2010, 84-101.

Constantelos, Steve. "George T. Stovall." In Jones, *Deadball Stars of the American League*, 663-64.

Cook, William A. *August "Garry" Herrmann: A Baseball Biography*. Jefferson NC: McFarland, 2008.

"The Cork Center Base Ball." In *Spalding's Official Base Ball Guide, 1911*, 141–43. New York: American Sports Publishing, 1911.

Curcio, Vincent. *Chrysler: The Life and Times of an Automotive Genius*. New York: Oxford University Press, 2000.

Deane, Bill. *Award Voting: A History of the Most Valuable Player, Rookie of the Year, and Cy Young Awards*. Kansas City MO: Society for American Baseball Research, 1988.

DeValeria, Dennis, and Jeanne Burke DeValeria. *Honus Wagner: A Biography*. New York: Henry Holt, 1995.

Dewey, Donald, and Nicholas Acocella. *The Biographical History of Baseball*. New York: Carroll & Graf, 1995.

——. *Total Ballclubs: The Ultimate Book of Baseball Teams*. Wilmington DE: Sport Media, 2005.

Dickson, Paul. *The Dickson Baseball Dictionary*. 3rd ed. New York: W. W. Norton, 2009.

——. *The Joy of Keeping Score*. New York: Walker, 1996.

——. *The New Baseball Dictionary*. New York: Harcourt Brace, 1999.

The ESPN Baseball Encyclopedia. New York: Sterling, 2007.

Finkel, Jan. "Honus Wagner." In Simon, *Deadball Stars of the National League*, 153–56.

Fischer, Leo. "The Superman of Baseball." *Esquire*, October 1941, 53, 158–60.

Fleitz, David L. *Silver Bats and Automobiles: The Hotly Competitive, Sometimes Ignoble Pursuit of the Major League Batting Championship*. Jefferson NC: McFarland, 2011.

"The Folly of Baseball Figures." *Baseball Magazine*, June 1911, 24.

Foster, Patrick. "The Birth of Hudson: 1909–1929." *Hemmings Classic Car*, November 1, 2005.

Fultz, David L., ed. "The Stovall Case." *Baseball Magazine*, July 1913, 72.

Georgano, G. N., and Thorkil Ry Andersen. *The New Encyclopedia of Automobiles: 1885 to the Present*. New York: Crescent Books, 1986.

Gietschier, Steve. "A Good Piece of Hitting: The 1910 American League Batting Race." *Timeline*, October–December 2010, 20–35.

——. "Scandal in St. Louis." *Cardinals Gameday Magazine*, no. 5 (2010): 92–94, 97–99.

——. "The Strange Case of the Courts, a Car, and the 1910 Batting Title." *The Confluence*, Fall/Winter 1910, 4–15.

Ginsburg, Daniel E. *The Fix Is In: A History of Baseball Gambling and Game Fixing Scandals*. Jefferson NC: McFarland, 1995.

——. "Ty Cobb." In Jones, *Deadball Stars of the American League*, 546–50.

Gould, James M. "Why Not Make Official Scoring Really 'Official'?" *Baseball Magazine*, March 1930, 437–38, 471–72.

Graham, Michael. "Record Books Still Wrong on Cobb's Career Hits Total." *Baseball Digest*, June 1985, 43–44.

Grahek, Mike. "Davy Jones." In Jones, *Deadball Stars of the American League*, 553–54.

Hammond, David C. *Hugh Chalmers: The Man and His Car*. Mountain View CA: Shoreline Printing, 2005.

Hample, Zack. *The Baseball: Stunts, Scandals and Secrets Beneath the Stitches*. New York: Anchor Books, 2011.

Hatcher, Harlan. *Lake Erie*. Indianapolis: Bobbs-Merrill, 1945.

Holtzman, Jerome. *Jerome Holtzman on Baseball*. Champaign IL: Sports Publishing, 2005.

Huhn, Rick. *Eddie Collins: A Baseball Biography*. Jefferson NC: McFarland, 2008.

———. *The Sizzler: George Sisler, Baseball's Forgotten Great*. Columbia: University of Missouri Press, 2004.

Hyde, Charles K. *Riding the Roller Coaster: A History of the Chrysler Corporation*. Detroit: Wayne State University Press, 2003.

Imhoff, Kevin. "Maxwell & Chalmers." Cyclopaedia.net. http://www.de.cyclopaedia.net/wiki/Maxwell-Chalmers.

Ivor-Campbell, Frederick, Robert L. Tiemann, and Mark Rucker, eds. *Baseball's First Stars*. Cleveland: Society for American Baseball Research, 1996.

James, Bill. *The New Bill James Historical Baseball Abstract*. New York: Free Press, 2001.

Jensen, Don. "Tris Speaker." In Jones, *Deadball Stars of the American League*, 434–37.

Johnson, Willis E. "Into His Own." *Baseball Magazine*, April 1910, 69–70.

Jones, David, ed. *Deadball Stars of the American League*. Washington DC: Potomac Books, 2006.

———. "Dode Paskert." In Simon, *Deadball Stars of the National League*, 212–14.

———, and Steve Constantelos. "Napoleon Lajoie." In Jones, *Deadball Stars of the American League*, 657–61.

Kavanagh, Jack. *Walter Johnson: A Life*. South Bend IN: Diamond Communications, 1995.

Klinetobe, Charles, and Steve Bullock. "Complicated Shadows: Ty Cobb and the Public Imagination." *NINE* 18, no. 1 (Fall 2009): 21–36.

Koppett, Leonard. *Koppett's Concise History of Major League Baseball*. New York: Carroll & Graf, 2004.

Kossuth, J. "How Cobb Played the Game, Part 3: His Batting Abilities, The Cobb-Lajoie Race of 1910." http://wso.williams.edu/~jkossuth/cobb/lajoie.htm.

Kuenster, Bob. "These Were the Majors' Closest Batting Races Ever!" *Baseball Digest*, July 1988, 60–65.

Lamberty, Bill. "Sam Crawford." In Jones, *Deadball Stars of the American League*, 537–39.

Lane, F. C. "Behind the Scenes in Organized Baseball." *Baseball Magazine*, January 1913, 49–54.

———. "A Day with Ty Cobb." *Baseball Magazine*, April 1916, 47–58.

———. "The Inside Facts of the Great Lajoie Deal." *Baseball Magazine*, June 1915, 51–62.

———. "Ty Cobb, the King of Ball Players." *Baseball Magazine*, July 1911, 3–8.

———. "Where the Baseball Records Fail to Tell the Truth." *Baseball Magazine*, June 1913, 39–49.

———. "Why the System of Batting Averages Should Be Changed." *Baseball Magazine*, March 1916, 41–47.

Lee, Bill. *The Baseball Necrology: The Post-Baseball Lives and Deaths of 7,600 Major League Players and Others*. Jefferson NC: McFarland, 2003.

Lewis, Eugene W. *Motor Memories: A Saga of Whirling Gears*. Detroit: Alved, 1947.

Lewis, Franklin. *The Cleveland Indians*. Kent OH: Kent State University Press, 2006.

Lieb, Frederick G. *The Detroit Tigers*. Kent OH: Kent State University Press, 2008.

——. "Napoleon Lajoie: The King of Modern Batters." *Baseball Magazine*, August 1911, 53–56.

Longert, Scott. *Addie Joss: King of the Pitchers*. Cleveland: Society for American Baseball Research, 1998.

"Looking On." *Baseball Magazine*, July 1910, 86–87.

"Lot 31: 1909 Chalmers-Detroit Thirty Touring." Motorbase.com. http://www.motorbase .com/auctionlot/by-id/646142032/.

Louisa, Angela. "Elmer Flick." In Jones, *Deadball Stars of the American League*, 649–51.

Lowry, Phillip J. *Green Cathedrals: The Ultimate Celebration of Major League and Negro League Ballparks*. New York: Walker, 2006.

Lynch, Michael T., Jr. *Harry Frazee, Ban Johnson and the Feud That Nearly Destroyed the American League*. Jefferson NC: McFarland, 2008.

——. "A Question of Ownership." Seamheads.com, February 26, 2010. http://www.seam-heads.com/2010/02/26/a-question-of-ownership/.

Lyons, M. V. B. "The Problem of Official Scoring." *Baseball Magazine*, November 1912, 55–60.

Macht, Norman L. *Connie Mack and the Early Years of Baseball*. Lincoln: University of Nebraska Press, 2007.

McCallum, John D. *Ty Cobb*. New York: Praeger, 1975.

McMahon, Thomas. "Old Scout Expired as Protégé Won in '59 Playoff." *Baseball Research Journal*, no. 13 (1984): 17–18.

Moreland, George L. "Need of a Better Scoring System." *Baseball Magazine*, November 1908, 15–16.

Morris, Peter. *A Game of Inches: The Stories behind the Innovations That Shaped Baseball*. Vol. 1, *The Game on the Field*. Chicago: Ivan R. Dee, 2006.

——. *A Game of Inches: The Stories behind the Innovations That Shaped Baseball*. Vol. 2, *The Game behind the Scenes*. Chicago: Ivan R. Dee, 2006.

Mulford, Ren. "The Chalmers Baseball Trophy." *Baseball Magazine*, April 1914, 79–82.

Murdock, Eugene C. *Ban Johnson: Czar of Baseball*. Westport CT: Greenwood, 1982.

——. "The Tragedy of Ban Johnson." *Journal of Sport History* 1, no. 1 (1974): 30–31.

——. "The Youngest 'Boy Manager.'" *Baseball Research Journal* 4 (1975): 29–32.

Murphy, Cait. *Crazy '08: How a Cast of Cranks, Rogues, Boneheads, and Magnates Created the Greatest Year in Baseball History*. New York: HarperCollins, 2007.

Murphy, J. M. "Napoleon Lajoie: Modern Baseball's First Superstar." *The National Pastime: A Review of Baseball History* 7, no. 1 (Spring 1988): 1–82.

Nemec, David. *The Rules of Baseball*. New York: Lyons & Burford, 1994.

Okkonen, Marc. *Baseball Memories, 1900–1909*. New York: Sterling, 1992.

——. *The Ty Cobb Scrapbook*. New York: Sterling, 2001.

Phillips, John. "John Joseph O'Connor." In Ivor-Campbell, Tiemann, and Rucker, *Baseball's First Stars*, 122.

——. *The Story of Larry Lajoie*. Kathleen GA: Capital Publishing, 2006.

Reach Official Baseball Guide [1911]. Philadelphia: A. J. Reach, 1911.

Reisler, Jim. *A Great Day in Cooperstown: The Improbable Birth of Baseball's Hall of Fame.* New York: Carroll & Graf, 2006.

Ritter, Lawrence S. *The Glory of Their Times: The Story of the Early Days of Baseball Told by the Men Who Played It.* New York: William Morrow, 1984.

———. *Lost Ballparks: A Celebration of Baseball's Legendary Fields.* New York: Viking Penguin, 1992.

Rogers, C. Paul, III. "Hugh Jennings." In Jones, *Deadball Stars of the American League,* 555–58.

Rose, William Ganson. *Cleveland: The Making of a City.* Cleveland: World, 1950.

Saccoman, John. "August 'Garry' Herrmann." In Simon, *Deadball Stars of the National League,* 235–36.

Sallee, Eric. "Harry Howell." SABR Baseball Biography Project, SABR.org. http://sabr.org/bioproj/person/b8aabfeb.

———, and David Jones. "Harry Howell." In Jones, *Deadball Stars of the American League,* 780–81.

Sanborn, Irving E. "Some Needed Changes in the Baseball Records." *Baseball Magazine,* August 1922, 401–3, 421.

Santry, Joe, and Cindy Thomson. "Byron Bancroft Johnson." In Jones, *Deadball Stars of the American League,* 390–92.

Schaefer, Robert H. "The Legend of the Lively Ball, 1850–1920." *Base Ball: A Journal of the Early Game,* Fall 2009, 88–98.

Schechter, Gabriel. "Fred Snodgrass." In Simon, *Deadball Stars of the National League,* 65–66.

Schiff, Andrew J. *The Father of Baseball: A Biography of Henry Chadwick.* Jefferson NC: McFarland, 2008.

Schneider, Russell. *The Cleveland Indians Encyclopedia.* 2nd ed. Champaign IL: Sports Publishing, 2001.

———. *Tribe Memories: The First Century.* Hinckley OH: Moonlight Publishing, 2000.

Schoor, Gene. *Ty Cobb: Baseball's Greatest Player.* With Henry Gilfond. New York: Julian Messner, 1952.

Schul, Scott E. "Bobby Wallace." In Jones, *Deadball Stars of the American League,* 776–77.

Schuld, Fred. "Charles W. Somers." In Jones, *Deadball Stars of the American League,* 393–94.

Schwarz, Alan. *The Numbers Game: Baseball's Lifelong Fascination with Statistics.* New York: Thomas Dunne Books, 2004.

Seaver, Tom. *Great Moments in Baseball.* With Marty Appel. New York: Carol Publishing, 1992.

Selter, Ronald M. *Ballparks of the Deadball Era: A Comprehensive Study of Their Dimensions, Configurations and Effects on Batting, 1901–1919.* Jefferson NC: McFarland, 2008.

Seymour, Harold. *Baseball: The Golden Age.* New York: Oxford University Press, 1971.

Simon, Tom, ed. *Deadball Stars of the National League.* Washington DC: Brassey's, 2004.

———. "Sherry Magee." In Simon, *Deadball Stars of the National League,* 193–96.

Smiley, Richard. "Matthew 'Matty' McIntyre." In Jones, *Deadball Stars of the American League,* 544–45.

Smith, Dave. "A Number of Changes." *Memories and Dreams* 33, no. 3 (Summer 2011): 36–39.

Solomon, Burt. *The Baseball Timeline*. New York: Dorling Kindersley, 2001.

Spatz, Lyle, ed. *The SABR Baseball List and Record Book*. New York: Scribner, 2007.

Spink, Alfred H. *The National Game*. 2nd ed. Carbondale: Southern Illinois University Press, 2000.

Stang, Mark. *Indians Illustrated: 100 Years of Cleveland Indians Photos*. Wilmington OH: Orange Frazer, 2000.

Stanton, Tom. *Ty and the Babe: Baseball's Fiercest Rivalry; A Surprising Friendship and the 1941 Has-Beens Golf Championship*. New York: Thomas Dunne Books, 2007.

Steinberg, Steve. "Robert Hedges." In Jones, *Deadball Stars of the American League*, 768–69.

——. "Robert Hedges." SABR Baseball Biography Project, SABR.org. http://sabr.org/bioproj/person/b91246d7.

Stout, Glenn. *Fenway 1912: The Birth of a Ballpark, a Championship Season, and Fenway's Remarkable First Year*. New York: Mariner Books, 2011.

Strohl, Erik. "The Ultimate Loving Cups." *Memories and Dreams*, Spring 2011, 28–31.

Stump, Al. *Cobb: A Biography*. Chapel Hill NC: Algonquin Books, 1994.

Swift, Tom. *Chief Bender's Burden*. Lincoln: University of Nebraska Press, 2008.

Thorn, John, and Pete Palmer. *The Hidden Game of Baseball: A Revolutionary Approach to Baseball and Its Statistics*. With David Reuther. Garden City NY: Doubleday, 1984.

Thorn, John, Pete Palmer, Phil Birnbaum, Bill Deane, Rob Neyer, Alan Schwarz, Donald Dewey, Nicholas Acocella, and Peter Wayner, eds. *Total Baseball: The Ultimate Baseball Encyclopedia*. 8th ed. Wilmington DE: Sport Media, 2004.

Thornton, Patrick K. *Legal Decisions That Shaped Modern Baseball*. Jefferson NC: McFarland, 2012.

Vass, George. "It's Time to Quit Fiddling with the Record Book." *Baseball Digest*, January 1992, 28–34.

Voigt, David Q. "Charlie Radbourn's Record-Setting Season." *Baseball Research Journal* 39, no. 1 (Summer 2010): 141–42.

——. "Fie on Figure Filberts: Some Crimes against Clio." *Baseball Research Journal*, 1983, 32–38.

Waggoner, Glen, Kathleen Maloney, and Hugh Howard. *Spitters, Beanballs, and the Incredible Shrinking Strike Zone: The Stories behind the Rules of Baseball*. Rev. ed. Chicago: Triumph Books, 1990.

Ward, Geoffrey C., and Ken Burns. *Baseball: An Illustrated History*. New York: A. A. Knopf, 1994.

Wertheim, Jon L. "The Amazing Race." *Sports Illustrated*, September 20, 2010, 76–86.

Wiggins, Robert Peyton. *The Federal League of Base Ball Clubs: The History of an Outlaw Major League, 1914-1915*. Jefferson NC: McFarland, 2009.

Wirkmaa, Andres. *Baseball Scorekeeping: A Practical Guide to the Rules*. Jefferson NC: McFarland, 2003.

Wukovits, John F. *The 1910s*. San Diego: Greenhaven Press, 2000.

Index

Illustrations are indicated by *fig. 1*, *fig. 2*, and so forth.